RACISM IN THE
POST-CIVIL RIGHTS ERA

SUNY SERIES IN
AFRO-AMERICAN STUDIES

JOHN HOWARD AND ROBERT C. SMITH,
EDITORS

RACISM IN THE POST-CIVIL RIGHTS ERA

NOW YOU SEE IT, NOW YOU DON'T

ROBERT C. SMITH

STATE UNIVERSITY OF NEW YORK PRESS

Published by
State University of New York Press, Albany

©1995 State University of New York

For information, address State University of New York Press,
State University Plaza, Albany, N.Y. 12246

Production by M. R. Mulholland
Marketing by Theresa A. Swierzowski

Library of Congress Cataloging-in-Publication Data

Smith, Robert Charles, 1947-
    Racism in the post civil rights era : now you see it, now you
don't / Robert C. Smith.
      p.   cm. -- (SUNY series in Afro-American studies)
    Includes bibliographical references (p.   ) and index.
    ISBN 0-7914-2437-5 (HC : acid-free). -- ISBN 0-7914-2438-3 (PB :
acid-free)
    1. Racism--United States.   2. United States--Race relations.
I. Title.   II. Series.
E185.615.S5825   1995
305.8'00973--dc20   94-21493
                                                              CIP

10 9 8 7 6 5 4 3 2 1

To my beautiful bird.
Don't fly away.

Contents

Tables

Acknowledgments

I would like to thank my wife, Scottie Gibson Smith, for her patient assistance in the research and writing of this book, without which it could not have been written. The late Professor Aaron Wildavsky of the University of California at Berkeley rendered a detailed critique of the conceptual chapter. Mack Jones of Prairie View A & M and Joseph McCormick of Howard made useful comments on Chapter 6. My longtime friend Larry Mason brought a layman's eye to his detailed reading of the entire manuscript. His comments and suggestions led to clarification of several important historical and conceptual points. The three anonymous reviewers for SUNY Press made comments and suggestions that led to improvements, especially in the Epilogue. I am also grateful to the Academy of Political and Social Science for allowing me to quote generously from the elegant study by Theodore Hershberg and his colleagues that appeared in volume 441 (1979) of *The Annals*.

The ideas in this book were initially tried out on the students in my black politics classes at Howard and San Francisco State Universities. I am grateful to those many students for listening and questioning. I owe a special debt to the students in my Howard black politics class of spring 1987 for conducting the project on Washington, D.C., cab drivers discussed in Chapter 4. At Howard, I also benefited from the work of three able research assistants, Bernice Taylor, Sadu Sowa, and Abraham Poole. At San Francisco State, Paul Anderson was an able and diligent research assistant. This study and a related one were supported by modest grants from the faculty research committees at Howard and San Francisco State.

I am grateful for permission to quote or adapt material from the following:

Theodore Hershbert, et al, "A Tale of Three Cities: Blacks and Immigrants in Philadelphia, 1850–80, 1930," *The Annals of the American Academy of Political and Social Science* 441 (1979): 55–81. ©The Academy of Political and Social Science. All Rights Reserved.

Linda Sharpe, "In Latest Recession, Only Blacks Suffered Job Loss," *Wall Street Journal*, September 14, 1993. ©Dow Jones & Company, Inc. All Rights Reserved Worldwide.

But the basic thing I want you to see is that while this period [the protest phase of the civil rights movement] represented a frontal attack on the doctrine and practice of white supremacy, it did not defeat the monster of racism. And this is very important, my brothers and sisters; if we are to see what is wrong we will have to face the fact that America has been and continues to be largely a racist society. And the roots of racism are very deep in this country, started a long time ago. . . . And we got to admit and we got to say to the nation that racism is evil and we must see it for what it is, racism is a faith, a form of idolatry; it is the dogma that one ethnic group is condemned to eternal inferiority and another ethnic group is somehow given the status of eternal superiority. This is what racism says, that some ethnic groups are innately inferior, worthless and defective. And don't let anybody fool you, racism is not based on any kind of empirical generalization; it is not based on going out and studying the facts and then coming back out of it and saying as a result of experimental studies that these people are behind because of environmental conditions. Racism is based on an ontological affirmation. It is the contention that the very being of a people is inferior. And the ultimate logic of racism is genocide. . . and the other thing, it is the ultimate arrogance of saying God made a creative error. This is the evilness of racism.

—Martin Luther King, Jr. (1968)

Introduction

This is a complicated book to write, dealing as it does with the nature of racism in the post–civil rights era. Trying to get a handle on this problem involves complex issues of concept formation and operationalization, methodology, data availability, empirical testing, logic, and interpretation related to the appropriate drawing of inferences from a mass of amorphous material ranging from systematic surveys to personal anecdotes. There are two basic problems that are not unique to the study of racism.[1] First, social science knowledge has not developed to the point that any consensus has emerged on how to define and give operational meaning to racism and its various modes or types. Second, putting aside the conceptual problems, social scientists have not developed a systematic way to collect even crude data longitudinally on indicators of racism; a particularly vexing problem for this book given its concern with the phenomenon in the last twenty-five years.

The best data on racism in the United States deals with its historical and attitudinal modes or dimensions. Historical studies of the phenomenon have long been conducted. And while unexplored areas of inquiry remain and interpretation differs in areas where the research has yielded a near definitive body of knowledge, compared to social scientific knowledge of racism, modern historiography is quite well advanced. While many reasons for this disjuncture may be suggested, Ruth Benedict's notion advanced more than fifty years ago that racism cannot be scientifically investigated or demonstrated but must be studied historically is probably overstated, especially given postwar advances in social scientific methodologies.[2] For example, we have reasonably good data on the attitudinal basis of racism, based on more than forty years of systematic social surveys. Although there are problems with this survey material, it does suggest the possibility of scientific progress given the investment of the necessary time and resources. In any event, we must do the best we can with the conceptual and methodological tools available. If nothing else, it is my hope that this study will modestly contribute to clarification of the conceptual and methodological problems in the empirical study of racism because the subject is too important; too critical for the well-being of the society in the here and now to be left to history and the historians or to philosophy, literary criticism, or popular writings.[3]

My procedure is first to present a historical analysis of the origins and evolution of racism in the United States, with a particular focus on the development of its justificatory ideology, the doctrine of white supremacy. This historical analysis is reasonably straightforward given the abundance of the available material, and it provides an ideational context for the conceptual and empirical analysis. I follow this historical analysis with a discussion of the concept of racism employed in the study, a concept derived from Carmichael and Hamilton's *Black Power*. Carmichael and Hamilton explicitly identify two modes or types of racism and implicitly a third. The two explicit modes are individual and institutional and the implicit mode is internal inferiorization—the inculcation by some blacks of attitudes of inferiority and self-hatred. Thus, the concept of racism used here is multidimensional, focusing on its historical development as a set of ideas, on its individual and institutional modes, and on its manifestations in attitudes and behavior internally or in the black community. This is a more adequate conception of the phenomenon than usually found in the literature because it focuses on its historical, cultural, economic, and political spheres.[4] Given an adequate concept of racism and its various types or modes, my principal aim in this study is to see what has happened to racism in the post–civil rights era.

At the outset I will briefly sketch out the broad outlines of the conceptual, methodological, and data problems that may hamper the development of knowledge and understanding of the realities of racism in the post–civil rights era. Carmichael and Hamilton define racism as the "predication of decisions and policies on considerations of race for purpose of *subordinating* a racial group and maintaining control over that group" (emphasis in original).[5] Although this concept is delinked from the justificatory ideology of white supremacy, I believe it is otherwise theoretically, empirically, and politically relevant. The problem is therefore largely methodological rather than conceptual. In other words, in view of the theoretical adequacy of the Carmichael and Hamilton concept, how do we empirically observe over time the extent to which decisions and policies, individually and institutionally, are predicated on considerations of race for the purposes of subordinating black people and maintaining control over them?

At the individual level, the problem is largely one of data on individual acts of racism. Subsumed under this category is the attitudinal component—the extent to which individual whites hold antiblack or racist attitudes that *may* predispose them to engage in racist behavior.

The data here in the form of sample surveys are reasonably good, allowing us to track this dimension of racism from the 1940s to the present with some precision. What we do not have are systematic data on behavior, the extent to which individual whites engage in overt, intentional acts of racism. Here I have to rely on amorphous material, including press reports, court cases, selected government and privately collected statistical data, and anecdotal material.

At the institutional level and in terms of internal inferiorization, we confront complex conceptual, methodological, and data problems. I address these problems in the chapters that follow, but in terms of the institutional type a critical problem is how to draw inferences from the body of available data that may constitute manifestations of institutional racism. In this regard, I argue as a principal thesis that the existence of the so-called black underclass is a major piece of evidence or indicator of institutional racism. This inference (and, to some extent, the very concept of institutional racism) is rejected by Wilson in his influential treatise, *The Truly Disadvantaged*, where he argues that the underclass is only a manifestation of historical racism. Thus, I render a detailed critique of Wilson and related underclass literature in order to advance this thesis about institutional racism.

The analysis proceeds in the following sequence. Chapter 1 presents a historical analysis of the development and evolution of the doctrine of white supremacy. This is followed in Chapter 2 by further explication of the concept of racism, especially the nettlesome institutional or indirect mode. Chapters 3 and 4 analyze the available data on individual and institutional racism in the post–civil rights era. Chapter 5 deals with the problem of internal inferiorization both conceptually and empirically. Here I rely extensively on the classical and more recent psychological studies dealing with the problem of the internalization of negative stereotypes, race group, and individual low self-esteem and self-hatred, in addition to drawing on scattered other data that might shed some light on this problem. Finally, Chapter 6 provides a critique of the underclass literature in order to advance the thesis that it is a major manifestation empirically of institutional racism.

As indicated above, there is no systematic body or even bodies of data that one might draw on to deal with the problem of scientifically demonstrating the existence and the extent of racism except at the attitudinal level. This is unfortunate given all the talk in the popular and academic media about the "declining" or "inclining" significance of racism since the 1960's civil rights revolution. Absent such a systematic repository of racism indicators, I have spent the last several years trying to identify and piece together the broadest array of material that may be helpful in dealing with a major question in American society today—the extent of racism in the post–civil rights era

Among the sources of data used are court cases, press reports, scholarly reports and studies on race and racism, various government and privately collected statistical data, as well as my own personal and professional observation and experiences as an African-American. A review of court cases dealing with race yielded a surprising amount of data on both individual and institutional racism. The courts have unrivaled data-gathering or fact-finding capacities, the envy of any scholar or journalist. And when they deal, as they often do, with allegations of racism in the United States they often find evidence of both the individual and institutional types of racism. Indeed, when the courts impose an affirmative action remedy it is often based on a finding of institutional racism, although the courts have not formally adopted this concept for purposes of judicial scrutiny. The media frequently report incidents of individual racism and occasionally institutional racism, as in the remarkable investigative report by the *Atlanta Journal-Constitution* on racial disparities in mortgage loans discussed in Chapter 4. The Community Relations Service in the Department of Justice, state and local human relations agencies, and private antidefamation groups often report on incidents of individual racism. There are also several scholarly reports on differential access by blacks and whites to employment, education, housing, and health care.

The problem with these varied sources of "data" is how to use them in order to draw valid and reliable inferences about the patterns of racism in the post–civil rights era. Use of this material in the manner proposed here raises serious methodological and interpretative problems largely ignored in the methodology of the social sciences. But success should be measured by the ends achieved as well as the methods employed. Therefore, it seems appropriate to try to delineate as precisely as possible the post–civil rights era pattern of racism, methodological limitations notwithstanding.

1

Historical Considerations on the Doctrine of White Supremacy and Its Status in the Post–Civil Rights Era

In an effort to develop a theory, or what he called a "frame of reference," for black politics Mack Jones argues that "one should begin by searching for those factors which are unique to the black political experience, for this is the information which will facilitate our understanding of blacks in the American political system."[1] Jones argues that those factors unique to the black political experience, that distinguish it from that of other ethnic or political communities, are racism—the ruthless subordination of blacks on the basis of their skin color—and the doctrine of white supremacy that is employed as its justificatory ideology. He writes, black politics is "essentially a power struggle between blacks and whites, with the latter trying to maintain their superordinate position vis-à-vis the former."[2] But this formulation is inadequate for distinguishing the phenomenon. Jones states:

> However, we need to add one other specifying condition to further distinguish black politics from other extensions of the universal power struggle. That condition is the stipulation that the ideological justification for the superordination of whites is the institutionalized belief in the inherent superiority of that group. This condition cannot be overemphasized. It says that it is not their late arrival, their patterns of migration, their numerical strength, nor their cultural patterns which, beginning with Jamestown and continuing to the present, have underlain the differential treatment of blacks; it says further that any attempt to explain the black political experience in terms of any one or any combination of these will be insufficient.[3]

Racism and the doctrine of white superiority are thus two of the three essential components or distinguishing features of the black political experience in the United States and indeed everywhere that the African and European encounter each other—Europe, the Americas, and Africa itself.[4]

It is clear that the notion of black inferiority has deep historical roots in this country. Kovel, for example, in his grimly pessimistic volume *White Racism: A Psychohistory* proposes "to delineate in depth what many know intuitively, that racism, far from being the simple delusions of a bigoted and ignorant minority, is a set of beliefs whose structure arises from the deepest levels of our lives. . . . Racism was an integral part of a stable and productive cultural order."[5] Or, as Lawrence, a legal scholar, has written more recently, "Racism in America is much more than either the conscious conspiracy of a power elite or the simple delusions of a few bigots. It is part of our common historical experience and therefore a part of our culture. It arises from the assumptions we have learned to make about the world, ourselves and others as well as the patterns of our fundamental social activities."[6] Kovel's and Lawrence's observations call attention to the importance of Jones's idea that the ideology of white supremacy is institutionalized, emanating from the base and structure of the society, widely distributed throughout such that it exercises a continuous influence, conscious or unconscious, on attitudes and behavior. Thus, an effort to assess scientifically the status of racism today requires some inquiry into its historical development and institutionalization, what West calls "a genealogical inquiry into predominant European supremacist discourse—Judeo-Christian, scientific and psychosexual."[7]

My purpose here is not to present anything like a full-scale genealogy or history of the origins and evolution of white supremacist doctrine. There are many competent studies in that regard.[8] Rather, I rely on these studies in order to sketch the major doctrinal components of the ideology, show its relationship to European attitudes toward Africans and to the American doctrine of the equality of man. This accomplished, we are in a better position to assess the status of white supremacist doctrine in the post–civil rights era.

In his monumental study of the origins and development of white attitudes toward the Negro from the sixteenth century to the early years of the Republic, Jordan identified several of what he calls "first impressions" that ultimately structured relations between white and black. They include: (1) extremely negative attitudes toward the color black and a tendency to explain it, ultimately, in terms of God's curse; (2) the notion that Africans were defective; (3) that the Africans were savages; (4) that Africans perhaps were little more than apes; and (5) that African men were "libidinous."[9] Although these negative attitudes or "first impressions" were later to be employed in the development of a systematic ideology to rationalize slavery and, to some extent, colonialization, it is not at all clear that most Europeans, even the English, believed them and it is certain that these negative attitudes about African color, religion, or culture were not determinative in the initial decision to enslave the African. Frederickson, for example, cites Davis's research to show that "distaste for blackness was not unanimous" and that indeed some early English and Dutch observers expressed admiration for African physical beauty.[10] And Fields writes:

> Even if these same Europeans were capable of writing, then or in retrospect, in terms of their superiority over their African hosts, they knew better . . . no trader who had to confront and learn to placate the power of an African chief could in practice believe that Africans were docile, childlike or primitive . . . traders afforded civilized amenities in the compounds of their African patrons could speak of African savages, white missionaries whose acquaintances included both Muslims and Christians could speak of pagan Africans; and later white slaveowners who lived in fear of insurrection could speak of docile Africans. Attitudes toward physical characteristics thus provide a poor starting point for understanding how groups of people define themselves in relation to other groups.[11]

Thus, what is important for purposes of my analysis here is not whether these attitudes were accurate, whether they were believed to be accurate, whether they were held widely among English elites or masses, or whether they were casually bantered about to describe Africans or others. The point is instead to show how, after the decision was made to subordinate Africans through slavery and colonialism, these attitudes were resurrected in the United States in order to create and institutionalize a set of ideas that would rationalize and justify this historically extraordinary instance of the exploitation and degradation of one people by another. I emphasize "resurrected in the United States" because while these same general attitudes were current in South Africa and in Latin America they did not later give rise to an elaborate doctrine of race supremacy in those places as they did in this country.[12] This is so in part because of the doctrine of the equality of man that animated the founding of the Republic and is to this day an integral part of its creed. It is probable that, without the saliency of the ethos of equality, slavery and race subordination could have developed with less attention doctrinally to African inferiority and with a more uneven pattern of institutionalization. But Thomas Jefferson in the Republic's founding document justifying the invention of America wrote, "We hold these truths to be self-evident, that all men are created equal, that they are endowed by their creator with certain inalienable rights and that among these are life, liberty and the pursuit of the happiness." Given the self-evident equality of men and their God-given right to liberty—a right that cannot be surrendered and ought not be taken—the obvious question is how one can simultaneously sanction slavery, the taking of the liberty of millions of men, women, and children. Logically, rationally—the inventors of America were quintessential rational men of the Enlightenment—one, of course, could not, except by denying their fundamental humanity. Thus, simultaneous with the elaboration of the doctrine of equality initiated with the Declaration began the elaboration of the ideology of black inferiority or black subhumanity as expressed in the Constitution's three-fifths clause, Article I, Section 2.[13] The ideology of white supremacy as it evolved over the centuries was constituted by three major elements: the idea of the white man's burden, the notion of God's curse, and the concept that there was scientific proof of black inferiority. The first two of these elements maybe traced to the initial attitudes or "first impressions" of the English toward the Africans and were most influential in the eighteenth and the nineteenth centuries. The so-called scientific basis for the doctrine has been and remains most salient in this century. I first examine the basis for the white man's burden and God's curse and then turn to the alleged scientific component of the ideology.

The notion that slavery and colonialization were the white man's burden derives from the complex of early attitudes that viewed the African as a heathen, savage, purely sensual people more akin to the apes of Africa than to the civilized English. Again, Jordan and others note that these attitudes were "first impressions" that long pre-dated slavery; however, once slavery was institutionalized, these early attitudes were in a sense rediscovered by white supremacist ideologues in order to justify the "peculiar institution" in the context of the nation's egalitarian ethos. Thus, slavery could be understood not as evil, not as the exploitation of a people but rather as a burden to be borne by the European and as a benevolence to be bestowed on the African. Ideologically, then, the institution was turned on its head in that the burden of slavery was now on the slavemaster rather than the slave. As Rudyard Kipling wrote:

Send forth the best ye breed/
go bind your sons to exile/
To serve your captives need/

To wait in heavy harness/
On fluttered folk and wild/
Your new caught, sullen peoples, half devil and half naked.[14]

Numerous accounts of African society and culture were reiterated so as to establish the European's burden to civilize the savages. One of these has its origins in Christianity's universalistic, proselytizing ethos, which requires that non-Christians, savage or not, be brought into the fold. It was this monotheistic notion that there was only one true, universal religion and that the duty of all good Christians was to spread the "word" throughout the world that lay at the core of its aggressive racism. Forrest Woods writes in his aptly titled *The Arrogance of Faith*, "Herein lay the fundamental component of the Christian's racism, his inherent inability to leave other people alone."[15] But while Christianity may have been hostile to all other religions (Islam, Judaism, Hinduism, and so on, it was most extreme toward the religions of Africa and the Native Americans, arguing that they were either defective or indeed not religions at all. Jordan claims, "Englishmen were ill prepared to see any legitimacy in African religious practices. Judged by Christian cosmology Negroes stood in a separate category of men."[16] Jordan, quoting some of the earliest English accounts of African culture in terms of religion, says they "were a people of beastly living, without a God, law, religion or commonwealth," or, in the words of another, "Negroes in color and condition are little more than devils incarnate . . . the devil . . . has infused prodigious idolatry into their hearts, enough to relish his palate and aggrandize their tortures when he gets power to fry their souls, as the raging sun has already scorched their cole black carcasses."[17]

Thus, one important part of the white man's burden was to Christianize the heathen, but Jordan states, "heathenism was for the Englishmen one inherent characteristic of savage men."[18] Consequently, the Christian impulse aside, a further component of the white man's burden was related to the notion of civilizing the savage through the processes of slavery and colonialism. "Evidence" of savage behavior include reports of polygamy, infanticide, ritualistic murder, and food and dress patterns (the fact that men and women in certain parts of Africa wore very little apparel compared to the English). Interestingly, in light of late nineteenth-and twentieth-century stereotypes about blacks, Jordan reports that, a couple of hundred years before, the English described the Africans as "libidinous men, incapable of controlling their appetites sexual or otherwise." Africans were described as "very greedie eaters and no less drinkers," as large propagators of children, as "treacherous and thievish," and as "much addicted to uncleanness." Africans were said to "lie constantly," to have a "vicious humor," and that "another innate quality they have is to steal anything they can lay their hands on, especially from whites."[19] Variations on these negative stereotypes have characterized racist discourse about blacks from slavery to this day, but they have their origins in inconsequential "first impressions" that were resurrected, elaborately distorted, and institutionalized as an essential component of racism's justificatory ideology.

The most pervasive of these stereotypes is undoubtedly the sexual one. Jordan and other students of racist discourse have repeatedly remarked on the European fascination with African sexuality.[20] As shown below some of this fixation is rooted in the alleged sexual nature of the offense that led to God's curse of Ham, but, as Jordan observes, it runs throughout much of the early commentary. The sexual aggressiveness of black women was especially noted, as in this eighteenth-century observation about black women possessed of a "temper hot and lascivious, making no scruples to prostitute themselves to Europeans for a very slender sum, so great is their inclination to white men."[21]

The most dastardly lie about African sexuality was the attempt to link it to bestiality. As Jordan writes, "If Negroes were likened to beasts, there was in Africa a beast which was likened to men. It was a strange and eventually tragic happenstance of nature that the Negro's homeland was the habitat of the animal which in appearance most resembles man. The animal called the 'orang-outang' by contemporaries (actually the chimpanzee) was native to those parts of western Africa where the slave trade was heavily concentrated."[22] This led to a series of speculations and assertions that there occurred in Africa a "bestial" copulation between apes and Africans. Although it was rarely asserted that the African himself was a beast, an offspring of this copulation, Jordan quotes the eminent sixteenth-century French political theorist Jean Bodin as stating categorically, "A promiscuous coition of men and animals took place, wherefore the regions of Africa produce for us so many monsters."[23] This absurd idea fits not only the stereotype of blacks as a lewd and lascivious people but takes to its ultimate logic the notion of the African as a subhuman being.

Throughout the eighteenth and nineteenth centuries various of these notions purporting to show African savagery were employed by the propagandists for slavery in their efforts to provide justification for the manifestly unjustifiable. Similar rationales were employed to justify the colonialization of Africa and, to a lesser degree, the subordination of the native people of the Americas. But during this period the idea of slavery as the will of God was probably more influential than this secular notion of the white man's burden. Religion—specifically

Christianity—was much more influential in the thinking of both elite and mass in the early years of the Republic than was secular thought. And while it may seem paradoxical that adherents of a faith committed to the universalistic principle that all men share a common bond in Christ could embrace slavery, it only seems so, for as Wood writes, "English North Americans embraced slavery *because* they were Christians, not in spite of it."[24] That is, "Christianity in the five centuries since its message was first carried to the people of the new world—and in particular to the natives and the transplanted Africans of English North America and the United States—has been fundamentally racist in its ideology, organization and practice."[25]

The resolution of the apparent contradiction largely involved a theologically contorted interpretation of a story not in the Christian New Testament but in the King James Version of the Judaic Old Testament and earlier Talmudic writings.[26] Jordan traces this interpretation of the African as the divinely cursed people to the attempt by the early English to explain the African's black skin. This nexus between the curse, blackness, and slavery provides a parallelism, given the historic animus of the English toward blackness. Jordan notes that to the English "the most arresting characteristic of the newly discovered African was his color."[27] Long before the English knew there were black people they held profoundly negative attitudes toward blackness in the abstract. Jordan quotes from the sixteenth-century Oxford English Dictionary definition of black:

> Deeply stained with dirt, soiled, dirty, foul . . . . Having dark, deadly purposes, malignant, pertaining to or involving death, deadly; baneful, disastrous, sinister . . . . Foul, iniquitous, atrocious, horrible, wicked . . . . Indicating disgrace, censure liability to punishment, etc.[28]

Given the intense meaning of blackness to the English obviously they would seek an explanation of its cause(s) so as perhaps to understand its nature and significance. Jordan observes that the first explanation was in terms of climate; the extraordinary heat of equatorial Africa had literally turned the African black. This explanation was soon set aside as it became clear that skin color was invariant, a genetic characteristic. The explanation then turned to the Bible. In Genesis 9:10 the story is told that after the flood Ham had looked upon his father's nakedness as Noah lay drunk, but the other two sons covered their father without looking at him. When Noah awoke he cursed Cannan, the son of Ham, saying he would be "servants of servants." The theological contortion here is that this story may logically imply slavery but it says nothing about color.[29] However, in Jewish folklore and the Talmud the story of Noah and his sons is told in a way that specifically makes black skin a curse. There are many versions of the story in Jewish tradition but the following makes the relevant point:

> . . . therefore, it must be Cannan, your first born, whom enslave. And since you have disabled me . . . doing ugle things in black-ness of night, Cannan's children shall be borne ugle and black. Moreover, because you twisted your head around to see my na-kedness, your grandchildren's hair shall be twisted into kinks and their eyes red; again because your lips jested at my misfortune, theirs shall swell; and because you neglected my nakedness, you shall go naked and their male members shall be shamefull elongated.[30]

From the justification of slavery at the founding of the Republic to defense of segregation during the civil rights era, this notion of the curse has been a frequently invoked element of the doctrine of white supremacy and black inferiority and the consequent imperative of black subordination. This element of the doctrine resonated particularly well among white Christian fundamentalists in the south. (As a young person growing up in rural Louisiana in the 1950s and early 1960s, I often heard this notion of the curse and the idea that blackness denoted inferiority invoked by white radio preachers. This latter notion was explained by noting that most successful blacks at the time—Adam Clayton Power, Robert Weaver, and Ralph Bunche—had light skin color and thus "white blood" accounted for their relative success.) It was also not without influence throughout the country. But in the late nineteenth century and especially in the twentieth century science begin to replace God as the most influential component of the doctrine of white supremacy.

The ideology of white supremacy as the justificatory basis for the subordination of the African really turns on the basis less of evidence of European or, in the United States case, Anglo-Saxon superiority and more on arguments for the inferiority of the African. If one views this ideology as constituted by the three principal components identified here, then it is possible to locate the influence of each component temporally. That is, it appears that the first two components were most influential in the United States during the eighteenth and nineteenth centuries while the last has been most influential in this century. To be sure, each component has been influential throughout the country's history even now, thus it is a matter of the saliency of a given component at a particular time. The white man's burden and God's will were the principal rationales offered to justify the slave trade and slavery, while the scientific rationale came into prominence late in the nineteenth century as a justification for the overthrow of Reconstruction and the imposition of the system of racial segregation.[31] Each component, therefore, may be associated with a particular mode or type of racial subordination. In addition, it is probable that the persuasiveness (at least at the elite level) of the arguments embodied in the white man's burden began to wane somewhat, constituted as it was by such obvious misconceptions, distortions, prejudices, and unsustainable assumptions. Similarly, the saliency of God's curse probably began to lose some of its power to persuade as the nation's culture became more secular (again this would perhaps especially be the case among the nation's liberal establishment centered in the northeast). Related to this is the progress of science itself, which contributed to the decline of religious doctrines as explanatory devices and made science the last word in the explanation of social as well as natural phenomena.

In any event, certainly by the dawn of the twentieth century so-called scientific proof of black inferiority was offered as the central rationale for their continued subordination. Rhett Jones's short but cogent essay suggests that this scientific "proof" may be divided into three "ideal types" or, in terms of academic organization, disciplines: sociological, physiological, and psychological.[32] The sociological analysis sought to prove black inferiority on the basis of comparative analysis of statistical data on the social organization of black and white communities in terms of such things as unemployment, housing conditions, educational attainments, family dissolution's, out-of-wedlock births, alcohol abuse, and crime. On the basis of this type of analysis, sociologists concluded that blacks' moral attitudes were inferior to those of whites.[33] They also sought to demonstrate a "natural aversion" between the races that precluded equality and that those blacks who had achieved a measure of status in the United States were mulattos, thus proving again the superiority of "white blood."[34] The physiological approach usually dealt with brain or, more precisely, skull sizes, arguing that the average black brain was smaller than the average white brain and that there was a direct correlation between skull size and intelligence. Jones, for example, cites the work of Robert Bean, a professor of anatomy at the University of Michigan, that purported to show the following pattern: the largest brains were those of white males, followed by white females, black females, and black males in descending order.[35]

It was, however, the discipline of psychology, not sociology or biology, that eventually became the principal means by which "evidence" of black inferiority was established.[36] This is so in part because sociological explanations are inherently variable, given changes in the social environment, and the proponents of black inferiority were more interested in establishing an invariant, genetic basis for race group differences. Advances in sociological methods also undermined the validity of this work because the simple evidence of statistical disparities is not sufficient to establish race-based differences. For example, W. E. B. DuBois, in his classic sociological study *The Philadelphia Negro* (1899), also showed statistical disparities between the races but argued that they were to be explained on the basis of environmental rather than genetic differences between the races. And the physiological data on skull size, for example, was fairly easily discredited. Jones, for example, notes that Bean's results were based on flawed data. He used unclaimed bodies in order to measure skull sizes, which meant, as Jones writes, "The worse of whites were being compared to the entire black population. Bean argued that the lowest type of white person left a body unclaimed while all classes of blacks did so."

From the 1900s to the 1930s or 1940s (and, of course, as discussed later in this chapter, to some extent even today) psychology was, as one observer said, "the most powerful weapon in the arsenal of the racist." The fundamental premise of the research that sought to show that blacks were inherently inferior may be stated in terms of the "hereditarian doctrine," which asserted that given the obvious inherited differences in physical traits between the races—skin color, hair texture, facial features—and the manifest differences in levels of social and economic development between the races, it might be that these latter differences were also inherited. This, of course, is but a statement of one side of the familiar "nature vs. nurture" debate with respect to explanation of human behavior. On the one hand, the "nurture" school of thought views most differences in human behavior, especially at the group level, as a function largely of differences in environmental conditions that would change with changes in those conditions, while the "nature" school of thought views these group differences as invariant, a function of inherited, genetic differences between the races. Given its fundamental organizing assumptions about the source of group differences, the intelligence quotient (IQ) test became the principal tool to establish empirically the proposition of black inferiority.

The IQ test has a long, disgraceful, and by now largely discredited history as an instrument of ethnic and social class discrimination.[37] As Chief Judge Robert Peckham of the U.S. District Court for the Northern District of California wrote in *Larry P. vs. Riles:*

We must recognize at the outset that the history of the IQ test . . . is not the history of neutral scientific discoveries translated into educational reform. It is at least in the early years, a history of racial prejudice, of social Darwinism and of the use of scientific "mystique" to legitimate such prejudices.[38]

Many problems with the test in terms of race may be identified. It is beyond the scope of this analysis and my competence to review them all, but it is important to discuss the more significant ones. First, the key variables—race and intelligence—are not definable in an objective, universalistic way. With respect to the latter "most authorities agree that we can not define, much less measure intelligence and virtually all agree that standardized tests of whatever sort do not measure innate capacity. The tests measure the skills tested."[39] And with respect to race Karen Fields is correct that "with a few well publicized exceptions, no one holding reputable academic credentials openly adheres to the view that race is a physical fact. Most now understand that, from a scientific standpoint, race can be no more than a statistical description of the characteristics of a given population—a description, moreover, that holds good only as long as the members do not marry outside the group."[40] Although it is commonly held that humanity may be neatly divided into three races—caucasoid, mongoloid, and negroid—most scientists view these categories as more sociological rather than biological. Generally, homogeneous populations do not exist and traits are not discontinuous between populations, therefore a particular race can be classified only in terms of the relative frequencies of various traits. Moreover, it has been found that differences between individuals of the same race are often much greater than the differences between the "average" individuals of different races.

Second, as Wechsler wrote in 1944, "We have eliminated the colored vs. white factor admitting at the outset that our norms can not be used for the colored population of the United States. . . . We omitted the colored population from our first standardization because we did not feel that the norms derived by mixing the population could be interpreted without special provisos and reservations."[41] Yet the results were presented and interpreted to establish the case for the inferiority of blacks. A final point of manifest bias is in terms of how disparities in test results between males and females and blacks and whites were treated. Early versions of the Stanford-Binet test were modified because the results were different for males and females and the designers assumed such differences were not valid. However, no such modifications to take account of racial differences in results have been tried by the various testing companies. As Professor Leon Kamin testified in *Larry P. v. Riles*:

> If one looks at what happened, it is perfectly clear the testmakers have a pre conception that males and females do not differ in intelligence. It seems quite clear from the fact . . . that they continue to include in the test items which do discriminate between races or social classes . . . [that] at least they do not have a preconception that races and social classes are equal in intelligence.[42]

Indeed, it is reasonable to assume the contrary; that the testmakers assume race differences in intelligence.

Apart from these rather obvious conceptual and methodological problems (and there are others, including problems in statistical analysis and interpretation), a brief inquiry into the history of the use of the test in the United States will serve to make the point that the so-called scientific proof of black inferiority has little more credibility than the notions of the white man's burden or God's curse. First, when Alfred Binet developed what was to become in this country the Stanford-Binet test he insisted that while it was useful in distinguishing between "backward" and "normal" children it did not measure a fixed, innate, or genetic characteristic. However, several years later, when Lewis Terman at Stanford developed his version of the test, he argued that it measured a fixed, innate ability and that it "will ultimately result in curtailing the reproduction of feeble mindedness and in the elimination of an enormous amount of crime, pauperism and industrial inefficiency."[43] We also now know—thanks to the skillful detective work of Kamin— that the work of Cyril Burt, the English psychologist who did much to establish the notion of the inheritability of intelligence, was a fraud, with Burt going so far as literally to falsify data to support his conclusions.[44] But perhaps the most telling evidence of the bankruptcy of the IQ test as it relates to ethnicity and race is the results of its use, viewed historically, which show quite clearly its ethnic and class bias, and, contrary to the hereditarian school, that (as measured) intelligence is a function of environmental or situational factors rather than some fixed, innate quality.

In the early part of this century, various versions of the IQ test were administered to selected ethnic and racial groups in the United States. The results mirrored almost exactly the ethnic status hierarchy in the country and the relative socioeconomic status of the ethnic groups studied, with people of white Anglo-Saxon Protestant (WASP) and Nordic descent testing high and Slavs, Jews, and blacks testing low.[45] For example, Carl Brigham in his 1923 book *A Study of American Intelligence* concluded that 83 percent of Jews, 80 percent of Hungarians, and 79 percent of Italians were "feeble-minded." Brigham then generalized in the following language:

> The Nordics are . . . rulers, organizers and aristocrats . . . individualistic, self reliant and jealous of their personal freedom. . . . As a result they are usually protestant . . . The Alpine race is always and everywhere a race of peasants. The Alpine is the perfect slave, the ideal serf . . . the unstable component and the lack of coordinating and reasoning power so often found among the Irish . . . we have no separate intelligence distribution for the Jews . . . [but] our army sample of immigrants from Russia is at least half Jewish. . . . Our figures, then, would rather tend to disprove the popular belief that the Jew is intelligent . . . he has the head form, stature, and color of his Alpine neighbor.[46]

Nothing more clearly demonstrates the environmental rather than hereditary basis of intelligence as measured by these tests than the foregoing. In the early part of this century Jews, for the most part, were concentrated in poverty-stricken ghettos and *consequently* scored relatively low on the tests. Today, Jews are near the top of the social class structure and *consequently* score near the top in the various tests of intelligence. By contrast, blacks fifty years later remain near the bottom of the class structure and *consequently* continue to rank near the bottom in IQ scores.

Unlike with the other two elements of the ideology of white supremacy-the white man's burden and God's will—I have gone to considerable length to refute the scientific component. This is because the other components are based on obvious lies or distortions, myths, and religious prejudices that do not require refutation or are in their nature beyond rational discourse. Yet, in spite of the anemic status of the IQ tests as proof or evidence of black inferiority, they held near complete sway over mass and elite thinking and dominated scientific research until about World War II, institutionalized in the pages of the leading quality magazines and the curriculum of the nation's leading universities.[47]

By the 1930s and 1940s the dominance of the view of scientific proof of black inferiority was under effective challenge within scientific and intellectual communities. Even during its heyday and within the discipline of psychology, there were scholars who challenged the notion of black inferiority, but it was a new generation of sociologists and anthropologists (particularly the latter's use of culture as a powerful explanatory concept) who as "cultural environmentalist" gained ascendancy over the geneticists.[48]

By the end of World War II most social scientists (including psychologists) had come to the following rough consensus regarding the relationship between race and intelligence: If there are significant racial differences in intelligence, it is beyond the competence of science to demonstrate them. Thus, without evidence to the contrary science assumes equality of the races although this too cannot be scientifically demonstrated. Although there was ongoing work by scores of scholars that served to undermine the scientific basis of white supremacy,[49] perhaps no single work was more influential in the United States then Gunnar Myrdal's *An American Dilemma: The Negro Problem and American Democracy*, published in 1944.

Although Myrdal's work has been subject to extensive criticism by black scholars—in terms of its origins and inspiration, the selection of Myrdal and his team of scholars, which subordinated black scholars, and its use of the flawed moral dilemma notion as a conceptual framework—fifty years later its two volumes remain the most exhaustive, comprehensive study of race ever undertaken in the United States. The study was inspired by liberal, internationalist elements of the white power structure who, concerned about America's post war role, saw a need to abolish legalized racism if the United States was to be an effective competitor with the Soviet Union in the cold war battle for the support and allegiance of the third world. Familiar with the growing body of research that cast doubt on the scientific rationale for racism, these powerful white men thought that the most useful thing they could do at the time was to present the American people with the facts as a first step in the long struggle to abolish legal distinctions based on race. The Carnegie Corporation commissioned Myrdal, a relatively unknown Swedish economist and member of parliament with no interest or experience in research on race, to direct the research project. Myrdal was selected rather than one of the many well-qualified white American students or an African-American because it was thought he would bring a tone of neutrality and objectivity to the study that would enhance its credibility.[50] Myrdal then assembled a distinguished team of black and white students of race and American society and with ample time and money examined virtually every aspect of the "Negro problem"—physiological, historical, psychological, cultural, economic, and political— and its findings and conclusions demolished the hereditarian explanation of the status and condition of blacks and replaced it with

environmentalism. Immediately recognized as a classic, the work became the point of departure for postwar research on race.

In the introduction to volume 1 Myrdal succinctly stated the environmentalist thesis. He wrote that the "Negro problem" is really a "white
problem," and "If the Negro was a 'failure' as he obviously was by
every criterion that white society recognized as valid, then he was a
failure because white America made him so." And then, noting the
comprehensive character of his inquiry, he continued, "All recent attempts to reach scientific explanations of why the Negroes are what
they are and why they live as they do have regularly led to determinants on the white side of the race line."[51] In other words, it was not the
Negro's skull size, the measure of his genetically endowed intelligence,
or the retention of his African cultural heritage that accounted for the
relatively low level of development of the race; rather, it was the environment of systematic subordination imposed and sustained by white
people and the institutions of American society they controlled. This
view slowly became dominant in intellectual circles in the United States.
Thus, the last leg of white supremacism's three-leg stool of the white
man's burden, God's curse, and science was broken.

On the Status of the Doctrine of White Supremacy in the Post–Civil Rights Era

Doctrinal expressions of racism in terms of the ideology of black
inferiority have definitely declined in the post–civil rights era. Racism,
in this sense, is no longer respectable. Formerly open white supremacists such as Governor George Wallace, Senator Strom Thurmond, or
Rev. Jerry Falwell have repudiated the doctrine's three components, and
even a virtually unreconstructed racist like Louisiana's state senator,
David Duke, does not choose to justify his antiblack rhetoric and policies openly in terms of the ideology of white supremacy. Public persons
simply do not express in public racist ideas of supremacy (what is said
in private by whites, I, as an African-American, am not of course privy
to).[52] And when there is the occasional slip, as with remarks by Agri-
culture Secretary Earl Butz, television personalities Howard Cosell,
Jimmy "the Greek" Snyder, and Andy Rooney, or Los Angeles Dodgers
Vice President Al Campanis, there is usually a quick denial or an apol-
ogy and frequently the censure or dismissal of the person, all amid much
public handwringing about ethnic and racial sensitivities.[53] At the mass
level openly white supremacist ideas are more frequently heard, yet as
the attitude data analyzed in Chapter 3 reveals, there has been a substantial decline in expressions of black inferiority since the 1940s. Thus,

a canvas of material on the status of the doctrine in the post–civil rights era is sparse.

In terms of the uncivilized, savage, or animal-like character of blacks that burdens whites, one still occasionally reads echos of Kipling's ode. For example, during the Reagan administration, Marianne Mele Hall was nominated for a minor post in the federal bureaucracy. In the course of Senate consideration of her nomination, it was learned that she had coauthored a volume called *Foundations of Sand: A Hard Look at the Social Sciences.* The book suggested that the problems of the so-called black underclass could be traced to the several hundred-year-old stereotypes of black inferiority in terms of laziness and sexual promiscuity, arguing that as long as "blacks insist on their jungle freedoms, their women, their avoidance of personal responsibility and their abhorrence of the work ethic" there was nothing the government could do to solve their problems.[54] Frederick Goodwin, director of the Alcohol, Drug Abuse, and Mental Health Administration in the Bush administration's Health and Human Services Department, made similar remarks linking the behavior of young black men in the cities to jungles, apes, and hypersexuality. At a 1992 conference at the department dealing with inner-city violence, Goodwin said:

> If you look, for example, at male monkeys, especially in the wild, roughly half of them survive to adulthood. The other half die by violence. That is the natural way of it for males, to knock each other off, and in fact there are some interesting evolutionary implications of that because the same hyper-aggressive monkeys who kill each other are also hypersexual, so they copulate more and therefore they reproduce more to offset the fact that half of them are dying. . . . Maybe it isn't just the careless use of the word when people call certain areas of certain cities jungles, that we may have gone back to what might be more natural, without all of the social controls that we have upon ourselves as a civilization over thousands of years in our evolution.[55]

Such expressions of black inferiority by whites in the elite are relatively infrequent in the post–civil rights era but at the mass level such expressions are quite frequently reported during incidents of neighborhood turf conflicts between blacks and whites (see also the survey data discussed in Chapter 5).[56]

There is, as has been the case historically, a psychosexual undertone or overlay to these expressions. The use by the 1988 Bush campaign of the now infamous Willie Horton ad was an indirect, subtle appeal to this racist stereotype. For twenty-eight days during the 1988 fall campaign an ad showing a picture of Horton, a person very dark in skin color and in a photograph that he himself said pictured him as "depraved and maniacal" and as "the devil incarnate" (Horton says at the time the photograph was taken he had not been permitted a shave or haircut for six months or more) was shown on national television.[57] A convicted murderer sentenced to life in prison, Horton was released on a weekend pass under the Massachusetts furlough program during which time he was accused of brutally raping a white woman and assaulting her husband (he proclaims innocence in both the murder and the rape). The ostensible purpose of the ad was to show that the Democratic nominee, the Massachusetts governor, was "soft on crime" but a clearly intended by-product, if not its primary purpose, was to arouse racial fears by appealing to the stereotype of the savage black wantonly raping a white woman.[58] As the Washington political scientist and commentator William Schneider observed at the time, "The fear of crime originates in racial fear . . . fear of crime is associated with blacks. I don't argue he is running strongly because he is racist. He is not a racist. But there is a racist component."[59] This component of racism in terms of the psychosexual was given its most explicit expression in terms of post–civil rights sensitivities on race in a column by Patrick Buchanan, the influential conservative columnist, television commentator, Nixon and Reagan administration functionary, and 1992 candidate for the Republican presidential nomination. In a column written in the immediate aftermath of the alleged gang rape of a young white woman in New York's Central Park by a group of young black men, Buchanan wrote a column dripping with the language and symbolism of the white man's burden.

> How does a civilized, self-confident people deal with enemies who gang rape their women? Armies stand them up against a wall and shoot them, or we hang them. . . . If . . . the eldest of that wolf pack were tried, convicted and hanged in Central Park by June 1 and the 13 and 14-year-olds were stripped, horse whipped and sent to prison, the park might soon be safe again for women. Historically, civilized nations have put an end to savagery by traditional means. With their conquering armies they put fear of death into the barbarians, then, with religious conversion, they instilled

fear of God. Thus, did self confident nations "civilize" the barbarians.[60]

A final example of the persistence of the psychosexual dynamic in post–civil rights era racism is the story of the eventual desegregation of the Forrest City, Arkansas, schools. In 1970 when Forrest City, Arkansas, was required to desegregate its schools it abolished the senior prom and did not reinstate it until 1988. At the first public meeting after the schools were ordered to be integrated, "The hall was packed with angry men shouting things like 'I won't have some black boy looking up my girl's dress.' " Finally, once the prom was reinstated, strict rules to forbid interracial intimate contact were established by school authorities because, as one white parent said, "It's a secret, unspoken fear around here. Dancing leads to touching, touching leads to mingling. Parents worry if I let my child go to an integrated dance, does that mean she'll start dating someone of the opposite race." And one white male student said, "Sure, I'd go to a mixed prom. But I tell you one thing. If some black guy started messing around with a white girl, that would be it. I'd be stroking heads."[61] This would be a trivial and somewhat humorous commentary to most blacks on what Langston Hughes used to refer to as "the ways of white folks," but for familiarity with the deep-seated history of these remarks and their consequences for black access to education, employment, and housing, not to mention the consequences for the life of the African-American male caught in the wrong place at the wrong time.

A few quotations, columns, books, or news accounts do not suffice to establish a pattern. In fact, in isolation the anecdotes cited above might be viewed as innocuous compared to the earlier virulence of the expressions of the doctrine of white supremacy.

This may be so, but to be able to find "isolated" documentary material today is evidence of the tenacity in the minds of many Americans of their ancestors' "first impressions" of the Africans.[62] It also strikes me (and this may be just a personal idiosyncrasy) that the role of black athletes in mass consumer sports—especially football and basketball (less so in baseball, where blacks are less dominant)—reinforces aspects of this component of white supremacist ideology.[63]

Especially at the college level at places like Duke, Georgetown, or Georgia Tech, where black students and faculty are nearly as scarce as a black face in the United States Senate, it seems incongruous to see young black boys running up and down the floor or field for the fun and profit of white people.[64] There is also an incongruity in watching the even relatively well paid professional athletes in football and basketball do the same thing while virtually all the owners, coaches, and highly paid sportscasters are white. This may contribute to or reinforce what one commentator refers to as the "pseudo-scientific prattle" about blacks excelling in athletics because of genetically distinct physical features.[65] As the coach of an American Olympic team was quoted as saying, "The Negro excels in the events he does because he is closer to the primitive than the white man."[66] Or as Underwood wrote in *Life*, "Even as the racial imbalance distorts the black youngsters, perception of sport as the most accessible avenue up and out, it reinforces the white man's unholy stereotype of the one-dimensional black gladiator. . . . The picture of the exuberant, intimidating, posturing, preening, trash talking black kid doing his end zone disco after a TD is the image of big money sport. It also happens to be the image of inner city youth."[67]

This "unholy stereotype" is given further currency by the relatively low graduation rates of black athletes, the occasional press stories about black athletes in college who are unable to read, and by the sense that many are in college because of their muscles, not their minds. For example, when the National Collegiate Athletic Association instituted Proposition 42/48 requiring that students score a relatively modest 700 on the Scholastic Aptitude Test or 15 on the American College Test and earn a C average in specified courses more than 80 percent of those disqualified were black.[68] This stereotype even finds its way into the positions blacks have traditionally played. Ira Berkow, the *New York Times* sports columnist writes, "The prejudice was that blacks might be able to run, but they couldn't think, or even play under pressure. And quarterback was the ultimate thinking and pressure position."[69] Berkow notes that this barrier has now been broken, with a number of successful black quarterbacks and middle-linebackers but "now, however, there is another whispering refrain around college campuses' 'well, they can play all the positions but they still can't do it in the classroom.' "[70]

Again, the view that the disproportionate representation and frequent exploitation of blacks in mass consumption sport represents symbolically stereotypical images of blacks incorporated in the white man's burden may be idiosyncratic and relatively inconsequential, but the foregoing suggests that my perspective is shared by respected sports commentators, who are white and therefore perhaps more conversant with what white people really think as they cheer "Magic," "Kareem," "Bo," and all the rest.

In the media one hears or reads relatively little about the second component of the ideology—the notion of God's curse.[71] Many white churches and church leaders in the wake of the civil rights revolution explicitly repudiated the doctrine. Jerry Falwell, the influential leader of the Christian right's political action network, renounced the doctrine although he initially denied having ever embraced it. But after he was given a tape of a 1958 sermon in which he espoused segregation on the basis of Genesis 9:18–27, he admitted that he had once preached the doctrine of the curse but now says, "he was wrong, that he knew [even in 1958] in his heart that segregation was wrong but he was influenced by his Bible college teaching."[72] In the late 1970s the Elders of the Church of Jesus Christ of Latter-Day Saints (the Mormons) repudiated their doctrinal teachings on the inferiority of blacks, in part as a result of pressure from Mormon politicians (such as Michigan Governor George Romney) with national political ambitions. And in 1990 even the dominant church authorities in South Africa moved officially to change their teachings on the biblical basis of apartheid. Thus, formally the doctrine of black inferiority on the basis of God's curse is largely extinguished, although not completely, as evidenced by the Bob Jones case decided by the Supreme Court in 1983, in which the Court held that the university's authorities apparently had a sincere religious belief that the Bible required racial discrimination.[73] Not so with the third component of the ideology—science which has experienced a modest resurgence in the post–civil rights era.

As in the past the IQ test is the principal tool of the racist ideologue in the post–civil rights era, but controversial research on skull size and its relationship to intelligence and social behavior also continues. At the 1989 meeting of the American Association for the Advancement of Science, Professor J. Phillipe Rushlon, a psychologist at Canada's University of Western Ontario, presented a paper on this subject. The paper argued that Asians have larger and heavier brains, Europeans fall in the middle, while Africans are last in brain size and weight, and that on over fifty different behavioral measures a correlation between race and brain size is observed, with Asians at the top in socially acceptable behavior, Caucasians in the middle, and Africans at the bottom. As examples, Rushlon noted that Asians mature more slowly, are less impulsive, more sexually restrained, law abiding, and stable in health and marriage. And again all this is said to be a function of relative differences between the races in terms of their brain sizes. Overall the paper concludes that the African is lowest on the "evolutionary ladder."[74]

But the key work in science remains the IQ test. In 1969 Professor Arthur Jensen, an educational psychologist, published in the *Harvard Educational Review* the results of a study he had conducted among children of different races. The article contended that intelligence is hereditary and is not susceptible to material alteration by the environment and that because blacks tend to inbreed, their genetic potential is depressed more than whites.[75] Although Jensen's study was vigorously refuted in a subsequent issue of the *Review*, [76] it became the most widely publicized and arguably most influential of the post–civil rights era treatises offering a scientific rationale for black subordination. Yet as Professor Jerry Hirsch shows in his aptly titled monograph "To Unfrock the Charlatans," it was Stanford University's William Shockley, a Nobel laureate, who played the crucial role in restoring the IQ test to a measure of respectability in scientific circles.[77] With substantial support from wealthy individuals and organizations devoted to overturning the *Brown* school desegregation decision and undermining the intellectual and legal rationales for the civil rights movement, Shockley engaged in a decade-long campaign to get the scientific community and policymakers to accept the proposition that blacks are genetically inferior to whites.[78] As Hirsch writes:

> He [Shockley] had taken up the segregationists' cause and carried their fight to the inner sanctum of the country's highest tribunal of science, onto the pages of its most prestigious journal and also onto those of the most influential and widely circulating journal (*Science*), to the Congress of the United States and onto the pages of its influential and widely circulating *Congressional Record*, and into the White House in the person of the advisor to President Nixon for Science and Technology . . . and through presidential advisor Moynihan . . . even into a meeting of President Nixon's cabinet.[79]

At a 1967 meeting of the National Academy of Science, Shockley presented a paper urging the Academy to adopt his proposal for what he called a eugenics approach to our "national human quality problems." The paper titled "Try the Simplest Cases Approach to the Heredity Poverty-Crime Problem" sought answers to such questions as "To what extent are urban slums the result of poor heredity? Is the genetic quality of the human population being eroded by differential birth rates in various social, economic and educational groups? Are genetic factors responsible for a significant part of the racial differences in educational and economic development."[80] The Academy accepted Shockley's proposal and appointed a committee on "Human Genetics and Urban Slums." However, in its report the committee rejected the substance of Shockley's argument, noting that it did not state a scientific problem that could be addressed by any existing data or methods.

There is no scientific basis for a statement that there are or that there are not substantial hereditary differences in intelligence between Negro and white populations. In the absence of some now-unforeseen way of equalizing all aspects of the environment, answers to this question can hardly be more than reasonable guesses . . . [the report of the committee then expressed] the conviction that none of the current methods can produce unambiguous results. To shy away from seeking the truth is one thing; to refrain from collecting still more data that would be of uncertain meaning but would invite misuse is another.[81]

This, of course, was but a restatement of what had been the emergent consensus in the scientific community since the late 1940s. Yet five years later the Academy reversed itself in part on the basis of the influence of Jensen's article and pressure from those concerned about academic freedom and the right of scholars to pursue a line of inquiry, notwithstanding how the results might be misused. Thus, the Academy's 1972 report said, "Investigation of the nature and significance of . . . racial hereditary differences in the human species is a proper and socially relevant subject . . . to the extent which methodology gives promise of reasonable progress, the investigation should be encouraged."[82]

Thus, although it is controversial and probably a minority view in the scientific community, the ideology of white supremacy is nevertheless clearly alive and well in the post–civil rights era, insofar as its scientific component is concerned. In a 1988 survey of 400 randomly selected high school science teachers (94 percent of whom were white) 26 percent said they believed (and perhaps therefore taught the children, black and white) that it was definitely or probably true that "some races are more intelligent than others."[83] And in 1991 in spite of criticism even from some of his conservative colleagues, Charles Murray, author of *Losing Ground: American Social Policy, 1950–1980,* a book that provided an influential intellectual rationale for the Reagan administration's anti social welfare philosophy and policies, is working (in collaboration with Richard Herrenstein, the Harvard psychologist) on a study to determine whether there are differences in intelligence between blacks and whites that might help explain differences in their social and economic standings (I would bet my tenure as to what the ultimate results, conclusions, and recommendations will be).[84] There is thus in respectable intellectual and policy-making circles today the view that the terrible conditions of a large segment of the African-American community is a function not of centuries of racial subordination and exploitation but rather of their nature, their very being; doomed to be forever at the bottom of the social structure. In today's argot there is a "permanent underclass" for which government ought not—because it cannot—do anything to change. They still say about black people, incredibly, that "God made a creative error."

2

Racism: Toward Conceptual Clarification of the Institutional Mode

Having dealt with the historical development and evolution of racism's justificatory ideology, we are now in position to deal with racism itself. Although the literature contains many definitions or concepts of racism, I employ Carmichael and Hamilton's because it is delinked from the justificatory ideology of white supremacy, because it is linked to the possession and exercise of power—a central concern in any analysis of racism—because of its relevance to the post–civil rights era policy debate on affirmative action and because of its multidimensional character. In *Black Power* racism is defined as the predication of decisions and policies on considerations of race for the purpose of subordinating a racial group and maintaining control over it. This definition says nothing about why this is done, its purposes, or rationales, thus it does not infer anything, about the superiority or inferiority of the groups involved. It does not say, as many definitions and concepts of racism do, that racism involves the belief in the superiority, inherent or otherwise, of a particular group and on that basis policies are implemented to subordinate and control it. Rather, it simply indicates that whenever one observes policies that have the intent or effect of subordinating a racial group, that phenomenon is properly identified as racism, whatever, if any, the justificatory ideology.[1]

As is well known scientific concepts are neither true nor false, rather they are only more or less useful theoretically and empirically. The central aspect of the Carmichael and Hamilton concept's utility is its focus on power as an integral aspect of the phenomenon. In order for racism to exist one racial group must have the relative power—the capacity to impose its will in terms of policies—on another relatively less powerful group. Without this relative power relationship, racism is a mere sentiment because although group A may wish to subordinate group B if it lacks the effective power to do so then it remains just that, a wish. Racism may be exercised and analyzed, as Carmichael and Hamilton point out, at both the individual and institutional levels, but the latter is by far the more important because, as Mills and other students of power in America have observed, "No one . . . can be truly powerful unless he has access to the commands of major institutions, for it is over these institutional means of power that the truly powerful are, in the first instance, powerful."[2] This is why it is important to get an empirically relevant handle on the institutional mode of racism. Conceptual and methodological clarity aside, the implications of this definition are important in ordinary discourse and in the effective struggle against racism in the post–civil rights era. This may be illustrated by examining the case of Carolyn Pitts, an affirmative action officer for the New York State Insurance Fund.

In 1987 Pitts as part of her work was asked to design a training manual for supervisors and others in authority positions so that they might be more effective in dealing with matters of race. In the thirty-eight-page document she prepared, she employed the Carmichael and Hamilton definition to make the case that blacks because of their relative powerlessness vis-à-vis whites in the United States today could not be racist. Specifically, she wrote:

> In the United States at present only whites can be racists since whites dominate and control the institutions that create and enforce American cultural norms and values. . . . Blacks and other Third World people do not have access to power to enforce any prejudices they may have so they cannot by definition be racists. . . . All white individuals in our society are racists. Even if a white is totally free from all conscious racial prejudices, he remains a racists, for he receives benefits distributed by a white racist society through its institutions. Our institutional and cultural processes are so arranged as to automatically benefit whites, just because they are white.[3]

After a New York State Assemblyman called attention to these passages, Mrs. Pitts found herself involved in a firestorm of controversy in which she, in Orwellian fashion, amid calls for her dismissal, was accused of being racist. Although many academic students of race, black and white, as well as black academic, professional, and political organizations sent letters and telegrams to the State Insurance Fund and Governor Mario Cuomo indicating that Pitts was using a concept of racism that was widely accepted in the academic literature, the manual was nevertheless withdrawn, and Pitts was forced to issue a statement of regret and was formally reprimanded "for making an error in judgment in utilizing and disseminating inflammatory, insensitive and offensive material."[4]

Unless one is prepared to say that dissemination of widely current academic concepts and ideas is "inflammatory, insensitive and offensive" then clearly Pitts was the victim of a politically inspired, misinformed lynch mob.[5] Properly conceptualized blacks cannot be racist (except attitudinally) in the United States except in isolated individual cases where they may be in a more powerful position than individual whites.[6] And, as I shall show in Chapter 6 many American "institutional processes are so arranged as to automatically benefit whites, just because they are white." This will be shown to be the case in everything from buying a house or car, to getting a kidney transplant, to getting a cab, or to being punished for drug use.

Another value of the Carmichael and Hamilton concept of racism is its utility for policy discussions on race. This is because it provides a clear-cut conceptual rationale for why taking race into consideration for purposes of affirmative action is not racist. One of the principal currents underlying the political attack on Pitts's manual was its implications for the state's affirmative action personnel policies. In its editorial the *New York Post* said Ms. Pitts dismissal was "essential" because "There is no other way of adequately signaling that unvarnished racism of the kind she expressed won't be tolerated" because "counting by race has to be defended intellectually. And racial goals—which inevitably become quotas-have to be defended. And the only way to do that is to assert that an ongoing and all embracing racism remains the order of the day in American life."[7] What the *New York Post* and other conservative scholars and politicians object to in the institutional racism concept is the view expressed by Justice Blackmun in the *Bakke* case, in which he argued that to overcome racism it may be necessary to take race into consideration, not for the racist purpose of subordination but for the purpose of ending subordination and its consequences.[8] What conservatives argue is that any taking of race into consideration for any purposes including overcoming past racism is racist.[9] The concept as employed by Carmichael and Hamilton undermines the intellectual basis of the conservative argument by calling attention to the fact that a policy use of race is not racist unless its intent or effects are to subordinate and maintain control over a racial group. Using the Carmichael and Hamilton concept it becomes nonsensical to see affirmative action as "reverse racism" since it is inconceivable that the white-dominated policy process would use race in order to subordinate its own racial group. Thus, this academic concept becomes the axis of bitter policy and political debates (as in the unfortunate case of Ms. Pitts) precisely because the concept is not "just academic" but profoundly political, and social scientists in the ebony and ivory towers cannot in their work isolate themselves from these debates; nor indeed should they even try.

The final value of the concept is its multidimensional character, focusing explicitly on individual and institutional modes of racism and implicitly on internal inferiorization. My concern in this chapter is to explicate the institutional mode. Although Carmichael and Hamilton were the first to use the concept, they did little more than lay it out in the most rudimentary way. This in part is because the concept and the book itself was forged in the anvil of political struggle as the manifesto of the emergent black power movement. Combining the perspectives of an activist academic and the movement's charismatic leader the book is part academic treatise and part political propaganda. Consequently, there is relatively little attention to the technical requirements of concept formation in terms of abstraction, classification, specification, measurement, and logical and empirical relations.[10] The concept of institutional racism, however, gained rapid acceptance among academic students of race and racism both in the United States and England who in time did much to clarify it and give it operational content.

In laying out the notion of institutional racism, Carmichael and Hamilton after defining racism write:

> Racism is both overt and covert. It takes two, closely related forms: individual whites acting against individual blacks, and acts of the total white community against the black community. We call these individual and institutional racism. The first consists of overt acts by individuals, which causes death, injury or the violent destruction of property. This type can be reached by television cameras; it can frequently be observed in the process of commission. The second type is less overt, far more subtle, less identifiable in terms of specific individuals committing the acts. But it is no less destructive of human life. The second type originates in the operation of established and respected forces of the society, and thus receives far less public condemnation than the first type.[11]

Except providing a couple of illustrative examples, this is all they do with the concept. An incident in which white terrorists in Birmingham bomb a black church and kill five black children is offered as an example of individual racism, while the death in that city of five hundred black infants each year because of inadequate food, shelter, and medical care is an instance of institutional racism. The other example cited is when a black family is driven through intimidation and violence out of a previously all-white neighborhood as a case of individual racism; it is institutional racism, they argue, that keep blacks locked in dilapidated slum tenements.[12]

What appears clear in the distinction drawn between the types and in the examples is a difference in visibility, intent, and, since the 1960s civil rights revolution, legality.[13] That is, individual racism is observed when an individual or group *overtly* takes into account the race of another individual or group and takes action *intended* to subordinate that individual or group. Such acts by blacks against whites have always been illegal, and since the civil rights legislation of the 1960s such acts by whites against blacks are also illegal. This is clearly the logical implication of the examples of the Birmingham white terrorists and of the whites who used threats and violence to force blacks to move out of a neighborhood. By contrast, institutional racism is observed when the normal, accepted, routine patterns and practices of society's institutions have the *effect or consequence* of subordinating an individual or group or maintaining in place the *results* of a past practice of now illegal overt racism. It is covert and unintended because to achieve the results the individuals involved need not consciously take into account race but need simply go about the normal routines of their work as required by an institution's standard operating procedures. Thus, institutional racism, as will become clear in our analysis of relevant post–civil rights era court cases in the next two chapters, conforms to custom and law. This is the logical inference to be drawn from the Carmichael and Hamilton examples of the high black infant mortality rates and their forced ghettoization. Without this critical conceptual distinction between the types in terms of intent and consequences, meaningful operational content and empirical data collection are forfeited. Indeed, without this conceptual distinction the concept's principal contribution to post–civil rights era discourse on racism is obscured. The classical social science model of racism during the civil rights era, which influenced the movement to some extent, was that the principal causal agent of race subordination was individual attitudes and behavior and that with the withering away of such attitudes and actions racism itself would disappear. In effect, Carmichael and Hamilton articulated a new perspective for analyzing race issues. The concept of institutionalized racism as articulated in *Black Power* suggested that racially invidious consequences might not reflect consciously malicious intent, but might stem from institutional practices, seemingly neutral in character, which result in systematically negative outcomes for blacks and other minorities.[14]

Yet in spite of these reasonably clear-cut distinctions between the two basic types of racism, the concept, especially as employed in the still sparse empirical literature, has about it a barren quality, as Williams writes, being often used as a "catch all phrase to cover any situation where racial discrimination has been practiced or racial disparities are observed."[15] Thus, even accomplished scholars in Afro-American studies have tended to dismiss, in far too facile fashion, the concept as useless.[16] The concept clearly is not marked by the kind of precision one would wish for in scientific discourse, but as I indicated in the Introduction this is not a problem unique to discourse on racism; on the contrary it is characteristic of most of the basic concepts in social science (such as class, culture, and power) and even middle-range working concepts in the discipline of political science.

Although scholars have used the concept in a variety of ways, there is one point of common agreement: institutional racism is to be understood in terms of its consequences.[17] Feagin's working definition reflects this consensus when he refers to institutional discrimination as "actions or patterns carried out by members of dominant groups, or their representatives, which have an adverse impact on members of subordinate groups."[18] The tricky problem, given this consensus, is, if the concept is to be operationalized in terms of its consequences or adverse impact does any policy or practice having adverse consequences on subordinate groups constitute institutional racism? Or, more broadly, does any observed racial inequality in a society point to the existence of institutional racism? On both points conceptual and operational clarity suggests that the answer is no. Let us address the last point first. Some observed racial inequality in discrete social sectors (education, health, the professions, etc.) may be a function of distinctive group cultures that may predispose individuals in different race or ethnic groups to pursue differential paths of behavior.[19] Second, cultural predilections aside, observed racial inequalities today may be a function of racism; not the individual or institutional modes, but, rather, the historical one. That is, black-white inequalities in the United States today in part result from past patterns of subordination—a pattern difficult to overcome today even though its continuation is not necessarily a result of ongoing individual or institutional racism.[20]

On the second point, any policy having an adverse impact on blacks should not be conceptualized as institutionalized racism because of the intersection of race and class in the United States. Blacks in the United States are disproportionately lower class, and in any class-stratified society most institutional arrangements have an adverse impact on the poor and dispossessed whatever their race.[21] For example, the Scholastic Aptitude Test (SAT) and other examinations designed to select persons for college and advanced study have often been called institutionally racist because of their adverse impact on blacks. Yet, the tests also have an adverse impact on white members of the lower class, thus one might argue that the SAT reflects class, not race, bias; "institutional classism," to use an awkward phrase.[22] Thus, my approach to the matter operationally is to view as institutionally racist those policies and practices that have an adverse impact on blacks, *controlling for social class*. Any use of the concept requires comparisons of whites and blacks, either all blacks with all whites or some strata of each group to each other. I believe the most useful methodological approach to follow is to attempt to hold class constant in empirical analysis of the phenomenon.[23] Strictly speaking, the empirical analysis that follows takes this approach, although more general cases of race disparities are also examined.

3

Individual Racism in the Post–Civil Rights Era

The Attitudinal Dimension

Individual racism has two dimensions—attitudinal and behavioral. I first focus on the attitudinal. Many surveys and studies have been conducted on the attitudinal component of individual racism in the post–civil rights era, with the results usually showing a decline in white racist attitudes and negative stereotypes toward blacks.[1] Yet, as the *Washington Post* reported in a 1981 survey of white racial attitudes, "Hard core racism is still alive in America but it is not growing as many blacks fear. At the same time racial stereotypes still pervade white attitudes toward blacks—stereotypes that may be less malicious than the old white supremacy but are still damaging to blacks."[2] In most surveys this "hard care" of racist sentiment is measured at about a fourth to a third of

TABLE 3.1

White Supremacist Attitudes in the Civil Rights and Post–Civil Rights Eras

	1963	1967	1978
Blacks less ambitious	66$*	70%	49%
Blacks prefer handouts	41	52	36
Blacks more violence prone	42	34	NA**
Blacks more crime prone	35	32	29
Blacks less intelligent	39	46	25
Blacks care less about family	31	34	18
Blacks inferior	31	29	15

Source: Louis Harris, *A Study of Attitudes Toward Racial and Religious Minorities and Toward Women* (New York: National Conference of Christians and Jews, 1978).

*Percentage of white respondents agreeing

**Not available

respondents in nationwide surveys. For example, Table 3.1 reports data from the 1978 Harris survey for the National Conference of Christians and Jews on the pre– and post–civil rights eras white attitudes toward blacks were grounded in terms of historical white supremacism. In 1963, at the height of the civil rights protest era, 66 percent of whites said that blacks preferred to live on handouts, 35 percent thought blacks were more prone to crime, 42 percent that blacks were more violence prone, 39 percent that blacks were less intelligent, and 31 percent agreed that blacks cared less about family and in an overall sense that blacks as a people were inferior to white.

During the fifteen-year period from 1963 to 1978, one observes a steady decline in each of these racist attitudes (except the item on black ambition, which increased from 66 percent in 1963 to 70 percent in 1967 and then declined to 49 percent in 1978). For example, in 1978 only 25 percent of the respondents agreed that blacks were less intelligent, 29 percent that they were crime prone, and only 15 percent that they were inferior. Thus, there has clearly been a substantial decline in the willingness of white Americans to express white supremacist attitudes to survey researchers.

I should emphasize, however, that this decline is not necessarily a decline in such attitudes, but perhaps a decline in the willingness to express such attitudes in the quasi public forum that is a sample survey. That is, in the post–civil rights era it has become less socially acceptable to express racist attitudes openly. Thus, it is possible, I would argue even likely, that there is more real attitudinal racism than is revealed in the extant survey data. That is, in the privacy of one's peer group with no blacks around one is likely to find more expression by whites of ideas of black inferiority. As a black person I of course am not privy to such intimate conversations among whites. We may infer evidence of some degree of hidden racism in the exit poll data on elections where blacks are candidates for high visibility offices. In such elections black candidates usually receive more white voter support in public opinion surveys and exit polls than they do at the ballot box, and this is explained in terms of the unwillingness of some white voters to admit their opposition to a black candidate for fear of being thought of as racist.[3] This is not to diminish the importance of the fact that it represents considerable progress in the post–civil rights era that the climate of discourse on race has changed to the extent that whites in America are reluctant or ashamed to be openly racist. This certainly makes for a climate more conducive to the black psyche if not material well-being in that blacks, especially children, are not assaulted on a daily basis with the rhetoric of inferiority in the nation's media, on the Senate floor, and in ordinary discourse, as was the case when I was growing up in the 1950s and early 1960s. Nevertheless, it must be concluded that attitudinal racism is probably greater by some unknown factor than the data show.

For example, the most recent data on racist attitudes show a somewhat higher percentage of antiblack attitudes among whites.

TABLE 3.2

White Attitudes toward Blacks, 1991

	Blacks tend to be lazy	Blacks prefer welfare	Blacks violence prone	Blacks unintelligent
All whites	46.6%*	58.9%	53.7%	30.7%
By Education:				
Less than high school	58.1**	69.2**	52.2**	35.5**
High school graduate	50.3	62.3	55.6	33.9
Some college	40.5	58.7	58.4	29.5
College graduate	38.8	47.9	49	24.4
By Age:				
18–24	35.2**	49.5**	53.3	26**
25–24	42.7	56.8	54.4	28.3
55+	57.8	65.6	52.5	36.5
By Region:				
South	44.1**	56.9	53.3	29.3
Non-South	51.8	62.9	54.7	33.5

Source: National Opinion Research Center 1991 General Social Survey.

*Percentage Agreement

**Indicates differences arc statistically significant.

Table 3.2 displays the results of the National Opinion Research Center's 1991 General Social Survey, with controls for education, region, and age. Forty-seven percent of whites said they thought blacks tend to be lazy, 53 percent that blacks tend to be violence prone, 59 percent that they prefer to live off welfare; and 31 percent said that blacks tend to be unintelligent. As expected, these negative attitudes about blacks are more widespread among the elderly and less educated. Interestingly, however, the expected regional difference is not so great; except for the item on laziness, where northern respondents are more likely to embrace this racist stereotype than are southerners.

Again, this most recent survey on white attitudes toward blacks

shows a much larger proportion of whites expressing anti black stereotypes than in 1978. It is difficult to account for this rather large discrep-
ancy between the 1978 and 1991 findings. There are of course, modest
differences in the wording and ordering of the questions, in the sam-
pling process and in the stated purposes of the surveys but these factors normally are not enough to account for differences of this magnitude.[4] It may be that the 1991 results, represent, as some observers have
suggested, a rather sharp increase in racist sentiments during the 1980s
Ronald Reagan era of conservative reaction on race.[5]

Two attitudes measured in the survey data—intelligence and sex—
are central components of the doctrine of white supremacy. In the modern era the idea that blacks are somehow less intelligent than whites
has been central to the notion of black inferiority. The National Opinion
Research Center has measured this attitude periodically since 1942. In
that year more than half (53 percent) of whites disagreed with the statement "In general, Negroes are as intelligent as white people—that is
they can learn things just as well if the are given the same educational
training." By 1963 this percentage had declined to 21 percent, and by
1968 it was 23 percent.[6] In the post–civil rights era, then this historically
pervasive notion of black inferiority has apparently stabilized at around
25 percent of the white population, depending on how the question is
worded (particularly whether the question specifically suggests that the
racial gap in intelligence is inborn or genetic). For example, the *Washington Post* survey found that 23 percent of whites agreed that blacks
had worse jobs, income, and housing than whites because they have
"less inborn ability to learn."[7] This attitude, like more racist stereotypes,
tends to be anchored in the lower class. Jackman and Jackman, for example, found that 29 percent of poor whites accepted a genetic explanation for the lower socioeconomic status of blacks, 19 percent of the
middle class, and 17 percent of the upper middle class.[8] It is probable
that this hard-core racist minority will persist for some time and constitutes an important psychological barrier to interracial coalitions of blacks
and working-class whites.

Frequently during the civil rights era, when white liberals would
urge upon southern segregationists racial equality in terms of schools,
public accommodations, and voting, the latter's ultimate rejoinder
would be "Ah, but would you want your daughter to marry one," thus
suggesting that no matter how liberal or egalitarian a white person might
be he would ultimately recoil from the idea of interracial sexual intimacy and marriage. In 1963 90 percent of whites said they would be
"concerned" if their teenage child dated a black and 84 percent said
they would be concerned if a close friend or relative married a black.

By 1978 these percentages had declined to 79 percent and 60 percent respectively.[9] Therefore, the ultimate taboo on sexual intimacy remains pervasive in the post–civil rights era despite changes in attitudes toward racial integration in more public spheres such as schools, transportation, and housing.[10]

Before turning to the limited data on the behavioral dimension of individual racism, I examine one final attitudinal component of an explicitly political character and then discuss what we know in general about the relationship between attitudes and behavior. The explicit political measure deals with the extent to which whites say they would not support an otherwise qualified black candidate for president. In 1958 the Gallup organization found that 58 percent of whites would not vote for a qualified black presidential candidate, by 1965 this number had declined to 42 percent, in 1970 29 percent and by 1988 to 20 percent.[11] Keeping in mind that these post–civil rights era figures probably underestimate the extent of the actual antiblack vote at the presidential level (in terms of our discussion earlier of the "hidden" racist vote), this 20 percent plus handicap poses a near insurmountable barrier to Jesse Jackson, Colin Powell, or any other would-be black candidate for the presidency. As Williams writes, "To secure a majority . . . a black presidential candidate would have to win the votes of 65 percent of that part of the electorate that did not automatically reject black candidates (including roughly 60 percent of the white vote). Yet, no presidential candidate since the dawn of the two party system has won more than 61 percent of the entire vote, racist and nonracist."[12]

To conclude this analysis of the attitudinal dimension of individual racism, clearly there has been an appreciable decline in antiblack attitudes since World War II, a decline that accelerated during the 1960s civil rights era. Yet the key question is what the effect of these attitude changes is on behavior. Blacks, after all, are less concerned with what whites think about them than what they do to them. There is an extensive psychological and sociological literature on the attitude—behavior linkage, and although the problem is controversial a review of the literature suggests that certainly there is no one-to-one relationship between attitude changes and changes in behavior; that the relationship is probably reciprocal and that it is probably more likely that attitudes will be unrelated or only modestly related to overt behavior rather than the contrary.[13] Research on white racial attitudes and behavior tends to support this general absence of an attitude—behavior linkage. Schumann, Steeth, and Bobo, for example, show that among whites attitudinal support for desegregation and equality differs significantly from support for specific policies to translate these attitudes into action.[14] And Jackman and Crane show that whites with egalitarian racial attitudes and even close black friends and acquaintances persist in opposing government attempts to promote equality. They conclude, "If prejudice derives not from feelings of personal animosity but from an implicit sense of group position, then dominant groups will seek to defend their privilege no matter how they feel toward subordinates. . . . The corollaries that discriminatory orientations need not rest on feelings of personal animosity. Indeed, if circumstances are conducive, discrimination can rest as comfortably on a friendly disposition as on a hostile one."[15] Thus, while one should not gainsay the progressive changes in white attitudes toward blacks, since clearly absence of overt racist attitudes contributes to a more enlightened and humane discourse on race, one also should be mindful that, as always, actions speak louder than words and nonracist attitudes do not necessarily translate into nonracist actions.

The Behavioral Dimension

Given that there is no necessary relationship between racist attitudes and racist behavior, we know next to nothing about the trend lines of racist actions by individuals in the post–civil rights era. There is no systematic data on individual racism—when individual whites take race into consideration in order to inflict injury, harm, or in other ways take actions calculated to subordinate blacks. Such data simply are not systematically collected. In 1969 the Department of Health, Education, and Welfare recognized this problem in *Toward a Social Report*, in which it stated, "The nation has no comprehensive set of statistics reflecting social progress or retrogression. There is no government procedure for periodic stocktaking of the social health of the nation."[16] The report recommended the development by the federal government of a comprehensive social report with emphasis on the development of social indicators that would measure social change and facilitate the establishment of national social policy goals.[17] Although some progress has been made since the 1960s in the development of social indicators in the areas of health, the environment, educational attainment, and income poverty, little has been done in the area of measuring racism. The 1969 report alluded to the problem of racism and racial conflict, however, the distinguished group of social scientists (headed by Daniel Bell and Alice Rivlin) who prepared the report failed to call for the development of indicators of racism. As a result while we can speak with some confidence about the nation's progress in health, education, and the environment since the 1960s, in the area of racism, arguably the nation's most pressing domestic problem, we are left to rely on sporadic data collected by private individuals or groups or, more frequently, simply anecdotal material reported in the press.

In recent years some attention has been given to the systematic collection of data on individual racism as it is manifested in acts of violence or harassment by whites against blacks and other minorities. This interest was sparked by certain well-publicized incidents of individual racism, such as the murder of young black men in the boroughs of Queens and Brooklyn, which gave rise to a sense that racism was on the increase in the 1980s. In a 1987 paper Howard University Professor Ronald Walters pulled together the scattered data on individual acts of racial violence and harassment in the post–civil rights era. Reports of human relations commissions in California, New York City, Montgomery County, Maryland, and from the Justice Department's Community Relations Service show a steady increase in incidents of racially motivated harassment and violence since the late 1970s.[18] During this same period, there have been reports of increased incidents of individual racist harassment and violence on the nation's college and university campuses.[19] Many observers see the rise of individual racist violence in the 1980s as an aberration—an interruption of a previous pattern of decline in such acts in the post–civil rights era as a result of a climate of intolerance or resurgent "white nationalism" fostered by the Reagan administration.[20] Others suggest that the figures may reflect not an increase in such incidents but rather an increase in the reporting of such incidents or simply better data collection efforts.[21] In conclusion, we are back to where we started, we simply do not know the extent to which individual acts of racially motivated violence have increased, decreased, or simply stayed the same in the post–civil rights era. All we may properly infer from the available information is that racism of this type has not been completely eliminated in the post–civil rights era, which suggests once again the need for more systematic data collection.[22]

Other forms of individual racism are just as difficult to make sense of empirically. For example, in the area of employment blacks have a widespread perception of racism on the part of individual employers.[23] But we are hard-pressed to know the extent to which this perception is correct except for when the occasional case reaches the courts or is otherwise reported in the press. This is so in part because more than half the persons who perceive employment discrimination do not report it.[24] Second, as Brooks points out:

> discrimination does not exist, at least not in a legal sense, until a court (and, really the Supreme Court) says so. A judicial finding

of discrimination, however, has an uncertain quality about it. The finding is empirical (a question of fact), analytical (a question of law applied to the facts), and policy driven (a question of who bears the burden of proof). In addition, a lower court's finding of discrimination is subject to reversal on direct appeal or years later when and if the issue comes before the court again in another case. Thus, a careful review of judicial determinations (the 'best' evidence available) is inconclusive evidence of the existence of even a legally controlled concept of discrimination.[25]

Given these difficulties in judicial determination of racism, Brooks and his colleagues relied in their research not on judicial proof of racism but the filing of claims of job discrimination in court or with government agencies, whether proved or not, as well as personal perceptions of discrimination.[26] Brooks concludes that these sources "offer compelling evidence that complex racial discrimination faced by middle class African Americans [who are more likely than the lower class to report their perceptions of discrimination] is more than an intermittent phenomenon. They provide at least prima facia proof that such discrimination is regular and systemic in places of middle class employment"[27] Brooks's "juri-statistical" research on racism in employment is further substantiated by the occasional egregious "case study" reported in the press. The two cases discussed below were widely reported in both the national print and electronic media. They are useful to discuss because they illustrate not only cases of individual racism but also how these individual acts become so embedded in systemic practices that it becomes all but impossible to disentangle the individual from the institutional type of racism.

The first is the seven-year ordeal of Donald Rachon, an African-American FBI agent. Since the FBI is the government's principal agency for the investigation of racism, especially the manifestly unlawful individual type, the Rachon case is a quite compelling example of the persistence of racism in the post–civil rights era. While assigned to the FBI's Chicago and Omaha offices in the early 1980s, Rachon reported a consistent pattern of racial harassment by his white colleagues, and after the incidents were reported, a systematic effort by Bureau supervisors' to cover them up. In charges that were upheld in administrative inquiries by the Justice Department and the Equal Employment Opportunity Commission, Rachon indicated, amount other things, that his wife (who was white) received obscene, threatening telephone calls that often included lurid references to interracial sex; photographs were placed on his desk with an ape pasted over his son's head and in his mailbox with the image of a badly bruised black man. Another incident included a forged death and dismemberment policy taken out in his name by one of his colleagues.[28] As a result of incidents of this sort, Rachon reports that he became physically ill and the emotional toll eventually broke up his marriage. In an out of court settlement, the FBI agreed to pay Rachon $1 million, his wife $150,000, and his lawyers a half million dollars, although the Bureau refused to concede any wrongdoing. Rachon, who as part of the settlement agreed to resign from the Bureau, claims his case was not, as the director said, an isolated case, but represented a systematic pattern of internal discrimination, harassment, and intimidation of black agents by their white colleagues. As with most instances of individual racism that come to light in court or the press, the analyst has little basis for making a judgment but the *perception* of systematically sanctioned racism by individuals in the nation's principal law enforcement agency is, on the basis of the Rachon case, not unwarranted.

The second case of individual racism involves four New York City employment agencies where employees under the direction of their managers systematically discriminated against blacks seeking jobs as low-level white-collar receptionists and secretaries in corporate offices. The case, reported on the CBS news program "60 Minutes" and in the *New York Times*, showed that the agencies routinely asked their corporate clients their racial preferences for employees and then used code words like "All American," "front office appearance," and "corporate image" to alert would-be employers to the fact that the prospective employee was white. Once this situation came to light and suit was filed by the New York attorney general, the agencies responded with the now expected post–civil rights rejoinder that this was "an aberration" that did not reflect institutional policies or practices.[29] The analyst has no way of knowing but, again, if this kind of discrimination can be documented for such low-level white-collar jobs as receptionist, then this reinforces Brooks's argument that perceptions matter and that discrimination in white-collar employment may be widespread.[30] This perception is supported by one systematic study of entry-level white-and blue-collar jobs. In a study for the Urban Institute Turner, Fix, and Stryck conducted a "hiring audit" to determine the degree of racial discrimination in entry-level employment in Washington and Chicago. The research involved selecting black and white "job testers" carefully matched in terms of age, physical size, education (all were college educated), and experience, as well as such intangible factors as poise, openness, articulateness, and sending them to apply for entry-level jobs identified in newspaper ads. The results found what the authors call "entrenched and widespread" discrimination at every step in the process, with whites three times as likely as blacks to advance in the hiring process to the point of being offered a job.[31] Again, the data here are limited, but the cases discussed should at least caution those who facilely dismiss racism in the post–civil rights era as a causal factor in black unemployment and the associated problems of the so-called black underclass.

On the day I was compiling material for this chapter in preparation for writing the first draft, the videotape of the brutal beating of Rodney King, a young black man, by officers of the Los Angeles Police Department was first broadcast. I watched the tape with ambivalence, revolted by the atrocity and feeling pain for the young man, yet clearly pleased that the tape provided unambiguous "data" for my planned discussion of racist violence by the police in the post–civil rights era. I was neither surprised nor shocked by the tape (as I was by the jury's subsequent verdict of not guilty) because, having resided in Los Angeles during the late 1960s and early 1970s, I lived in constant fear of the police and as a frequent visitor to the city since then, I knew that black residents, especially young men, still lived in fear of being stopped and harassed, if not beaten by the police. Los Angeles, in this sense, is somewhat unique. In the 1950s and 1960s charges of harassment and brutality were frequently made against the police. The 1969 *Report of the National Advisory Commission on Civil Disorders* (the Kerner Report) found that police misconduct was one of the leading grievances of urban blacks against the local authorities and frequently a precipitant cause of the ghetto riots. Yet students of big city politics in the post–civil rights era have reported a decline in police misconduct in the last twenty-five years, in part as a result of the election of black mayors, the appointment of black police chiefs, and the racial integration and reform of many departments. In all cases except Los Angeles, that is, where, in spite of the election of a black mayor and some degree of racial integration, the perception remained that its police department was effectively out of control.[32] This is certainly my perception as an individual who has lived for the last two decades in big cities—New York City, Washington, D.C., Houston, San Francisco, and Oakland, as well as Los Angeles—the latter is the only city where I approached the police with a palpable sense of fear and dread. The Rodney King videotape thus came as an unexpected piece of "data" in the analysis of individual racism by the nation's police in the post–civil rights era.[33]

Although anecdotal and scattered systematic data (systematic data are not routinely collected on a national basis on incidents of police conduct, although after the Rodney King incident Congress considered legislation to require the FBI to include such statistics in its Uniform crime Reports) suggest a decline in police brutality since the 1960s, there are still ample anecdotes and statistical data to suggest that this form of individual racism is by no means a thing of the past. Indeed, in the post–civil rights era police violence has probably replaced the Ku Klux Klan and other white terrorist groups as the most pervasive racist threat to the individual security of blacks. In every major American city, every year or two an incident occurs to convince the black community, official findings notwithstanding, that the police murdered a black woman, child, or man.[34] Richard Pryor's humor provides some perspective on this problem, a perspective that resonates well throughout black America. On the album "That Nigger Is Crazy" Pryor tells the following story:

> Cops put a hurting on niggers, white folks don't believe it; they say, "I am tired of all of this talk about police brutality, those people were resisting arrest." That's because the police live in your neighborhood and when an officer pulls you over you say "Oh officer, glad to be of help" . . . a black doesn't say that. When he is pulled over he says, "I am reaching in my pocket for my license because I don't want to be no mother-fucking accident."[35]

The official statistics seem to bear out Pryor's observation in that when the police kill blacks it is often ruled "accidental"; because the officers claim they thought the victim had a gun, although when one looks at the data for any given year, in three out of four cases, the person killed was unarmed.[36]

Blacks, who are about 12 percent of the population, usually constitute more than half the persons killed by police, and in some years the figures are even higher. For example, Walters cites figures from the Police Foundation that show that 78 percent of those killed and 80 percent of those nonfatally shot were minorities. Apparently, the police use of deadly force increased in the early 1980s, up 43 percent in 1983 from 1980, according to the Police Foundation data.[37] Walters notes that the police shootings were rarely prosecuted and that "The only factors which appeared to restrain the growth of such official, racially motivated violence was not the criminal justice system itself, but the election of sensitive Black mayors who initiated new policies for the use of deadly force."[38]

In the aftermath of the King verdict, a study of reports of police brutality in fifteen major daily newspapers between January 1990 and May 1992 found that the majority of the civilian victims of police brutality were black. Of 131 such cases reported, during this period 87 percent were black, 10 percent Hispanic, and 3 percent white. By contrast 93 percent of the officers involved were white, suggesting a national pattern of misconduct by white police officers toward black citizens.[39] This form of individual racism under the cloak of authority must, however, be placed in the context of the extraordinarily high rate of violent crime in inner-city black communities. Just as in any given year half the persons killed by the police are black so in any given year half the murders committed in the United States are by blacks, usually blacks killing blacks. This form of communal violence has increased in the post—civil rights era in part as a result of changes in the structure of the urban economy.[40] Other reasons include the violence associated with intensification of the drug wars, the turf disputes among gangs, and the increased availability of more lethal weapons. Thus, in a real sense many police officers view inner-city black communities as war zones, where, like in Vietnam, everyone is a potential enemy and one shoots first and ask questions later because to do otherwise might put their own lives at risk. Consequently, some unknown number of the shootings and killings of blacks by white police officers are surely justified. Yet in other cases when the police kill blacks it is simply murder, as in the Thanksgiving incident in Brooklyn cited in note 34 or the widely publicized Miami case in the 1980s when several police officers wantonly beat a young black man to death, precipitating several days of rebellion in the Liberty City ghetto after the clearly guilty officers were found innocent.

This is the significance of the infamous Los Angeles videotape "data" because it unambiguously demonstrates individual racism by the police. The videotape not only clearly shows the persistence of this form of racist behavior by the individuals involved but it also suggests it was systematically or institutionally sanctioned. First, the two-minute beating occurred in full view of passing motorists and witnesses in nearby apartments, who shouted, "Don't kill him. Stop, don't kill him." One must infer here that the officers believed they could get away with it; the witnesses and the evidence of King's mangled body notwithstanding. Second, the fact that some twenty officers witnessed the incident but did not intervene suggests that this kind of individual racism had some peer sanction. Third, that this was more than an individual aberration is suggested by the fact that the officers casually joked over their radios about the beating with colleagues, leaving a record of racial slurs and intimations that this was not an unheard-of occurrence. As one officer said, "I haven't beaten anyone that bad in a long time"; another replied, "I thought you agreed to chill out for a while."[41]

As I have reiterated throughout this chapter, any effort to chart the course of racism in the last twenty-five years is fraught with many difficulties in terms of data and methods. Facts and figures are hard to come by, and when they are available they may be ambiguously interpreted; seen as isolated incidents or aberrations. The Los Angeles videotape and the transcripts of the officers' conversations in the immediate aftermath of the incident are useful precisely because their meanings are beyond doubt.[42] (I wrote this initially before the verdict was delivered in the case, on the assumption that no one, especially not a duly sworn jury—even if all white—could see the videotape and conclude that the police had not used excessive force. Thus, the jury verdict becomes an additional bit of data on the nature of individual racism in the post–civil rights era.)

White people—including social scientists—have better access to data on individual racism than do blacks. That is, in the course of their daily lives—personal and professional—whites have the opportunity to observe racist thinking and behavior that would probably be hidden given the presence of a black person. Perhaps, some white journalist or scholar ought to make a project of keeping a journal for several years on observed or reported racist behavior of white friends and colleagues. It might make a remarkable document. Skin color notwithstanding however, I conclude this chapter by discussing some personal encounters with individual racism in the post–civil rights era. While this maybe unusual in an academic treatise, it may also be useful, first, because in some sense it is the "data" I know best and, second, because all knowledge, even academic work, is in some sense personal. One's personal history exercises some influence, whether conscious or not, on even the most objective, quantitative analysis. I focus here not on minor irritants and slights that are a constant of an African-American's predicament in the United States but rather anecdotes that had or might have had a significant effect on the life chances of me and my family.[43]

My initial encounters with racism were in the rigidly segregated rural Louisiana of my youth; however, my encounters in the post–civil rights era have occurred in the urban north. On several occasions I have been arrested simply for being a black man in the wrong place at the wrong time. In 1971 I drove my wife to an appointment for a receptionist position at a Beverly Hills law firm (she didn't get the job). Dressed as usual in t-shirt and jeans, I casually window-shopped while waiting for her. When we returned to our car we were briefly followed by the police and then stopped. The car was illegally searched (apparently for drugs) and, as I told the officer he had no authority under the Fourth Amendment to search the car, he replied to his partner, "I am not searching Joe, do you see me searching?" I was then arrested and held for several hours on the spurious charge that there was an outstanding warrant for my arrest on murder chargers. On another occasion, in White Plains, New York, while shopping with my five-year-old daughter at a local supermarket I was arrested on the compliant of an elderly white woman that I had snatched her purse a week before. The charges were taken seriously, and if I had not had the good fortune to be on the faculty at the local university I might have been tried and imprisoned. As it turned out, the president of the university called the police chief and in effect told him, "you got the wrong nigger; he is a professor." I was immediately released with profuse apologies to "Dr." Smith.

Suburban Westchester County, like many other places, is segregated along race and class lines, which gave rise to two encounters with racism, one individual and one institutional. The individual incident involved my search for housing. A friend and colleague, Dale Nelson, a professor at Fordham University, informed me that there would soon be a vacancy in his apartment building and he would keep me informed so that I might make early application. Sure enough, a vacancy occurred, and my wife and I immediately applied, only to be told by the superintendent that there were no vacancies and none were anticipated. Knowing that he was lying, we informed the Nelsons, and when another vacancy occurred Dale offered to put a deposit to hold the apartment until we arrived within the hour. The superintendent angrily told him "never to send a nigger to him for an apartment again." Although we sought the assistance of the local Urban League office in filing a compliant, nothing came of this until a year or so later when we heard on the radio that the U.S. attorney's office had filed suit against the rental agency, and we and the Nelsons subsequently became principal witnesses for the government in the lawsuit. After much delay, the rental agency entered a consent decree in which it agreed to a rigorous affirmative action program of rentals to minorities and to pay modest damages to my wife and me and the Nelsons.[44] This was a case of individual racism buttressed, according to the government's suit, by an institutional pattern of racism.

The second case involves a variant of institutional racism. As I indicated, Westchester County consists of many towns and villages segregated along race and class lines. I lived in White Plains, a relatively large city with segregation by race and class but also racially integrated neighborhoods. The nearby town of Harrison is an upper-class community, possibly all white, with homes selling for more than half a million dollars. The town operated a beautiful park that was nominally open only to residents but was used by residents of White Plains, at least white residents. My next-door neighbors (whites) frequented the park without any difficulties, and my wife, daughter, and I once accompanied them. Immediately, we were approached by a park official asking for our residency cards. Our neighbors had never been asked to prove residency, yet immediately when a black family is involved residency immediately becomes an issue—skin color serving as an indirect indicator that I was not a resident of Harrison, either because no blacks lived there or because the park attendant was able to recognize all two or three of them. Thus, I was deprived of the right to use a public park on the basis of race as surely as I was in rural Louisiana during the days of official segregation, yet it was, of course, all perfectly legal.

Let me conclude this discussion of personal encounters with racism in the post–civil rights era with a discussion of racism in the academy. I have been around academic institutions all my life and, except for minor racial slights and slurs, I have rarely encountered individual, overt racism, although at the white universities where I have taught I have frequently heard students remark, "He is black, but he is good," as if being black and a good teacher somehow don't go together. But professionally my encounters with racism have been institutional, not individual, revolving largely around my interest in black studies, black politics, and black colleges. As Hanes Walton writes:

> Negro politics (as it was called as late as the mid 1960s) was long considered an "off beat field of political science," an academic graveyard for young scholars who sought academic respectability and an opportunity to rise to the forefront of the discipline. At best, it was viewed as an occasionally interesting subject—an intellectual toy that one might tinker with from time to time. But since it, like black people, was looked down upon by society and, therefore, academia, one could not afford to devote extensive time, effort and attention to the subject in any sustained and consistent fashion.[45]

This institutional hostility to black politics in the discipline of political science and in the academy as a whole has been a part of my career from graduate school to the present, although in 1990 the American Political Science Association recognized black politics as one of its valid twenty or so subfields. This notion that the study of the politics of race—the nation's most enduring and pervasive cleavage—is somehow a "backwater" not in the "larger world" is a myopic feature of the post–civil rights era academy that operates as a continuing institutional barrier to the society's capacity to understand and deal with racism and its consequences effectively.[46]

4

Institutional Racism in the
Post–Civil Rights Era

Conceptually, institutional racism is understood as policies and practices that, controlling for social class, subordinate blacks or maintain or "freeze" them in a subordinate position. Like the development of civil rights jurisprudence and affirmative action procedures since the late 1960s, the concept focuses on the effects of a decision, not its intent. A decision, policy, or practice that is nominally nonracist, sincerely so, may nevertheless be racist in its consequences or effects. The crucial distinction in my use of the concept compared to that of other scholars and to that used in civil rights law and affirmative action decision-making is that I *attempt* to take into account the effects of social class. Class subordination or, to put it more benignly, discrimination on the basis of social class is a widely accepted, legitimate feature of any capitalist social structure. And since blacks in the United States belong disproportionately to the lower class (about three times as likely to be poor compared with whites), much of what may appear to be institutional racism is simply the effects of routine class bias in a market economy.

Although the disproportionate location of blacks among America's poor and lower classes is the result of a two-hundred-year pattern of intentional racial subordination, the problem for the analyst of institutional racism is to separate out the effects of contemporary policies and practices that have a *racially specific* discriminatory effect. Thus, my usage of the concept breaks with that of Bullock and Rogers and other students of the phenomenon who contend that ultimately all forms of institutional racism "stem from inequality in the distribution of economic resources."[1] Instead, I seek to identify empirically those forms of racism that exist independently of the distribution of economic resources. This means that certain routine operations of institutions that have a negative effect on black life chances are not technically considered institutional racism. For example, the practice of red-lining by auto insurers and banks who use zip codes to identify low-income areas where higher rates are charged and home improvements and business loans are denied. Or the increasing refusal by banks, supermarket chains, drug-stores, and other crucial commercial outlets to locate in low-income neighborhoods. Or, finally, the reluctance of cab drivers in virtually all American cities to provide service to low-income areas.[2] Now, in all these examples the disproportionate, if not exclusive, effect is on blacks or Hispanics who are denied opportunities otherwise routinely available to whites. It is of small comfort to the victims of these kinds of discrimi-natory practices to say that they have been so not because they are black but because they happen to live in a low-income area. Nevertheless, this is the logic of the institutional racism concept, properly specified.

My procedure, given this specification, is to locate empirical ma-terial that shows a pattern or practice of institutional racism. Again, this procedure is not, cannot, be systematic. Rather, I rely on material that has come to my attention in several years of research during which I systematically monitored the press and academic journals for mate-rial that fits this notion of institutional racism. The bias is clear; I searched for material to confirm the existence of a pattern. Disconfirming mate-rial, by its very nature, is difficult to collect because if it did not happen it will not be reported. The material is organized under the following categories: education, employment, housing, health care, and consumer services.

Education

Racial inequities in elementary and secondary education during the post–civil rights era are well documented in the National Assess-ment of Educational Progress conducted annually, in the armed ser-vices aptitude tests, and in the college admissions test administered by the Educational Testing Service.[3] These inequities, however, constitute a classic instance of the problems involved in disentangling the effects of race and class bias, given the relationship between class status and educational achievement. In general, black achievement on various as-sessments of knowledge and skill attainment is roughly equivalent or only somewhat lower than whites with similar family socioeconomic backgrounds. As a consequence, the scandalous state of black educa-tion in inner-city and rural schools is probably best understood as in effect of class bias in American education rather than institutional rac-ism.[4] For example, the National Academy of Sciences, in a study of the SAT and other standardized educational and employment tests, strongly rejected the allegations that such tests are institutionally racist, point-ing to evidence that they predict black and white performance equally and that the lower black scores are a result of their socioeconomic status and the resulting inadequate educational preparation, not racial biases in the test.[5] Although the evidence is not clear-cut and there are technical problems in validation, particular for job-related tests, the Academy's conclusions are probably substantially correct, especially in terms of the SAT and related tests of basic knowledge.[6]

The general conclusion that racial inequities in education are not to be explained by institutional racism does not, however, mean that one cannot find evidence of bias in the process traceable to racism. For example, the tendency of many school districts to place the least qualified and experienced teachers in inner-city schools, intent notwithstanding, may indicate institutional racism, as may the disproportionately low pass rates of black teachers on standardized competence exams. Good teaching is difficult to define, let alone measure and quantify on a standardized instrument, thus serious questions of validity and reliability are inherent in their use. In addition, the class factor is held constant since teachers, black or white, have similar educational and income attainments. But since standardized teacher competence tests were introduced in the post–civil rights era (before 1978, only Georgia and South Carolina required such tests; today they are required in some form in every state except Alaska and Iowa), black teachers have failed at rates two to three times that of their white colleagues. A study of pass rates in New Jersey, Connecticut, and California showed that the white pass rate ranged from 71 percent to 96 percent while the range among blacks was from 15 percent to 50 percent.[7] Thus, at a time when black educational reformers speak of an urgent need for black teachers in part as a result of their high failure rate on these competence tests observers are writing that they are "vanishing."[8] In 1970—the first year of the first decade of the post–civil rights era—blacks constituted 9 percent of elementary and secondary school teachers, but by 1980 their proportion had dropped to about 6 percent.[9] Given the way I have conceptualized institutional racism, it seems possible to infer that the vanishing black teacher is in part an effect of the phenomenon.

But perhaps the clearest evidence of institutional racism in education is the continued use in the post–civil rights era of the IQ tests, not to measure acquired knowledge, as with the SAT and related tests, but to measure innate intelligence. This mismeasure of young men and women is used to classify blacks as mentally retarded. This classification is then used to place them in classes for the so-called educable mentally retarded (EMR). An examination of EMR placements for the period 1976–78 indicates that in 1978 black students constituted 38 percent of the EMR enrollment but were only 16 percent of the national school enrollment generally. Although by 1984 the data indicate a slight decrease in black EMR placements, at 37.3 percent blacks still are en-rolled in such classes at twice their proportion of the general school populations.[10] However, among whites "the EMR percentages have never exceeded the white national enrollment percentages."[11] The U.S. District Court for the Northern District of California found that use of the test to place black children in EMR classes is institutionally racist and a violation, arguably of Title VI of the Civil Rights Act of 1964 but certainly of the equal protection clause of the Fourteenth Amendment.[12] In a suit brought by black parents (and joined by the United States in an amicus brief arguing that IQ tests violated federal law) the court found that the use by California educational authorities of "standardized in-telligence tests" are "racially and culturally biased, have a discrimina-tory impact on black children and have not been validated for the pur-pose of essentially permanent placement of black children into educationally dead end, isolated and stigmatized classes for so-called educable mentally retarded."[13] As indicated in Chapter 2 the findings of the court were based on a 10,000-page trial transcript that includes the testimony of California educational authorities, a detailed review of the history of the test, testimony from various experts in the field, and detailed statistical analysis of EMR placements in California. Find-ing that black children were disproportionately placed in EMR classes, the court concluded, "If defendants [California education authorities] could have shown here that the disproportionate enrollment in EMR classes actually represented and tapped a greater incidence of mild mental retardation in the black children population and not 'cultural bias' then defendant's EMR placement process could have survived. . . . Further, if defendants could somehow have demonstrated that the in-telligence test had been validated for purposes of EMR placement of black children those tests could have been utilized despite their dispar-ate impact.[14] The court concluded that the state could meet neither test; the record showed no cases applying validation criteria to the tests had been developed and that the "Anglo child identified and placed in an EMR class tends to be significantly more handicapped [than the black child] and the probability of placing a mildly handicapped Anglo child who is not in fact retarded in an EMR class is very small . . . which is to say that if a white child has an average IQ score of 75 or 80 it is more likely to be accurate than if a black child has an IQ of 70–80."[15] In enjoin-ing the use of the test for purposes of EMR placement the court con-cluded that its "decision in this case should not be construed as a final judgment on the scientific validity of intelligence tests . . . whatever the general scientific merit of the tests, defendants have failed to show a valid, legal justification for their use for black EMR placement."[16]

Institutional racism, if the findings and judgment of the District Court are valid, is widespread in American education in the post–civil rights era since apparently all states except California and Massachusetts continue to use the IQ test to place black children in classes for the mentally retarded when in fact they may not be retarded.[17]

Employment

The historic post–World War II gap between black and white rates of unemployment has widened in the post–civil rights era. At no time since the passage of the civil rights acts of the 1960s has the black community experienced full employment, measured at roughly 4 percent of the civilian labor force, while for whites (especially males) this rate of unemployment has generally characterized their communities except in times of recession. But in good times and bad times the black unemployment rate has generally been at least twice the full employment rate, and since the civil rights era it has come to be accepted that the black rate of joblessness will be at least twice that of whites. Thus, for whatever reasons, in the post–civil rights era the unemployment situation of blacks—with all its pathological consequences for family and community life—has continued to deteriorate. Explanations of this phenomenon abound in the social science literature, especially in the growth industry of research on the underclass. Chapter 6 examines in detail the various explanations of black joblessness that emerge from the underclass literature but here I wish to focus narrowly on the institutional racism explanation as it relates to the problems of employment tests and other so-called bona fide employment qualifications. A fuller treatment of racism as an explanation for black joblessness is reserved for the subsequent critique of the underclass literature.

For a brief period in the post–civil rights era the Supreme Court appeared prepared to give judicial recognition to the concept of institutional racism and to fashion affirmative remedies to deal with it in the areas of employment and voting. But the Nixon-Reagan-Bush appointees to the Court failed to follow through on the halting start made in the late 1960s and in 1989 appeared to reverse course fundamentally in a way that would provide judicial recognition and relief only for individual racism.[18] A likely reason for the retreat of the Court is its understanding that recognition and remedy of institutionally racist practices would require major changes in the way jobs and joblessness are allocated in the United States.

The Supreme Court, while recognizing the validity of the concept of institutional racism, has never formally employed the concept, nor

has it, in its notes and references in its opinions, cited the literature dealing with the concept. Indeed, in its more than two-hundred-year history of cases and controversies dealing with racism in the United States
the Court has rarely, if ever, used the word formally in its findings and
opinions. Rather, it has preferred euphemisms. For racism in employment the preferred euphemism is racial disparateness. For individual
racism the term is "disparate treatment"—where the employer intentionally uses race as a criteria to treat persons unfairly, and for institutional racism the term is "disparate impact" where the question is not
intent but whether an employer practice has a significant adverse effect
on an identifiable class of persons of a particular racial group regardless of the intent or motive for the practice.[19]

Gaston County v. the United States is the earliest case in which the
Supreme Court dealt with the problem of institutional racism.[20] In the
1965 Voting Rights Act Congress suspended literacy tests as a qualification for voting in most of the south. The suspension was based on a
congressional finding that the tests were administered in a racially discriminatory manner, an instance of individual racism. Subsequently,
Gaston County, South Carolina, restructured its tests to make them scru-
pulously fair in both content and administration. The county then sought
to reinstate the tests by seeking a "bail-out" judgment from the federal
district court in Washington as provided by Section 4(A) of the 1965
Act. The district court, while agreeing that the new tests were fair on
their face, held that they nevertheless deprived blacks of equal voting
rights in violation of the Voting Rights Act. In its 7–1 judgment affirm-
ing the lower court decision, Justice John Harlan read the legislative
history of the act to mean that Congress had adopted the suspension in
order to deal with the "potential effects of unequal educational opportunities on the exercise of the franchise" and that Gaston County's history of racially segregated schools has "deprived black residents of equal
educational opportunities . . . which in turn deprived them of an equal
chance to past the test." Thus, the Court said that the civil rights statutes could reach and remedy not only individual, overt acts of racism
but also the effects or consequences of historical racism as it may be
manifested in nominally nonracist practices of American institutions.
The logic of the Gaston decision was clear: historical racism could render racially impartial practices racist in their effects or consequences.[21]

The Court next pursued the Gaston logic two years later in its seminal employment discrimination case, Griggs et al. v. Duke Power Company.[22] When Congress passed the Civil Rights Act of 1964 the Duke
Power Company abandoned its overtly racist policy relegating blacks
to jobs in the low-skill, low-wage laborer category. However, the com-

pany simultaneously introduced a diploma and successful completion of two general intelligence tests as requirements to transfer to any nonlabor category or for initial hiring in such categories. Neither the tests or the high school diploma had been validated by the company, that is, shown to be related to performing a particular job or categories of jobs. On the contrary, the evidence presented at trial showed that whites in the nonlaborer jobs who had not taken the tests or graduated from high school continued to receive satisfactory job performance ratings, suggesting that none of the new qualifications were related to or predictive of job performance. However, the tests resulted in a 58 percent pass rate by whites compared with only 6 percent among blacks, and while 54 percent of white males in North Carolina had graduated from high school only 12 percent of black males had received a comparable level of education. The tests and diploma requirement thus allowed Duke Power to continue to relegate blacks to the lowest job categories in a manner almost as effective as when it practiced overt racism. Employing the logic of *Gaston* a unanimous Supreme Court struck down the new requirements. In the opinion of Chief Justice Warren Burger the Court held that blacks in the state had long received an inferior education and that this resulted in their disproportionately low high school graduation rates and performance on the tests. And since neither the tests nor the diploma requirements had been validated the Court held that under Title VII of the 1964 Act such practices, procedures, or tests, while neutral on their face and even neutral in intent, cannot be maintained if they operate to "freeze" the status quo of prior discrimination. The Court's clear recognition of institutional racism in the *Gaston* and *Griggs* decrees were promising departures in the restructuring of institutional racist practices in the area of voting and employment with implications for other institutional arenas as well—implications that might have resulted in efforts to eradicate not only individual racism but the effects or consequences of historical racism. Unfortunately the Court's departure down this road ended up in a cul de sac.

As early as *Washington v. Davis* five years later, the Court began to turn away from the *Gaston* and *Griggs* reasoning. *Washington v. Davis* is complicated because it was decided under the Fifth Amendment's due process clause rather than Title VII and the Court is usually more deferential to administrative authorities in constitutional rather than statutory interpretations. The case involved a challenge by black applicants for the police department in Washington, D.C., to a test administered by the city to determine whether applicants for employment had acquired a particular level of verbal skill. The tests, which had not been validated in terms of job performance, resulted in a fail rate for blacks four times as high as that for whites. In a 7–2 decision the Court rejected the challenge, holding that the Constitution does not prevent a government from seeking to modestly upgrade its employees communication skills, especially where the job requires some ability to communicate orally and in writing. Unlike in *Griggs*, the Court noted that the police department had affirmatively sought to recruit blacks: that in spite of the low pass rate on the test blacks constituted 44 percent of the new police recruits, a figure roughly equal to the number of 20–29-year-old blacks in the area labor force. The majority opinion also noted that while the test had not been validated in terms of specific police job performance, it nevertheless was a useful indicator of how recruits would perform in training school, and this precluded the need to show validation in terms of the job.[23] The facts of this case did not show the clear-cut disparate effect of *Griggs*, thus the Court majority declined to extend the rationale of *Griggs*; in terms of the need for employment tests to be validated in terms of job performance, or the *Gaston* rationale, with respect to "side effects discrimination" resulting from the District of Columbia's history of racially segregated and inferior education.

There was an implication in *Washington v. Davis* that if the suit had been brought under Title VII the different level of scrutiny involved might have rendered the District of Columbia's policy invalid. However, in subsequent Title VII cases the Court never extended the *Griggs* logic. In fact in the 1980s in several cases it began to back away from *Griggs's* implied recognition of institutional racism, and in the 1991 *Wards Cove* case the Court in effect repudiated the *Griggs* logic altogether. Apart from unvalidated tests and educational requirements that have the effect of eliminating blacks from employment for which they are otherwise qualified, in the post–civil rights era the seniority system is the most pervasive form of institutional racism.

The intent of the seniority rule—long established in American labor-management relations—is obviously not racist in origins; rather its intent or purpose is to protect workers from arbitrary and capricious layoffs in times of recession and to gain a measure of job security for those workers who have invested greater time and energy in an employer. In addition, it is reasoned that more experienced senior workers are likely to be more productive. But it is also clear that its unrestrained operation in the post–civil rights era is institutionally racist. In general, blacks are, as the saying goes, "the last hired and the first fired," but more critically until Title VII was enacted blacks were in an overtly racist manner frequently denied employment opportunities in the more skilled, professional, and technical sectors of the work force. Thus, once such overt racism was prohibited, the normal operations of seniority, given the cyclical nature of the economy, have the racist effect of forcing blacks onto the unemployment rolls in a way disproportionate to whites (see the discussion in Chapter 7 of black job losses during the 1990–91 recession). The Supreme Court, however, has refused to recognize claims of discrimination with regard to seniority, holding first in *Teamsters v. United States* (431, US 324, 1977) that section 703(h) of Title VII "insulates bona fide seniority systems from attack *even though they may have a discriminatory impact on minorities*" (emphasis added). In a subsequent case the Court reaffirmed this interpretation and explicitly declined to apply the *Griggs* rationale to seniority systems. The findings of the case, which involved the American Tobacco Company, provide the "best evidence" empirically of the institutional racist nature of the seniority system. At trial it was uncontested that the company and its union had until 1963 engaged in overt racism, including segregated locals and the relegation of blacks to the lowest-paying jobs. When these practices ceased in anticipation of the Civil Rights Act's prohibitions, the company and union began to hire blacks in all job categories, but when layoffs became necessary the seniority rule was rigidly followed, with the result that virtually all the blacks were fired, leaving these job categories again virtually all white. Yet the Court, with the dissents of Justices Thurgood Marshall and William Brennan, declined to give judicial recognition to this reality, notwithstanding the clear disparate impact of the seniority rule in this case. Rather, the majority held, "To be cognizable, a claim that a seniority system has a discriminatory impact must be accompanied by proof of discriminatory purpose."[24] A similar clear-cut empirical case of institutional racism was presented in *Firefighters Local Union #1784 v. Stotts et al*. The facts presented at trial established that even after the Civil Rights Act the City of Memphis continued to engage in patterns and practices of overt racism in employing firefighters in violation of Title VII. Under a Court order the city began to employ black firefighters, but in 1980 budget problems required layoffs. In a consent decree the city declined to follow the seniority rule but instead adopted a plan to protect the newly hired blacks.[25] The white-dominated firefighters union sued, claiming "reverse discrimination." The Supreme Court, consistent with its prior rulings, invalidated the consent decree, once again holding that Title VII protects bona fide seniority systems whatever their racist consequences.

What the Court has said in plain language in these cases is that racism exists but neither civil rights statutes nor the equal protection clause of the Fourteenth Amendment permit a remedy because the racism observed is institutional, not individual, and to provide relief would require a major restructuring of labor—management relations, which the Court was not inclined to undertake.[26] This, as Brooks points out, is the major problem in judicial handling of racism in American life, even the best evidence available of its existence provides no remedy under the Court's legal concept of discrimination.[27]

Brooks's point was clearly demonstrated in the *Wards Cove* case, in which by shifting the technical burden of proof in employment discrimination cases from employer to employee, the Court effectively repudiated the *Griggs* logic and for purposes of judicial scrutiny virtually eliminated institutional racism, or, in its language, disparate impact cases. This does not mean that institutional racism has ceased to exist in American life, only that the Court has structured its rules and procedures in such a way as not to see it, or if it is seen the court concluded that it is too disruptive to institutional relations to do anything about it. Justice John Stevens in his dissent in *Wards Cove* wrote that *Griggs* was rightly concerned that childhood deficiencies in education and background or other institutional forces beyond the control of minorities "not be allowed to work a cumulative and invidious burden on such citizens for the remainder of their lives." Yet, the reluctance of the Court or other institutions to undertake fundamental institutional reform make it likely that the historical burden of racism, except for its most obvious, overt, intentional forms, will continue to burden many blacks for the rest of their lives and probably even their children's lives.

I should not conclude this analysis of institutional racism in employment on a wholly pessimistic note, since in the post–civil rights era some progress has been made in its recognition and remedy. Ironically, this progress in one area—what is called "race norming"—was undermined by the Civil Rights Act of 1991's effort to overturn the *Wards Cove* decision. First, progress has been made in the area of federal employment. For years the federal government used the PACE—the Professional and Administrative Entrance Examination—to select employees for more than a hundred entry-level professional and technical jobs. In 1979 black applicants filed suit in the U.S. District Count at Washington, D.C., alleging that the tests were racially discriminatory. In 1978 42 percent of white applicants passed the test but only 5 percent of Hispanics and 13 percent of blacks did so. Plaintiffs alleged that this racially disparate effect of the test results, coupled with the fact that it had not been validated, made a prima facie case that its use was discriminatory.[28] In the last days of the Carter administration the government entered a consent decree that stipulated the test was discriminatory and that until a fair test could be designed the government would develop procedures to select minority employees in rough proportion to their percentage of applicants. When the Reagan administration took office it tried to withdraw the government's consent to the decree, but the Court refused and directed the Civil Service Commission to continue to comply with its interim terms while developing a nondiscriminatory test or an alternative selection procedure. Until it could develop a written examination that could be validated for the range of jobs covered by the PACE, the administration abolished the written examination in favor of an applicant's grade point average and a job related skills test called the "Individual Achievement Record," which sought to measure the full range of relevant job skills as well as qualities like "ambition" and "ability to cooperate."[29] What is remarkable about this change in civil service personnel practices is that if the Carter administration had allowed the case to go to trial and it had reached the Supreme Court the black plaintiffs would probably not have prevailed given the Court's then emerging line of reasoning in such cases.

The other change in institutionally racist employment practices was, surprisingly, undertaken by the Reagan administration. For more than fifty years employers could request state employment agencies to require job seekers to take the Labor Department's General Aptitude Test, which assesses a broad range of abilities, from literacy to motor skills. On average blacks scored 16–20 percent lower than whites and Hispanics 5 to 10 percent lower. In a study of the test the National Academy of Sciences found that the test was "only modestly" useful in predicting job performance and tended to "screen out minority applicants who often proved as competent as the whites who were screened in."[30] Meanwhile in 1980 the Labor Department began quietly to encourage state employment services and some federal agencies to adjust scores by race—what is called "within-group score conversion"—so that the scores of black applicants would be ranked only with blacks, Hispanics with Hispanics, and whites with whites. Thus, a black who scored in the eighty-fifth percentile of black test takers was put on the same footing with a white applicant who scored in the eighty-fifth percentile among whites, although the black applicant's raw score would have ranked him much lower when compared with all applicants. The effects of this process, labeled by the press "race norming" was to eliminate the disparate effects of the test and qualify more blacks for entry-level employment. Again, this practice was quietly introduced in the Reagan administration and was implemented with little public knowledge or controversy. However, during the debate on the 1991 Civil Rights Act it became known (as a result of a letter to the editor of the *New York Times* from a University of Delaware sociologist) and was immediately the cause of much debate and controversy, with conservative critics charging it represented a perfect example of the quota issue that the

Bush administration had used to veto the 1990 version of the bill. In the compromise version of the 1991 Act both the president and the Democratic leadership in Congress agreed to language abolishing "race norming." As a result, this fruitful line of attack on institutional racism was blunted, paradoxically, in the name of civil rights.

Housing

Racism—individual and institutional—is a widespread, almost routine practice in the rental and sale of housing in the post–civil rights era, notwithstanding the command of the Fair Housing Act of 1968. As my personal experiences in Westchester County discussed in Chapter 3 suggest, racism in the housing market can be both overt and crude as well as covert and institutional, and as the periodic housing audits— where matched couples in terms of social class, race, and housing needs are sent to rent or purchase available housing—conducted by the Housing and Urban Affairs Department (HUD) and private groups show, it is widespread. Depending on the metropolitan area, blacks in the United States are denied available housing from 35 to 75 percent of the time.[31] The result of this widespread racism in the housing market is that despite passage of fair housing legislation, more tolerant attitudes of whites toward integrated housing and the emergence of a sizable black middle class with incomes sufficient to promote residential mobility, academic studies continue to indicate that the segregation of blacks in many large metropolitan areas has hardly changed in the post–civil rights era.[32] Controlling for the effects of class, blacks remain the most racially segregated of the nation's minorities, confined disproportionately to the nation's deteriorating central city housing markets at a rate much greater than that of Asian and Hispanic Americans.[33] Racism in the distribution of housing affects not only the quality and cost of shelter but also a family's capacity to generate wealth since for the average person a house in the United States is his or her principal investment and means of capital accumulation.[34] It also has an indirect effect on employment and education because job opportunities and a higher quality of education are found increasingly in the suburbs rather than the central cities.

Individual racism in the sale or rental of housing is fairly easy to document. The audit or site survey methodology is accessible to any group of interested black or white citizens. As I tell the doubting Thomases in my classes, all one has to do is organize a team of black and white house hunters, telephone a sample of local realtors and rental agencies about available units, and then in turn send the individuals in separate visits to inquire about the availability of the units. The results, again depending on the metropolitan area and the particular neighborhood, invariably show some degree of individual, overt racism. For example, the most recent HUD-sponsored national audit conducted in 1989 in twenty-five metropolitan areas (with a sample of 3,000 paired testers) found that blacks faced racial discrimination 56 percent of the time in rentals and 59 percent of the time when they tried to buy a house.[35]

But racism in housing—particular in purchase rather than rental—is more complex than the behavior of individual realtors or apartment managers. It is in its covert, institutional mode that racism probably has its most deleterious effects on the life chances of African-Americans. The complexity of institutional racism is revealed in a remarkable investigative report on racial bias in mortgage loans conducted by the Atlanta *Journal-Constitution* and subsequently in a more extensive report prepared by the Federal Reserve Board pursuant to the Home Mortgage Disclosure Act. Although evidence of institutional racism in mortgage loans has long been alleged, these two studies for the first time provide empirical data on the phenomenon. These studies also show the limitations and complexity of the institutional racism concept, even with good race—class data.[36]

The Atlanta *Journal-Constitution* analyzed the records of ten thou-

TABLE 4.1

Racial Differences in the Rejection of Mortgage Load Applications By Region

	Black	White
National	23.7%*	11.1%
West	25.1	14.4
Midwest	29.6	12.2
South	24.1	10.2
Plains	30.9	12.6
Northeast	13.4	6.1

Source: Bill Dedman, "Race Gap in Loans Uncovered," as reported in the Houston Chronicle, January 22, 1989. National figures are for 1983–88; regional figures for 1985–88.

*Percentage of black and white applicants rejected by savings institutions.

sand loan applications (value at $1 trillion) from 3,100 savings and loan institutions from throughout the country for the period 1983–86. The results reported in Table 4.1 show that black applications for mortgage loans were rejected nationwide at a rate more than twice as great as among whites. Although there are regional variations in this race disparity, in no part of the country is the race gap in mortgage loan applications nonexistent. And the article contends that if one includes withdrawn applications, loans pending, and no decisions, the overall rate of loan approval is 50 percent for blacks compared with 74 percent for whites. The concept of institutional racism used here requires more than a finding of racial disparity in particular institutional practices; it requires instead a showing that the disparity persists after controlling for social class. The newspaper reported, "Throughout the country high income blacks were rejected more often than low income whites in 85 of the 100 largest metropolitan areas in at least one of the past five years. . . . In 35 of these areas high income blacks were rejected more often than low income whites in at least three of the five years."[37] Thus, what is observed here is not a class bias operating under the mantle of race but an institutional racist practice. Bankers who are supposed to look at the bottom line nevertheless somehow find it more financially prudent to loan to poor whites rather than middle-class blacks. When asked to explain this situation, Barney Becksma, chairman of the U.S. League of Savings Institutions, could not. He told the *Journal Constitution*

> As for people being discriminated against because they are minority, I've never heard of that. They must be getting a higher percentage of unqualified applicants or many of those applications may be coming out of very depressed neighborhoods. On the other hand, most people who can't qualify don't even apply or they're weeded out by the realtor because they don't have the income. You're dealing here with people who think they can get a loan, who are willing to pay an application fee. I admit I probably don't have a good answer for that.[38]

These data seem to make a clear—cut case for institutional racism. Racial disparities exist in the approval of home mortgage loans, and these disparities persist even when social class (income) is taken into account. The fundamental assumption of the concept of institutional racism that I am using is that holding class constant (income of applicants or the aggregate income of racially distinct neighborhoods) effectively accounts for economic or class differences, and therefore the only possible explanation for the persistence of the racial statistical disparities is racism. But an analysis of the *Journal-Constitution* report (and

a similar report that appeared in the Detroit Free Press) prepared by the
Federal Reserve Board at the request of Senator William Proximire, chairman of the Senate Banking Committee, found that this explanation "may
not always be valid."[39] Rather, the report suggests that factors such as
differences in loan demand, credit history, savings, job security, and
heavier black reliance on government-backed loans may explain the
observed black—white, race—class differences.[40] In part as a result of
these news accounts and the controversy they generated, in 1989 congress amended the 1975 Home Mortgage Disclosure Act (HMDA) to
provide for more detailed information on the ethnic, class, and geo-
graphic bases of mortgage loans for virtually all lenders in the United
States. Preliminary findings from the first of these reports are reported
in Table 4.2 by ethnicity and income.

TABLE 4.2

Mortgage Loan Rejection Rates in the United States
By Ethnicity and Income, 1990

		Lowest Income Group	Highest Income Group
Whites	14.4%	23.1%	8.5%
Blacks	33.9	40.1	21.4
Hispanics	21.4	31.1	15.8
Asians	12.9	17.1	11.2

Source: "Home Mortgage Disclosure Act: Expanded Data on Residential Mort-
gages, "Federal Reserve Bulletin, November 1991, p.870.

These more extensive data show the same pattern of ethnic—class
disparities, black applicants are rejected most frequently, followed by
Hispanics, whites, and Asian-Americans. In terms of social class, strikingly the highest-income black applicants have a loan rejection rate that
resembles that of the low-income whites (21.4 percent and 23.1 percent
respectively) than their white high-income counterparts. That is, it appears from these data that poor whites have about the same chance of
getting a home loan as middle-or upper-income blacks. By neighborhood racial composition, the data indicate that the rate of rejection increases as the proportion of blacks increases. For the conventional loan,
for example, the denial rate is about 12 percent for areas with less than
10 percent minorities and rises to twice that in areas more than 80 percent black.[41]

Again the data here would appear to show a fairly clear-cut case of institutional racism, but the report declines to draw this inference. Rather, citing a host of other possible explanatory variables—down payment, debt ratio, value of appraised property, and the applicant's employment experience—the report concludes, "Thus, it is not possible to determine from the HMDA data alone whether loan applicants are being treated fairly and on a racially non-discriminatory basis."[42] The report calls for further research, controlling for these other variables, before accepting racism as an explanation for these disparities. These data on mortgage lending illustrate the complexity of trying to establish empirically racism in the post–civil rights era.[43] It is difficult to see racism—except in the overt, individual sense—in the post–civil rights era, and even when it is apparent, as in this case of statistical race—class disparities, we cannot be certain that that is what we see.[44] This problem is not limited to mortgage loans. We will encounter this same complexity in access to health care, in automobile purchases, clinical drug trials, and in the so-called war on drugs. Clear racial disparities are observed in each of the institutional arenas, even when class is held constant yet researchers are reluctant to call the phenomenon racist, contending that some other variables not yet examined (or perhaps even known) may account for the empirical realities. This, of course, is correct, but one also must be alert to infinite regress analytically as well as the need for definitive policy action before there is definitive knowledge.

For example, as the Federal Reserve report points out, loan applicants with the same income maybe strikingly different in other characteristics, assets, for example. Blacks and whites experience an enormous gap in financial assets,[45] and this gap may in part explain the race—class statistical disparities. But in a substantive or policy sense, this may be irrelevant. If the relative lack of assets means blacks cannot obtain loans to purchase homes and a home is the average American's largest asset, then blacks do not have homes because they do not have assets and they do not have assets because they cannot purchase homes. This is a classic vicious cycle or Myrdal's notion of cumulativeness in racial discrimination. Or as, Justice Stevens noted in *Wards Cove*, historical racism in this area is allowed "to work a cumulative and invidious burden on citizens for the remainder of their lives." The American economy is credit-driven not only in housing but also in other durable good purchases and in business development. To the extent that blacks cannot get credit because they are black or can get it only on inequitable terms compared with whites, this is a factor that should be taken into account to explain the post–civil rights era deterioration of inner-city black communities and the emergence of the so-called black underclass.

Health

In the post–civil rights era virtually everyone agrees that the health of the black population has substantially deteriorated; so much so that scholars and practitioners now routinely use the word crisis to describe the situation.[46] Two measures that frequently serve as summary indicators of the well-being of a people—the infant mortality and life expectancy rates—may be used to establish this point. Although the black-white infant mortality gap narrowed in the mid-1970s, since then it appears to be widening to the point where the black rate is now almost twice that of whites, 19.6 versus 10.1 (this indicates the number of deaths per 1,000 live births before the child reaches one year of age). Using this measure, black American health resembles that of a poor third world nation more than it does their fellow citizens in this country or the citizens of the major industrialized states.[47] Life expectancy for blacks has actually declined in the post–civil rights era. This is extraordinary since from the time recordkeeping began life expectancy has generally improved for both blacks and whites. Yet, the most recent data released by the National Center for Health Statistics show the continuation of a four-year decline in the black rate, dropping from 69.7 years in 1984 to 69.2 in 1988 (the comparable figures for whites are 75.3 and 75.6). Although these changes may seem modest, statistically the decline in the black rate was significant enough to cause a decline in the overall national rate, from 75 years to 74.9.[48]

Thus, blacks are not as healthy as whites and they never have been. The problem is to what extent this health gap can be accounted for in terms of racist practices within the health institution. Probably not much, given the way I have defined and operationalized institutional racism. Although there are some exceptions, much of the data suggests that the vast differentials in black and white health are to be explained on the basis of social class and public policy; in terms of the latter, primarily the absence of a comprehensive national health insurance program.[49] David McBride, in a fine sociohistorical study of the urban black community since 1900 and its relationship to health-care providers, writes that "the nation's health care apparatus, because of its institutional history and links with larger processes of socioracial stratification, continues to develop in directions opposite one in which it could serve as a fundamental factor in alleviating the AIDS epidemic and other health problems among poor blacks and similar minorities."[50] McBride identifies "racialism"—racially based explanations of black susceptibility to certain diseases—racism, cultural differences between the races, social class differences, and institutional policies and practices in the delivery of health care as explanatory factors in the racial health differentials. Yet, in the post–World War II period and especially the post–civil rights era he is hard-pressed to isolate and disentangle the racism effect from social class or the other possible explanatory factors.

Most of the recent studies point to social class, not racism, as the key explanatory variable in explaining the race gap in health. Schwarz and his colleagues examined Americans aged 15–54 who died between 1980 and 1986 from twelve illnesses that normally are not lethal if treated early (pneumonia, gallbladder disease, influenza, hernia, Hodgkin's disease, among others). During that period there was an average of 17,366 "excess" deaths related to these diseases, almost 80 percent of them black.[51] Again, most of these illnesses usually do not result in death, thus the study concludes that the fact that blacks died of these conditions almost four times more frequently than whites suggests that the principal explanation is the absence of routine medical care, which is traced to poverty, the absence of health insurance, the inadequate services of public hospitals and clinics, and other conditions related to inner-city impoverishment.[51] Similarly, a study by the National Cancer Institute of the incidence of cancer in three large metropolitan areas— Atlanta, Detroit, and San Francisco-Oakland—between 1978 and 1982 found that the overall black rate was between 6 and 10 percent higher than the rate for whites.[53] And for specific types of cancer the race gap is much greater: rates of lung and prostate cancer are 60 to 70 percent higher among blacks than whites, and cervical cancer is more than twice as prevalent among blacks. However, once controls for social class are introduced, the study found, the race gap disappeared. Indeed, the authors conclude that the effect of social class is so powerful that if the income differences between the races could be eliminated the race gap would be reversed: blacks would have lower cancer rates than whites.[54]

Multiple factors contribute to the disparity in sickness, health, and death between blacks and whites, but the disproportionately high black poverty rate is clearly the most profound and pervasive. Yet, there is some evidence that racism may play a role independent of class. For example, studies show that, controlling for the effects of socioeconomic status as well as such relevant factors as diagnosis, age, and gender, blacks are less likely than whites to have undergone various coronary procedures and transplant operations.[55] Held, for example, found that race and income were statistically associated with receiving a kidney transplant but rejects racism as an explanation, writing, "At this stage only hypotheses can be offered . . . but *conscious* discrimination against specific individuals seems unlikely."[56] Similarly, Kjellstrand, after calculating that blacks had two-thirds of the chance of whites of receiving a kidney transplant, is reluctant to embrace racism as an explanation, writing, "If there is bias, it is not possible to use our data to examine whether the bias exists in patient, family, society in general or in physicians and medical institutions. However, the most favored recipient of a transplant is similar to the physicians who make the final decision: A young white man."[57] But, again, medical scientists generally are reluctant to see racism in these glaring statistical disparities. Wenneker and Epstein studied racial differences in utilization of coronary procedures. They examined all admissions for circulatory diseases or chest pain to Massachusetts hospitals in 1985. Controlling for age, sex, type of insurance, income, and the number of secondary diagnoses, whites underwent significantly more coronary bypass grafting procedures than blacks (one-third more coronary catherizations and twice as many coronary artery bypass grafts).[58] Why this race—class disparity? Not because whites have a higher incident of heart disease; to the contrary, the evidence, the authors suggest, show equivalent if not higher rates of heart disease among blacks. Might racism be a factor? The authors are not sure. They write, "These differences may not be due entirely to race per se; they may be due in part to differences in income or disease severity that have not been adequately accounted for in this study. Nevertheless, race does seem to be important. If medical decisions are being made on the basis of race we need to understand more about the complex interaction between physician and patient that leads to this inequality and the implications of these patterns for the appropriateness and efficacy of medical care."[59] This studied ambiguity was too much for several of Wenniker and Epstein's colleagues, who wrote a stinging letter to the editor that might apply as well to mortgage loan applications as to access to coronary by pass procedures.

> We believe that the most likely reason for the inequities found is institutionalized and subconscious racism. But in the JAMA article, racism is considered only briefly, lastly, and politely as "sociocultural factors influencing physician and patient decision making." In subsequent national media coverage, the authors are quoted as saying they "don't know" (safe, and always true) and "don't understand" the reason for the observed inequities. We cannot understand why the authors of this study, which was published in the Martin Luther King commemorative issue of JAMA, have stopped shy of implicating racism. Their own article carefully documents the evidence in the medical literature.

How many more studies do we need before we can seriously consider this as a factor? Are they reluctant to confront the possibility that even their colleagues are not immune from prejudice? With nearly a century of collective experience in understanding racism, we believe Drs. Wenneker and Epstein are scientifically fence-sitting to avoid taking a stand that conceivably could offend. In doing so they have offended us. It is time to take a more courageous stand and help rid out nation of this terrible scourge.[60]

"Scientific fence-sitting" does seem to characterize much of the literature on institutional racism, whether we are dealing with race—class disparities in education, housing, health, drug use, or consumer services. Drug use, prescribed and proscribed, provides yet another example of this "now you see it, now you don't" phenomenon. There is extensive documentation in the medical literature of substantial racial differences in response to drugs, yet there is also substantial evidence of the underrepresentation of blacks in clinical trials. Sevenson, in an examination of such trials, found that in most cases blacks were not adequately represented, even in studies involving hypersensitive agents where racial differences in reactions have been amply documented.[61] This means that there is insufficient knowledge to assess adequately the safety and efficacy of many new drugs on blacks. Whey are blacks underrepresented in drug trials. Sevenson writes, "It is difficult to determine . . . and more studies are needed."[62]

If blacks are underrepresented in clinical drug trials, they are by contrast substantially overrepresented in the jails for the use of illegal drugs. Studies by the FBI and the National Institute for Drug Abuse both conclude that blacks are no more likely to use illegal drugs than whites but are more than twice as likely to be punished for such use and punished more harshly, sentenced on average to prison terms 50 percent longer than are whites.[63] In effect, the war on drugs has become a war on blacks, especially young black men. The result is the increasing criminalization of black America, with roughly 25 percent of young blacks in prison or on probation compared with 6 percent of young whites. Why this enormous disparity? One reason is that the black community is more frequently targeted by the authorities, and therefore blacks are more frequently arrested. But why the disparity in sentencing? One reason is that Congress and most of the states have elected to punish the drug of choice among blacks—crack cocaine—more harshly than powered cocaine, the drug of choice among whites. Under federal law possession of five grams of crack cocaine, worth about $125 requires a mandatory five-year jail term, while possession of 500 grams of powdered cocaine, worth $50,000, results in the same sentence. The rationale for this distinction between the two drugs is that crack is more dangerous and addictive than cocaine. The effect, however, is to create a huge racial disparity in sentencing. In Minnesota, for example, a 1989 law imposed a penalty of twenty years for possession of 3 grams of crack but only five years for a similar amount of cocaine. Ninety-seven percent of those arrested in Minnesota for crack were black while 80 percent of those arrested for cocaine possession were white. In 1991 the Minnesota Supreme Court declared this law unconstitutional because of its "racially disparate" impact and because, in the Court's judgment, the evidence was not sufficient to support the distinction drawn between the two types of drugs in terms of addictiveness or danger.[64] The sponsor of the law, Representative Randy Kelly, expressed shock at the Court's ruling, declaring "we never considered it was going to be applied unequally to people of color. Our major concern was potency, its absolutely devastating influence on people, its cheapness and its attractiveness in terms of selling to children."[65] Which, of course, is precisely the point of the concept of institutional racism—no racism was intended but a black person is punished at a rate four times greater than is a white based on his choice of drug.[66]

Consumer Services

The cocaine case discussed above may be seen as racism in the cost of consumer services and products, although in this case the product is illegal. This case demonstrates the disproportionate costs that blacks must pay in order to purchase a range of goods and services. Several years ago Richard Cohen, the liberal *Washington Post* columnist, wrote a column on blacks shopping in Georgetown and other upscale neighborhoods. Cohen reported that when blacks, even well-dressed middle-class persons, shop they are frequently eyed suspiciously by store personnel, followed closely, and often asked, "can I help you, can I help you," while whites are allowed to browse leisurely without the watchful eyes of store personnel. Cohen argued that while blacks viewed this as a form of racism, in fact it is not racism but a form of rational behavior, given the statistical probability that blacks are more likely to shoplift than whites. Thus, the differential treatment of blacks in situations such as this is a rational response to the differential crime rates of the two groups, which results in treating all blacks as possible criminals.[67] A similar kind of racism is observed in many public places in many American cities in the United States.[68] For example, cabdrivers, black as well as white, tend to avoid black passengers in favor of white fares. Observing this tendency in Washington, D.C., students in one of my undergraduate black politics classes at Howard University interviewed thirteen cabdrivers (all African or African-American) about whether this kind of racism existed and why. While vigorously rejecting the notion that this kind of behavior was racist (several wondered how a black man can be a racist against his own people), each of the individuals confirmed that the tendency did exist and said it was because of several factors, including the fact that blacks would more likely than whites wish to travel to low-income areas where the chances for a return fare was lower and the chances of being robbed greater. Several also indicated that blacks were less likely to tip, and consequently the average white fare was more remunerative than the average black one. But the most frequently cited reason—indeed it was universally cited—was the fear of robbery, assault, or murder (several of the respondents indicated that in the previous year every single robbery and assault in the past year in Washington was committed by a black person). Thus, all blacks maybe denied service, as in the Cohen case, because of their association with the misdeeds of a few. Brooks call this "smiling discrimination," mentioning such examples as when "the sales clerk in a suburban shopping mall waits on a white customer before waiting on a minority customer who was first and the nightclub owner who imposes a dress code designed to keep minorities out or who makes it a policy to play a certain type of music (for example country and western) when 'too many' African Americans are on the dance floor."[69]

These cases of "smiling discrimination" do not easily fit our concept of institutional racism because the class bias, real or perceived, is difficult to disentangle. Rather, they more nearly fit Downs's definition of institutional racism, in which race itself is not used as the discriminatory device, but, rather, other mechanisms indirectly related to race serve as the surrogate. In cases of smiling discrimination, the indirect mechanism is the association of a black skin with crime and poverty. There are, however, cases of institutional racism in consumer services that are both conceptually and empirically clear in terms of disentangling the effects of class.

The first deals with access to social security disability benefits. In what is described as the most comprehensive study ever undertaken of the relationship between race and disability benefits, the General Accounting Office (GAO) found that over a thirty-year period blacks with serious ailments have been much more likely to be rejected for social security benefits, controlling for the applicant's class (measured by education), age, and type of disability).[70] The second case involves car sales. A research team at Northwestern University headed by Ian Ayres, a lawyer and economist, sought to test for the existence of racial and gender bias in new car sales. Commissioned by the American Bar Association, the study was based on a yearlong study of 550 new car sales in the Chicago metropolitan area.[71] The study was carefully designed to control for the effects of social class. Prospective customers were trained in a uniform procedure. Black and white, male and female rehearsed the same negotiating tactics so as to extract the best bargain. They dressed casually and presented themselves as well-educated, urban professionals of the same age. They were told to tell the salespersons that they all lived in the same upscale Chicago neighborhood. The results of the research summarized below would seem to provide unambiguous evidence of institutional racism in this consumer market:

> White men received final offers that averaged about $11,362 on a new automobile. By contrast, white females were given a price of about $11,504, a markup forty percent higher than offered white men. The black male was given an average price of $11,783, more than double the markup offered to white men. The black woman was given an average price of $12,237, three times the mark up for white males.[72]

Ayres suggest that his findings indicate a pattern of both individual and institutional racism, although he uses the terms "animus"-based discrimination and "statistical discrimination" from the economic literature and disparate treatment and impact from the law. Although Ayres concludes that individual "animus" based racism might partially explain the results,[73] overall the findings point to institutional racism in that "sellers took race . . . into account and treated differently testers who were otherwise similarly situated. These terms are not meant to imply that sales people harbored any animus based on race or gender."[74]

This case is perhaps a fitting place to end this discussion of racism in the post–civil rights era. After a house, a new car is the largest consumer investment. The results of this study suggest another possible explanation for the continuing economic disabilities of the black community.[75] If institutional racism is as widespread as this car sales case indicates, it may also exist in other unregulated consumer markets— car repairs, household services, or other major purchases such as appliances. We do not know whether this is a reasonable inference. But if this inference is correct, this is surely an important part of any explanation of the continuing economic and social disparities between the races.

5

Internal Inferiorization in the
Post–Civil Rights Era

The previous chapters have shown how the ideology of white supremacy and racism—historical, individual, and institutional—have damaged and continue to damage the material conditions of African-Americans in education, employment, housing, health care, and consumer services, as well as their physical well-being and personal safety. Yet, it is frequently said that the most pernicious effect of racism is not material but psychological. Slavery and its progeny shackled not only the body but the mind, and as a consequence the black freedom struggle has always been twofold: to battle the structural conditions of material subordination and the psychological conditions of mental subordination. The two struggles are viewed as interrelated with an almost chicken-and-egg quality with respect to which must take precedence. Before an effective struggle can be waged against the material basis of racism, one must struggle to remove the psychological barriers that may inhibit the struggle against the structural ones. Thus, one must "free the mind" before one can "free the body." Yet it may be that a precondition for psychic well-being is some measure of material well-being, since psychic self-esteem is not unrelated to material well-being. Thus, which comes first—another enduring dilemma in the Afro-American freedom struggle. Indeed it is a dilemma of the struggles of all colonized peoples. In this chapter the focus is on the psychological aspect of the dilemma, which, following Fanon, I call internal inferiorization.

Students of the black experience—challenged only in the post–civil rights era—have long contended that the subordination of blacks by whites and its justification on the basis of the institutionalization of the ideology of black inferiority leads some, if not all, blacks to internalize the notion of inferiority or self-hatred and low self-esteem. The key variable is institutionalization, through the polity, church, media, schools, and popular culture, the notion of black inferiority exercises a pervasive and continuous influence, conscious and unconscious, on attitudes and behavior throughout the society. As a result, it is only normal for white persons growing up in such a society to think and act on the notion of black inferiority. To do otherwise would require a conscious break with the very base of one's being, even perhaps, as Kovel suggests, professional therapy to get at the subconscious roots of the malady.[1] The psychic problem for the black man, woman, and child may be more difficult and complex. The institutional mechanisms of society exert their influence, but human beings naturally reject their own denigration, however powerful and pervasive its institutionalization. Thus, it may be some blacks feel ambivalent; what DuBois in his famous formulation alluded to as a "peculiar sensation," a "double consciousness," this sense of always looking at one's self through the eyes of others, of measuring one's soul by the tape of a world that looks on in amused contempt and pity."[2]

An essential component of the ideology of white supremacy was the denigration of blackness. This negative evaluation of blackness and black people is deeply rooted in Anglo-American culture. Thus, it is common to read in the literature of race in the United States observations such as the following by the social scientists Anderson and Cromwell: "white Americans have devalued black skin color. Blackness in general has been associated with discouragement, despair, depression, coldness, the unknown, the haunting shadow and nightmare."[3] And, they continue, the "American Negro has long ago adopted this negative blackness concept. For several reasons he identified with the white ego ideal. Thus, for decades within the American black culture the owner of a black skin resigned himself to the fact that he was negative, inferior and less attractive."[4] An influential early statement of this perspective was Dollard's *Caste and Class in a Southern Town*. Dollard's perspective is useful in this context because he skillfully links the process of institutionalization, socialization, and caste domination to the phenomenon of personality development, arguing that they produce a "distinctive psychology," which limits the personal development of blacks. A defining characteristic of this distinctive black psychology is what Dollard called "its damaging effect on individual self-esteem," which is seen largely as a function of the social structure's denigration of blackness.[5] The psychological mechanisms at work are quite explicit in Dollard's analysis:

> We have learned from Freud that the first love object of the human individual is his own physical self . . . primary narcissism. . . . If this be true, a considerable achievement is demanded of Negro persons in adjusting themselves to white society. They must accept the narcissistic wound of learning to prefer white color and features to their own; all that is designative of the primitive Negro

self is judged "bad" by society. Most Negroes accept the superiority of white characteristics and the inferiority of their own, and
attempt to edge over toward the toward the white model. . . . These
types of action indicate acceptance of white standards and admissions of inferiority.[6]

Behaviorally, Dollard suggests, in an analysis akin to that of Fanon
(discussed below), that this "psychopathology" leads to frustration,
which should lead to aggression toward whites, but since the sanctions
for following that course are so severe, blacks either engage in passive,
accommodative behavior or release the pent-up hostility in aggressive
actions toward fellow blacks.[7]

This line of analysis was also followed by Kardiner and Ovesy in
their classic study *The Mark of Oppression*, in which the central thesis is
that racism generated low self-esteem.[8] But perhaps the single most explicit and influential statement of this relationship is in the work of
Fanon, work based not on the study of American blacks but on Africans
on the continent living under colonial domination. Fanon's analysis
parallels that of Dollard and Kardiner and Ovesy, but as a black man, a
trained psychiatrist and philosopher, and a revolutionary, he was much
better equipped to analyze the problem: "I hope by analyzing it to destroy it." Using a variety of "data"—literature, dreams, and case histo-
ries—Fanon developed what he called a psychopathological and philo-
sophical explanation of the "state of being a Negro" in a social structure
controlled by whites. In such a situation, without revolutionary change,
Fanon saw little reason for optimism because "The black man has no
ontological resistance in the eyes of the white man."[9] It is therefore not a
problem of mere low self-esteem or feelings of inferiority but of "being." Fanon wrote, "A feeling of inferiority? No, a feeling of nonexist-
ence. Sin is a Negro as virtue is white. All those white men in a group,
guns in their hands, cannot be wrong. I am guilty. I do not know of
what, but I know I am no good."[10]

Fanon analyzed several manifestations of this psychopathology
in language, in interracial sex, in light skin color preference, and in
intragroup violence. Unlike the more narrowly academic studies of
Dollard and Kardiner and Ovesy, Fanon's work became very influential among 1960s civil rights activists and provided important intellectual stimulus for the black power revolt. Fanon's books, along with *The
Autobiography of Malcolm X*, became the Bibles of the 1960s black power
activists, displacing the Bible and Albert Camus as required readings.
This is in part because of the elegance and eloquence of Fanon's writings compared to the academic studies, but most critically because Fanon

clearly grounded the problem in the racist social structure and called for and became involved in revolutionary change of the structure. In his earliest work on the problem, he wrote, "The analysis that I am undertaking is psychological. In spite of this it is apparent to me that the effective disalienation of the black man entails an immediate recognition of social and economic realities. If there is an inferiority complex, it is the outcome of a double process—primarily economic and social. Subsequently the internalization—or better the epidermalization—of this inferiority."[11] Later, Fanon made a more explicit call for political action:

> As a psychoanalyst I should help my patient become conscious of his unconscious and abandon his attempts at hallucinatory whitening, but also to act in the direction of a change in the social structure. In other words, the black man should no longer be confronted by the dilemma, turn white or disappear, but he should be able to take cognizance of the possibility of existence. In still other words, if society makes difficulties for him because of his color, my objective will not be that of dissuading him from it by advising him to "keep his place"; on the contrary, my objective, once his motivation has been brought into consciousness, will be to put him in a position to choose action or passivity with respect to the real source of his conflict—that is the social structure.[12]

Later in this chapter in my examination of the black power movement and its attempt to deal with the inferiority complex, the influence of Fanon's work on the black power activists' efforts to create a new black consciousness will be discernible. But before turning to black power, there is one other civil rights era work that exerted considerable influence politically and in the post–civil rights era has become a source of a conceptual and methodological dispute—technical in nature—but one that challenges the validity of the proposition that blacks suffer from low self-esteem, self-hatred, and an inferiority complex. I refer to Kenneth Clark's famous doll experiments.

The work of Clark (and his wife, Maime) did not explicitly reach the low self-esteem, self-hatred, inferiority complex conclusion, but it is strongly implied. The methodology of the Clark's seminal study was deceptively simple.[13] Black children, ages three to seven, were shown identical dolls, two of them brown and two white, and asked (1) Give me the white doll; (2) Give me the colored doll; (Give me the Negro doll. Seventy-five percent of the children correctly identified the color of the dolls. Then they were asked such questions as which doll they liked best, to give him the doll that looked bad, and to give him the doll they would like to play with. The majority of the children in all age groups indicated an "unmistakeable preference for the white doll and a rejection of the brown doll."[14] The inference drawn from this finding was that as a result of racism black children developed at an early age an awareness of the color hierarchy, and in their preferences for the white doll indicated a degree of self-hatred or rejection.[15] This inference and its statistical underpinnings have been the object of extensive methodological criticisms, which I review below, but at the time it was widely hailed as a landmark work that showed the pernicious effects of racism on the psychological development of black people.[16] Thus, the civil rights movement, as Dr. King frequently said, was a struggle not only to remove racism's structural barriers to black progress but also the psychological impediments. The psychological aspect of this struggle was most effectively waged by the advocates of black power during the late 1960s and early 1970s.

Black Power and the Struggle for
Race Identity and Consciousness

The civil rights movement was likely the result of and contributed to a rise in individual and collective self-esteem among segments of the Afro-American population. Martin Luther King and other protest leaders spoke frequently of how the movement had awakened a new found sense of self-worth and self-respect among "Negroes," and studies conducted during the period show that those blacks with a positive self-image of the group were more likely to support militant civil rights activism.[17] In his famous speech "Message to the Grass Roots" and in his posthumously published autobiography, Malcolm decried the notion of black self-hatred as it manifested itself in such things as light skin color preference, processed hair, and hatred of things black and African. Malcolm said, "Negroes hated themselves, hated how they looked, hated their hair and most of all hated Africa." Frequently he said that blacks had no respect for the ability or accomplishments of other blacks, except perhaps in entertainment, "to play some horn, make you feel good but in serious things . . . no.[18] Malcolm's life was a testament to the efficacy of the Nation of Islam's program of psychological reconstruction that resulted in his transformation from "Negro" to "black." The Nation emphasized individual and collective self-worth, identification with Africa and things African. Thus, as early as the 1950s adherents of the group derisively referred to "so-called Negroes" who had lost their identity and knowledge of "true self," calling on individuals to drop their slave names (becoming X or some other Islamic or African name) and on the group to refer to itself as black, Afro-American, or African-American. This emphasis on Africa and black identification in the United States was reinforced by the decolonialization struggles and the re-emergence of independent African states, beginning in 1957 with Ghana and accelerating throughout the 1960s as scores of new nations gained independence. The independence of the new African states inspired Africans in America to think that with political independence would come economic independence, cultural revitalization, and the restoration of Africa to a place pre-eminent in the family of nations. Although these hopes have yet to be realized, for a time they were both a psychological and political inspiration for Africans in America struggling for freedom and cultural integrity.[19]

The contribution of the civil rights movement, the Nation of Islam, and the African independence struggles were necessary but not sufficient conditions in the emergence of a new race consciousness among blacks. The integrationist-assimilitionist ideology of the liberal leadership of the civil rights movement was and always had been ambivalent on the issue of racial identity, consciousness, and action.[20] The Nation of Islam had a mass following, but it was small and generally limited to the poor and lower middle class and northern avant-garde intellectuals. And the African independence struggles, while inspirational, did not provide a model for mass action in the United States. These necessary conditions, however, became sufficient ones as they came together to influence the young activists in SNCC to develop what was to become the black power movement.

By the mid-1960s the young SNCC activists were increasingly influenced by the writings of Fanon, the African independence struggles, and the teachings of Malcolm X. As a result of these influences as well as growing disenchantment with the slow pace of the civil rights struggle, the brutality of southern whites, and the ambivalence toward the struggle by white liberals in the movement and in the government, in 1966 SNCC activists launched the black power movement. The black power movement had important effects on the Afro-American freedom struggle, altering its ideological, organizational, and strategic bases and facilitating its institutionalization.[21] But black power also had an important effect on black identity and consciousness, resulting to some extent in a transformation of the "Negro" psyche and community.

The black power advocates were quite explicit on these objectives of the movement. They wanted to create a "new Negro" and call him "black." Carmichael and Hamilton wrote, "we aim to define and encourage a new consciousness."[22] Why? Because "The social and psychological effects on black people of all their degrading experiences are also very clear . . . a pernicious self and group hatred . . . [and] a new consciousness, this is the vital first step. . . . It is absolutely essential that black people know their history, that they know their roots, that they develop an awareness of their cultural heritage."[23] Thus, from the outset black power as a movement sought not only ideological, organizational, and political change but also psychological and cultural changes. Indeed, the distinction here is an artificial one. The advocates of black power believed that one could not have the kind of ideological and political change desired in the black community without first or at least simultaneously having the psychological and cultural changes. Black power was thus at once a mass movement for social and political change and a movement for cultural revitalization.

A first step in the development of this new consciousness and revitalized culture was to revisit the names controversy, what should persons in the United States of African descent be called? Carmichael and Hamilton wrote, "There is a growing resentment of the word 'Negro' because this term is the invention of our oppressor, it's his image of us that it describes. Many blacks are now calling themselves African-Americans, Afro-Americans or black people because that is our image of ourselves."[24] Although as this quotation shows a variety of alternatives to Negro were initially acceptable—African-American, Afro-American, and black—eventually black became the name of choice. First, of the three it was the briefest, but more importantly since black had historically had been a term of denigration institutionalized in the racist social structure and internalized by at least some parts of the black community, to use the term *black* was to simultaneously reject the racist stereotype and to vindicate blackness and black people. For example, in the cosmology of the racist black was defined as ugly; a new consciousness would define it as the opposite. Thus, the popularity during this period of bumper stickers and other emblems declaring "Black is Beautiful" or James Brown's number one record "I'm Black and I'm Proud." Finally, in the ideology of the white supremacist blackness elicits fear and disgust among whites, thus it was an appropriate name for expressing this new militant consciousness and strategy. This was thought to be especially the case when the word *black* was linked rhetorically with power. [25]

The struggle to have the name *black* displace the name *Negro* was not an easy one and was perhaps the new movement's first major victory. This was not the first names controversy in Afro-American history (and not the last, as the more recent controversy discussed below about African-American as the appropriate name for the group in the twenty-first century). Blacks called themselves African until early in the nine-

teenth century (reflected today, for example, in the African Methodist
Episcopal Church). After the Civil War *freedmen* came into use followed
by *Afro-American, colored,* and *Negro*. Each shift was accompanied by
debates about the ideological and political implications of the old and
new names.[26] For example, in the 1930s *Negro* became the name of choice
among elements of the black intelligentsia, including DuBois, who defended its use against charges that it was a white man's word.[27] Although
embraced by such eminent yet ideologically diverse figures as DuBois
and Marcus Garvey, *Negro* was rejected as early as the 1940s by the
Nation of Islam's Elijah Muhammad and Harlem's congressman, Adam
Clayton Powell. However, it was not until the 1960s, black power rebellion that it was effectively challenged and displaced. Within two years
of the 1966 black power march in Mississippi, *black* was the preferred
term among students and intellectuals, was gradually displacing *Negro*
in the black press (*Ebony* and *Jet*, for examples), and was accepted by
most of the civil rights leadership, with the notable exception of the
NAACP's Roy Wilkins, who never reconciled himself to the word.[28]
Whites and the black mass public were slower to accept the term.[29] Initially white radicals and liberals began to use the term, and even Richard Nixon in his 1968 campaign embraced *black* and used it to advance
his program of "black capitalism" as the real route to black power. By
1970 the *New York Times* dropped use of the word *Negro* in favor of *black*
and the Associated Press revised its widely used style book replacing
Negro with *black*. These successes at the elite level soon transformed
black mass opinion. *Newsweek*, in a 1968 poll, found that 69 percent of
blacks favored the term *Negro* and only 6 percent *black*, but by 1974 a
substantial majority had changed its mind and embraced the new black
power nomenclature.[30]

The black power advocates' successful imposition of this name
change was not merely symbolic but part of the broader movement of
cultural revitalization. On the campus students inspired and sometimes
led by former SNCC activists organized Black Student Unions. These
organizations had two major goals: to increase the number of black students and faculty and to transform the curriculum by adding to it departments and programs in black studies. The black studies movement
on campus was an integral part of the larger black power movement
since one of its major goals was to provide an intellectual and institutional basis for the new black consciousness. Carmichael and Hamilton
had insisted in *Black Power* that the movement's success required black
people to recover their roots, learn their history, and become aware of
their cultural heritage. Black studies was a concrete effort to achieve
these objectives. As a result of a wave of strikes and demonstrations in

the late 1960s black studies programs were established at most of the nation's leading colleges and universities.[31] Beyond the campus black power stimulated a remarkable transformation in mass culture in terms of the arts, popular music, and fashions.

In black arts Larry Neal's influential essay in the summer 1968 issue of the *Tulane Drama Review* inspired an outpouring of new black poetry and drama by persons such as Leroi Jones (Amiri Baraka), Don Lee (Haki Madhubuti), and Sonia Sanchez. Neal was explicit in linking black arts and aesthetics to black power politics:

> The Black Arts Movement is radically opposed to any concept of the artist that alienates him from his community. Black Art is the aesthetic and spiritual sister of the Black Power Concept. As such, it envisions an art that speaks directly to the needs and aspirations of Black America. In order to perform this task, the Black Arts Movement proposes a radical reordering of the Western culture aesthetic. It proposes a separate symbolism, mythology, critique and iconology. The Black Arts and the Black Power concept both relate broadly to the Afro-American desire for self determination and nationhood. Both concepts are nationalistic. One is concerned with the relationship between art and politics, the other with the art of politics.[32]

In popular music a similar transformation is observed. Black popular music is traditionally apolitical, focusing on themes of sex and love, with rhythms suitable for dance, but in the 1960s for a brief period it took on an explicitly political character. A few popular artists such as Curtis Mayfield and long included messages on race consciousness and solidarity in their music, but coincident with the black power movement traditionally apolitical artists such as James Brown ("I'm Black and I'm Proud"), the Temptations ("Message to the Black Man"), Marvin Gaye ("Inner City Blues") and B. B. King ("Why I Sing the Blues") began to include such themes in their music.[33] In addition, newer artists such as the Last Poets became popular by explicitly focusing on music as an instrument of cultural and political change.

In a comprehensive study of black music as a cultural expression Walker carried out a content analysis of all 1,100 songs that appeared on Billboard's cumulative annual best-selling black (soul) listings from 1946 to 1972. Walker's hypothesis was that the events of the 1960s combined to produce a distinctive group consciousness and solidarity that was manifested in an increase in "message songs." Walker employed specialists in black music as "coders" to assist in the identification of the content of the music in terms of message and nonmessage songs. His data show a steady increase in message songs beginning after 1957 and that a sustained increase of "inordinate proportions" occurred between 1966 and 1969, the peak years of the black power movement. By comparing black to nonblack music in this same period, Walker was able to show that this increase in message songs was peculiar to black music.[34]

This new black identification and consciousness also manifested itself in changes in names, fashions, hairstyles, and cosmetics. All these changes illustrate a widespread, mass-based cultural revitalization movement and not simply a project of an activist elite. The natural hairstyle (best symbolized in the 1960s by Angela Davis's widely publicized photograph) became for several years not merely an aesthetic preference (although it was that as well) or a fad but a social and political statement that "Black is beautiful." As Malcolm X and others had noted, blacks (himself included) had been ashamed of their "nappy, kinky" hair and had used various chemicals and hot combs to process it; that is, to make it appear more like the hair of a European. Thus, to wear a "natural" was to suggest that blacks were no longer ashamed of their blackness. The natural became not merely a cultural expression but to some extent a statement of black militancy. It was often said in the late 1960s that "processed hair means a processed mind; that is those who wear their hair as the European also thought as the European." Many blacks changed their names as well, from the Anglicized names of their slaveowners to those with African or Islamic origins (Cassius Clay became Muhummad Ali, Lew Alcindor became Kareem Abdul Jabbar, and Stokely Carmichael became Kwame Toure), and African fashions—dashikis, bubas, and jewelery—became popular. Overall, then, the civil rights and black power movements combined in the 1960s to produce a relatively high degree of race consciousness and solidarity, compared to earlier years and other ethnic communities in the United States. Basically, the individualistic ethos of the integrationist ideology gave way to more of a communalist, nationalist ethos, which probably operated to enhance individual self-awareness, consciousness, and self-esteem as well as a collective group consciousness that cut across class and other cleavages in the black community.

In an analysis of this process of change at the individual level Cross, a black psychologist on the faculty at Cornell's Africana Studies and Research Center, hypothesized that the 1960s transformation from what he called "Negro to black" personality entailed a series of well-defined stages. Arguing that "few people can claim that they have always been black," Cross posited a five-stage developmental process in "becoming black." Linking these individual-level changes directly to the black power movement, Cross contends that the rhetoric and activism of the movement's advocates resulted in "a disassociation from white standards and values that promote black inferiority and [a] turning toward other non-white peoples in different parts of the world, particularly Africa, for a frame of reference to replace the one rejected."[35] The first stage is Eurocentric, self-hating. The second is one where the individual initially encounters blackness through contact with an individual personally or through a lecture, speech, or some consciousness-raising event or series of events. In the third stage, called "saturation," the individual becomes immersed in blackness in terms of friends, rhetoric, music, fashions, and so on. At this stage the individual would often take on a "blacker than thou" attitude toward "Negro" family and friends and express hostility toward whites. The fourth stage of internalization indicates that blackness is becoming a part of the individual's psychological makeup, and the fifth and final stage involves the transformation of this psyche of blackness into behavior as the individual becomes a committed activist in the struggle for social change.[36] Although these developmental stages were empirically confirmed by Cross, with tests administered only to a small sample of college students, they closely parallel personal recollections of my development of blackness in the 1960s as well as that of many of my friends and colleagues. They also mirror Malcolm X's description in *The Autobiography* of his transformation from "Negro to black" (see especially chapters 11–19).

The collective level also shows evidence of this emerging race group identification and solidarily. For example, Aberbach and Walker on the basis of data from the Detroit Area Survey conducted in the late 1960s reported that the black power movement contributed to the formation of a specifically black political culture that cut across class lines.[37] These changes were not ephermal, rather, they persist into the post–civil rights era. The black power activists brought about a fundamental change in black political thinking. The political scientist Warren Miller writes, "The appropriate dimension for understanding the political behavior of black citizens may have changed. Contemporary black leaders may have helped shape the political meaning of being black in ways the black leaders two decades before could not. Certainly, racial identity is now the most useful prescriptive measure of the political choices of many citizens.[38] Hagner and Pierce use national survey data that show that for the period 1960 to 1980 mass black identification with the interests of the race as a group increased from 26 percent in 1960 to 54 percent in 1980.[39]

The effects of black power on the collectivity of the black community are clear. A conscious *black* identity was nurtured and consolidated, and that consciousness persists to this day, despite increased class differentiation in the post–civil rights era black community. The effect of these changes at the individual level in terms of enhanced black self-esteem and psychic well-being is more problematic. Before I turn to this problem, it is first necessary to analyze a body of literature that challenges the conceptual and methodological foundations of the very notion of black self-hatred and low self-esteem—a challenge that itself is an ironic outcome of the influence of the black power movement on black psychologists.

Methodological Note: The Post–Civil Rights Era Challenge to the Black Self-Hatred Paradigm

Earlier I discussed a body of literature that suggested that some blacks had internalized the negative images of themselves propagated and institutionalized by white supremacists. I then sought to show how the black power activists, acting on the premise of black self-hatred, attempted to develop a movement to reverse what Carmichael and Hamilton called "a pernicious self and group hatred" and reassert a new positive black identification and consciousness. Later I will attempt to assess the long-term effects of black power and other post–civil rights era changes on individual black consciousness, identity and self-esteem. However, there is a problem. Psychologists, especially African-Americans, have increasingly challenged the very assumption that black self-hatred and low self-esteem is or indeed ever was a problem. Baldwin states the problem this way: "one version is that improvements in black socioeconomic status in conjunction with the 'black consciousness' movement have led blacks to view themselves more positively. . . . However, such a proposition seems to assume that previous evidence for black self-hatred actually represents accurate and valid findings.. . . . Given the nature of numerous fundamental problems in theory and methodology challenging that literature, such an assumption is not valid."[40] The purpose of this methodological discussion then is to review the theoretical and methodological critiques of the self-hatred literature. This is necessary both as a technical matter and substantively. Technically, because although the critics of the self-hatred literature have made important contributions in clarification of conceptual and methodological problems in the research, they nevertheless have not successfully rebutted the notion that the phenomenon exists or has existed in the black community. Thus, while some technical conceptual and methodological problems in the research literature call into question the validity of some of the findings, these problems should not be allowed to obscure or obfuscate the reality of the problem in the past and—despite some possible progress in the last couple of decades—its reality at present.

In a sense the new literature on black identification is a product of the black power movement. Before the 1960s virtually all research on black self-identification focused on its negative attributes. Thereafter, most of the published work focused on the positive aspects of black identification, directly attacking the assumption that there was any relationship between race, individual self-esteem, and group self-hatred. It appears, therefore, that the new black psychology is itself a part of the consciousness-raising and cultural revitalization processes set in motion by black power. This may be seen in Cross's work, which is discussed earlier in terms of the five-stage developmental process from "Negro self-hatred" to a "positive black consciousness and identification." Yet Cross's *Shades of Black* is the most comprehensive statement of the point of view that the evidence for black self-hatred is of questionable validity, which, of course, casts doubt on his earlier work on the positive transformation of the black psyche since it suggests that it was not negative in the first place.[41] What I am suggesting is that in the new black psychology we have an interesting case in the sociology of knowledge whereby ideological and political concerns exert a profound, transformative influence on the nature of knowledge itself. For example, in challenging the self-hatred literature, Bruce Hare writes, "The argument that to be black in a predominantly white culture produces self-hatred rests not only the racist assumption that America is an irresistibly powerful white culture, but also on the assumption that black Americans internalize the negative images that white America projects. Both of these notions are questionable."[42] While these notions may be questionable, they are neither racist nor naïve. On the contrary, they are quite consistent with social scientific understanding of the meaning of institutionalization as a social process. It is not the "irresistibility" of "white culture" that is at issue but rather the irresistibility, for most people, of any institutionalized value, which over time exerts a continuous influence on mass thought and behavior, whether it be black inferiority, capitalism, or constitutionalism.[43]

The new black psychology challenges the black self-hatred literature on conceptual, methodological, and interpretative grounds.[44] The major conceptual difficulty involves, as Jackson and his colleagues put it, "The assumption that disassociating one's self from one's blackness implied rejection of the self, that feeling pride about black people implied feeling pride in self. This is simplistic and without support."[45] That is, in principle, one could simultaneously hold negative images of black people in general but individually exhibit high personal self-esteem. Indeed, some of the recent empirical studies show this to be the case and, moreover, that some blacks have higher measured self-esteem than comparable groups of whites.[46] This is because black individuals may use referants other than their race—their families, jobs, sexual orientation, their appearance—to gauge their self-esteem. Thus, this challenge does not assert that some blacks may not have internalized notions of black race group inferiority; rather, it suggests that personal feelings of self-worth and group identification are empirically separable phenomena.

The second problem is more interpretative than conceptual and deals with the doll studies that have been so influential in establishing the proposition of black self-hatred. As Cross, Hare, and others argue, Kenneth Clark and others using the doll experiments made three fundamental errors.[47] First, they imposed their "racialized" conception of the universe on "preracialized" youngsters. That is, children may not attach the same significance to color, positive or negative, as adults, and therefore color preferences may have no social or psychological significance. Second, even if the children's preferences were significant a second error is made when the scholars involved invariably drew conclusions about adults from the results of research on children. Third— and this is related to the conceptual problem—measures about social attitudes toward the racial group were used as if they were measures of individual personality attributes in terms of self-esteem or self-hatred.[48]

The final error is narrowly methodological and statistical. First, it is suggested that the methods employed in the doll studies—projective techniques, sociometric interactions, and self reports—are not systematically interrelated, consequently, the results are ambiguous.[49] Second, on the basis of review of the statistical inferences drawn from the major self-hatred studies, Banks concluded that the predominant pattern of race preference among blacks toward white and black stimuli conformed to simple chance.[50] Banks concludes, "The predominant pattern of black choice responses has been at a chance level. Although it has been advanced that black preferences have changed with the advent of the 1960s, little actual evidence supports either the contention that blacks rejected their own race prior to that time period or have consistently preferred their own race since then."[51]

In summary, then, this is the status of the research on black self-hatred. It is difficult to do justice in a few pages to the subtleties and nuances of this extensive and technically complicated literature. But

what it seems to suggest is not a lack of evidence of black internalization of notions of inferiority but, rather, that the evidence is not conclu-
sive or unambiguous and that the evidence of negative images toward
the group does not necessarily translate into an *individual* sense of inferiority or low self-esteem. This latter proposition of the new black psychology seems clearly established. However, on the former, while methodological errors may have corroded some of the pre-1960s findings
and the evidence is not clear-cut, we have ample theoretical and empirical reasons to believe that in the past and probably today *some* blacks
have internalized attitudes of group inferiority and self-hatred.[52] Therefore, I examine next the available data and evidence on internal
inferiorization in the post–civil rights era.

Internal Inferiorization in the Post–Civil Rights Era

Here I want to examine what is known about the status of internal
inferiorization, black identification, consciousness, and solidarity in the
post–civil rights era. In a sense the basic question here is how long-
lasting the effects of the black power movement have been in terms of
its efforts to enhance positive race identification, consciousness, and
solidarity. Some effects of the black power movement have clearly en-
dured. For example, with few exceptions most black organizations operate today on the black power principle that black people should organize independently or separately from whites. Black power also sought
to foster race group solidarity and, at least ideologically and politically,
that legacy endures as well. In spite of a widening post–civil rights era
class schism in the black community, between a relatively secure and
prosperous middle class and a large lower class, the black community
tends to be homogeneously liberal ideologically and highly cohesive in
its voting behavior. Most blacks continue to identify with their racial
community, and relatively few cleavages are observed at the mass level
ideologically or politically in terms of such things as class, gender, age,
or region, differences that continue to structure ideology and voting in
white America.[53]

If these organizational, ideological, and political legacies of black
power are clear, what is less clear is its effects on the black psyche in
terms of what blacks think of themselves with regard to feelings of inferiority or what Kenneth and Maime Clark call the "burdens, symptoms,
and determinants of negative self image."[54] In an important article, published of all places in *Ebony* magazine, the Clarks revisit their classic
work on racial identity and self-image.[55] They write that, forty years
earlier, "We documented the disturbing fact that the majority of [black]

children accepted the white society's definition of themselves as inferior. . . . They ascribed positive characteristics to whites and negative
characteristics to themselves. It was clear from those feelings that American racism imposed a tremendous burden of deep feelings of inferiority in the early stages of personality development in Black children."[56]
Given the important changes resulting from the civil rights and black
power movements, the Clarks sought to assess in this article the
"amount, nature and depth" of progress in the development of a positive race group self-image. According to the Clarks, the basic questions
in the study were posed by John Johnson, the publisher of *Ebony*, who
commissioned the project. In addition to general questions on the perceptions of progress in the post–civil rights era, the Clarks asked about
skin color preferences, attitudes toward black facial features, and attitudes toward black professionals and businesses. A telephone survey
of a national sample of 1,200 blacks was conducted in 1980. Because of
what they described as the complexity and sensitivity involved in asking adults about their "egos, self-esteem, conflicts, self-protective de-
fenses and pretenses," it was decided that simple direct questions would
be misleading. Thus, the issues were pursued in what they call "quasi-
projective" questioning. That is, rather than asking respondents directly
what they thought of blacks they were asked instead what they thought
other blacks thought about blacks. In this way the Clarks reasoned they
could "avoid direct confrontation of respondents with what he or she
thinks of themselves as a black. Hopefully, this would reduce the number of direct self-protective responses. In agreeing upon this approach
we operated on the assumption that the image that blacks have of others is reflective of the image the individual black has of himself and his
race."[57]

     According to the Clarks, the results of the survey show that while
progress is discernible in the post–civil rights era "blacks in general
have not yet developed a consistently positive self image" and "the
majority of blacks still appear to be burdened with racial self doubt."[58]
In terms of a general perception of a positive black self-image and in
terms of attitudes toward black elected officials, civil rights leaders, and
business and professionals (I discuss attitudes toward black facial features and skin color preferences below) the data are ambivalent. For
example, while 90 percent of the sample believed that blacks are more
proud now than before, signs of ambivalence are displayed when questions are asked in a less general manner, particularly in terms of positive or negative images of traditional black features and skin color preferences. A relatively large percentage (27 percent) stated a preference
for a white lawyer rather than a black one. Perhaps most interesting in

the context of the Clark's previous work the survey found that a majority (71 percent) of blacks do not purchase black dolls for their children.
Overall, the results of the survey show that blacks with more education
and income have more positive images of the race, and "Blacks in the
far west, for reasons that are not entirely clear, seem to have more positive self concepts than blacks in other sections of the country."[59]

While the Clarks' *Ebony* study focuses on adults—a departure from
their classic work, which generalized about adults based on studies of
children—several studies in the post–civil rights era have replicated
the doll experiments. At the peak of the black power movement in 1969,
Hraba and Grant found that a majority of black children of all ages at
an interracial school in Lincoln, Nebraska, expressed a preference for
black dolls and that this preference increased with age.[60] They attribute
this result to the effects of the ongoing black power movement, but since
in the original doll studies a majority of black children may have also
expressed a preference for colored dolls the findings here are difficult
to interpret. Cross reviewed twenty-nine race group identity studies
and eighty-nine self-esteem studies conducted between 1968 and 1980.
Sixty-two percent of the race identity studies showed blacks with a positive group orientation, 28 percent showed a negative orientation, and
10 percent had varied results. However, "just as the earlier studies tended
to show Blacks exhibiting a split pattern favoring whites (subjects selected whites on average 60 percent of the time and Blacks 40 percent),
the new preference for black was also accompanied by a split pattern
(60 percent black vs. 40 percent white)."[61] The studies of individual personality or self-esteem follow a pattern similar to that of the group identification studies since black power: 54 percent found no differences in
self-esteem between blacks and whites, 20 percent showed blacks with
higher self-esteem, and 15 percent showed whites having higher self-
esteem.[62] At best, what these studies show is an ambivalence in race
group identification and black individuals' sense of self-worth, a pattern that may or may not reflect improvements in the post–civil rights
era. In the absence of reliable base-line data, specific comparisons are
difficult to make, especially since even those studies in the 1940s, 1950s,
and early 1960s that found evidence of widespread forms of racial rejection also found evidence to the contrary, although it was not emphasized. Thus, black racial identification has probably always been ambivalent, reflecting a diversity of attitudes from positive to negative to
ambiguous, depending on such things as family, community, class background, and individual personality.

Diversity in terms of social class is reflected in most of the general
survey data on black attitudes toward themselves in the post–civil rights

era. In the 1981 *Washington Post* poll, a substantial minority of blacks share the same negative stereotypes toward the race as whites. Blacks were grouped in the poll according to how they answered three questions: Whether blacks had less inborn nobility to learn, whether blacks would rather accept welfare than work, and whether blacks lacked the motivation and willingness to pull themselves out of poverty. Among the respondents 10 percent took what might be described as the "anti-black" position on all three questions, 45 percent on one or two, while 45 percent rejected all three propositions.[63] The poll showed that negative sentiments toward the race were concentrated among the elderly and lower class, especially those living in impoverished, highly segregated urban areas. However, the report states, "In general, when poor blacks disparage blacks they do not refer to themselves and their own families but they do talk in general terms about the poor people in their neighborhood or housing project."[64] This is consistent with the notion of the new black psychology that negative images toward the group—holding it in low-esteem—does not necessarily translate into negative attitudes toward the self or individual low self-esteem.

TABLE 5.1

Black Attitudes toward Themselves by Education, Region, and Age, 1991

	Lazy	Violent	Unintelligent	Welfare
All Education	19.3%	42.8%	11.7%	38.6%
Less H.S.	26.3	46.2	7.5	43.6*
H.S. grad.	27.3	40.9	9.1	43.2
Some college	6.9	46.4	18.5	35.7
Coll. grad	11.8	38.2	14.7	29.4
Region				
Non-South	14.5	47.3	9.3	30.9
South	22.2	40.0	13.2	43.3
Age				
18–24	21.1	57.9	5.6	42.1
25–54	19.5	44.7	15.1	39.5

Source: National Opinion Research Center, 1991 General Social Survey.

*Difference statistically significant.

Table 5.1 reports the results of the most recent survey tracing racial rejection among blacks conducted in 1991 by the National Opinion Research Center as part of its General Social Survey. The results show, first, that the great majority of blacks reject the negative stereotypes about the race projected in the questions. Although substantial minorities agree with the notions that blacks prefer welfare to work and are violence-prone, the items on laziness and intelligence are rejected by large majorities. There are class (education), regional and age differences in the responses, but only the educational difference on black preference for welfare is statistically significant, with those with less than a high school education more likely to agree with this stereotype than the college educated. But in contrast to most studies of this sort attitudes on these items do not vary in a statistically significant way in terms of education, region, or age. Most of the studies have shown, for example, that members of the lower class are more likely to embrace the notion that blacks are less intelligent; however, in this most recent survey the class differences, while not statistically significant, nevertheless point in the opposite direction: college-educated blacks were more likely to agree with the proposition than those with less than a high school education.[65] Again, the results are ambiguous. A decline *appears* to have occurred in negative race identification in the post–civil rights era, but it is difficult to gauge precisely. Most, but not all, of the survey data suggest that it is lower-class blacks who display negative racial group images. It is also clear that in the post–civil rights era a significant minority of blacks (ranging from 10 to 25 percent depending on the survey and the question) continue to tell survey researchers that they hold negative images of the race, despite the black power movement.

Many observers contend that these negative images of blacks are reinforced by the images of blacks portrayed in the media in the post–civil rights era; images of blacks killing one another at an extraordinarily high rate, images of idleness and welfare dependency in the black community, and the constant reports about the "performance gap" between blacks and whites on various standardized educational and employment examinations. Some black psychologists have suggested that these "Rumors of Inferiority" result in a withdrawal of blacks from intellectually competitive activities who fear that the rumors might be proved true.[66] Thus, black young people supposedly compensate for this fear of failure intellectually by concentrating instead on athletic and other endeavors where the images are ones of competitive excellence.[67] This is largely speculative, however, isolated research reports confirm this line of thinking.[68] An example is Fordham and Ogbu's study in the early 1980s of black high school students in Washington, D.C. They found among a significant number of the students a clash between their peer culture and educational achievement, fearing that academic achievement would risk their being called a "brainiac" or worse "white." They write that "what appears to have emerged in some segments of the black community is a kind of cultural orientation which defines academic learning as acting white and academic success as the prerogatives of white America."[69] Again, the data here are tentative and the cases isolated, but they are suggestive of this continued pattern of racial ambivalence among some segments of the black community in terms of race identification and its social and cultural referants.[70]

Skin Color Differences and Preferences in the Post–Civil rights Era

One of the aims of the black power movement with regard to race group consciousness was to effect change in what was believed to be pervasive skin color consciousness and privilege in the black community. It was argued in the 1960s that black people historically had internalized the negative images associated with black skin color and traditional African facial features (hair, nose, lips) propagated in the ideology of white supremacy. It was also argued that historically and in present-day society persons with lighter skin color were accorded greater privileges—socially, economically, and politically—by the external white society but also internally within the black community. Ample historical, social science, and anecdotal evidence supports both propositions. Historically, slave society was organized externally and, to some extent, internally on the basis of color, such that lighter-skin blacks were granted greater privileges, which resulted over time in their constituting a disproportionately large segment of the middle and upper classes and of the leadership strata in the black community. The actual quantitative correlation historically between class and skin color cannot be known, but at the time of emancipation, Myrdal writes, "What there was in the Negro people of 'family background,' tradition of freedom, education and property ownership was mostly in the hands of mulattos. . . . They became the political leaders of the freedmen during Reconstruction, as well as their teachers, professionals and leaders."[71] Similarly, Holden writes of civil rights era black leadership in terms of the Negro "Gentry, the color conscious descendants of free negroes and mulattos who exercised leadership during the Civil War and Reconstruction."[72] Forsythe writes in a similar vien that "of the twenty congressmen and two senators who represented Blacks during Reconstruction, all but three were mulattos and about thirty-two of the thirty-nine leaders noted for their protest against slavery between 1831–1865 are usually described as persons of mixed blood."[73] Finally, Bennett described the civil rights era black establishment as the "Black puritan class, the lineal and spiritual descendants of the ante-bellum and Reconstruction upper class."[74]

The social scientific research on this question is not as extensive as the historical evidence, but it points in the same direction.[75] In general, Ransford notes that the observation that "A higher proportion of dark Negroes are found in low status jobs is nothing new" and that "Negroes who have moved out of the ghetto and have more prestigious jobs tend to be light skinned"; results he attributes to "The white gatekeepers who have allowed more light skinned Negroes into prestigious jobs and neighborhoods."[76] In order to examine this proposition empirically Ransford in 1965 conducted a study in Los Angeles of 312 black males between the ages of 18 and 65, selected randomly.[77] The results, in general, support the hypothesis that skin color structures opportunity. Dark respondents were three times as likely to be unemployed and, holding high school education constant, there was a 25 percent spread on white-collar occupations between light and dark respondents. Further, only 9 percent of light-skinned high school graduates had incomes of less than $5,000 compared with 33 percent of those with dark skin.[78] Ransford's work confirms that the historic privileges of light skin color persisted into the civil rights ear.

A fairly extensive body of research going back to the 1940s shows that some blacks have consistently expressed a preference for light skin color, rated their own skin color lighter than it was, and expressed a preference for lighter skinned playmates or mates.[79] Anecdotal material supports this research, as shown by the frequently told stories of how certain black Greek organizations during the civil rights era would use the "brown bag" test to decide who could join (if one's skin color was not as light as that of a brown bag then one failed the test), with certain fraternities and sororities reserved for those with light skin, curly or "straight" hair, and a so-called good background. Spike Lee dramatized these color conflicts in his films "School Daze" and "Jungle Fever." According to Lee "School Daze" was a fictionalized version of his own years as an undergraduate at Morehouse. He writes, "The people with money, most of them have light skin. They have the Porsches, the BMWs and the good hair. The others, the kids from the rural south, have bad, kinky hair. When I was in school, we saw all this going on. . . . I remember thinking this stuff has to be in a movie."[80] Given this well-documented cleavage in the Afro-American community on the basis of color, the question becomes what effect has the 1960s black consciousness movement, with its "Black is Beautiful" emphasis had on this phenomenon in the post–civil rights era.

The evidence is ambiguous in terms of mass attitudes, however, in terms of social class one still observes in the post–civil rights era a nexus between skin color and socioeconomic status. The data reported

TABLE 5.2

Selected Social and Economic Characteristics by
Skin Color Differences in the Afro-American Community*

	Dark	Medium	Light
Education			
Less high school	51.1%	35.9%	37.9%
High school graduate	48.9	64.1	62.1
Occupational Prestige			
Low	55.3	37.7	32.1
Medium	41.6	48.8	59.0
High	3.1	13.5	9.0
Family Income			
Far below average	22.2	15.2	9.3
Below average	38.0	29.1	38.4
Average	35.1	48.3	43.0
Above Average	4.7	7.4	9.3

Source: Adapted from Richard Seltzer and Robert C. Smith, "Color Differences in the Afro-American Community and the Differences They Make," *Journal of Black Studies* 21(1991): 281.

*All differences statistically significant.

in Table 5.2 based on NORC's 1982 General Social Survey show that darker skinned respondents are less likely to have completed high school, had lower occupational prestige scores, and were more likely to report below-average family income. Thus, skin color still has its privileges. It is not clear whether these privileges are the result of the continued cumulative effects of historic economic opportunities on the basis of skin color or the effects of an active, ongoing structuring of economic opportunities on the basis of skin color or some combination of both. We simply do not know because there has been relatively little research in the post–civil rights era dealing with this problem.[81] While skin color in the black community makes a difference socioeconomically, it probably makes little difference politically. That is, once the effects of social class are removed, there are few differences between light, medium, and dark blacks in terms of the liberalism—conservatism ideological cleavage.[82]

Since the leadership of black America tends to be drawn disproportionately from the middle and upper classes, it is also likely that in the post–civil rights era, as in the past, it continues to be disproportionately light skinned. It is, however, very difficult to document this. In an earlier project dealing with post–civil rights era changes in black leadership, I used *Ebony's* annual list of the top 100 black leaders to document changes in the social background and institutional affiliations of black leaders since 1963.[83] I briefly considered use of the photographs that accompany the list to trace skin color trends. But they were too unreliable to permit objective color coding. Whatever color differences exist are probably not important except aesthetically, since black leaders, like the black masses, probably do not differ that much politically on the basis of color. However, aesthetically it crops up from time to time in black conversations. Roy Innis, the head of the Congress on Racial Equality for example, has chastised the leadership for its color snobbery, saying that whenever he visits the offices of national black organizations, he sees from the top to the bottom a sea of mulatto faces. (I heard barbershop scuttlebutt of this sort regarding President Clinton's nomination of Hazel O'Leary as energy secretary and Lani Guinier as assistant attorney general.)

Several studies have been conducted on the extent to which the color preferences of blacks have changed since the black power movement. The Clarks' *Ebony* study found evidence of a more positive race identification in terms of a decline in light skin color preference and a decrease in the importance of skin color in mate selection. Yet they conclude "an unfortunately high percentage (41 percent) indicated either ambivalence or rejection of traditional black features."[84] Other studies show similar results, endorsement of the idea of positive identification with blackness, but still some ambivalence, with a preference for "light brown" rather than black or light skin colors.[85] In summary, the black power movement probably resulted in a long-lasting change for the better in black group identification, although there remains a degree of ambiguity or ambivalence among some blacks, which is probably to be expected since the culture constantly bombards blacks with the message that "white is beautiful" and that Anglo-Saxon features are to be emulated. (It was entirely predictable, for example, that the first black Miss America also was decidedly white-looking in her facial features and color.)[86] This progress is all to the good because it provides a more realistic basis for group solidarity and struggle since, unlike the question of individual self-esteem, which deals with the psychodynamics of personality (which may or may not be related to group identification and struggle), group identification is broadly politically, dealing with, as Cross writes, "questions of value, philosophic orientation, concepts of beauty, art, literature, musical preferences, sex role constructs, political behavior—these are all subtopics in the complex field of reference group theory."[87] It is because of this fundamentally political character of race group identity that, a   generation after the cultural revitalization movement sparked by black power, the black intelligentsia has once again returned to the problem of group identification and cultural integrity. It is this problem that I address in the final part of this chapter.

From "Black" to African-American:
Cultural Revitalization in the Post–Civil Rights Era
or an Empty Symbol

Whatever the documented effects of the 1960s black power movement on race group identity, consciousness, and solidarity, for a significant segment of the black intelligentsia they apparently were not enough because in the 1980s it attempted to launch yet another movement of cultural revitalization. In late 1988 at a Chicago meeting of national black leaders convened to discuss plans for a new black agenda and strategy, Ramona Edelin of the National Urban Coalition persuaded the group to adopt *African-American* as the preferred name for the race. At a press conference announcing the change Jesse Jackson said *African-American* had "cultural integrity. It puts us in our proper historical context. Every ethnic group in this country has a reference to some land base, some historical cultural base. African Americans have hit that level of cultural maturity. There are Armenian Americans and Jewish Americans and Italian Americans; and with a degree of acceptance and reasonable pride, they connect their heritage to their mother country and where they are now."[88] Jackson indicated that the term *black* should now be rejected because it "does not describe our situation. In my household there are seven people and none of us have the same complexion . . . we are of African heritage."[89] Thus, African heritage rather than blackness is said to be the key to race group identity. How does one account for this emergence of *African-American* in the post–civil rights era?

Historically, when blacks have sought to change the names by which they are called this change has presaged or been accompanied by a rise of militant nationalist sentiments in culture and politics. These periods of heightened nationalist expressions in culture and politics have also usually coincided with particularly difficult and disappointing times for the race. Thus, the question becomes does *African-American* signal the rebirth of a new nationalism in politics and culture, or is it, as some have suggested, an empty symbol artificially invented by a leadership that has little of substance to offer its constituents.[90]

The answer is that we do not know. The material basis for another cycle of militant nationalism is certainly present as *African-Americans* approach the new century with a growing sense of disappointment approaching despair. After a generation of optimism about the prospects for integration and acceptance in American society, blacks now increasingly experience a sense of alarm, of the clock's turning back, a renewed sense of apartness, of being outsiders in an increasingly hostile world that looks with amusement and contempt at the continued deterioration of the African-American community. In a sense this is paradoxical because, on the one hand, the last twenty-five years have seen blacks make enormous progress in integrating into American social, economic, and political institutions. A fairly secure and prosperous middle class has emerged; figures like Bill Cosby, Michael Jackson, and Oprah Winfrey dominate popular culture, and blacks have sat at the apex of such important institutions as the New York City government, the Ford Foundation, the Joint Chiefs of Staff, and the Virginia state government.

But these images of progress are dwarfed by the realities of a third of the race living under conditions of unspeakable poverty, immiseration, and degradation. These realities impinge on the psychic if not material well-being of all strata of the community, making the news of a Douglas Wilder or a Colin Powell seem almost trivial. Contributing to this sense of despair are the beliefs that the larger society does not care; that the ongoing Reagan revolution in social policy continues to turn back the clock on the quest for racial justice; that blacks are to blame for their own condition. Feeling increasingly ostracized and demeaned, blacks may increasingly turn inward toward the nationalist principle that blacks must depend mainly on themselves, their own resources, their own culture if they are to survive in a hostile land. Thus, the adoption of the new name by the African-American intelligentsia, this time with little controversy, may be emblematic of a new direction in black society, culture, and politics. Alternatively, the name may reflect a desperate attempt by the middle-class intelligentsia to use the symbolism of a new name with "cultural integrity" to cover over its inability to deal with the continued deterioration of black American society and culture.

Relatively little evidence of a renewal of militancy or nationalist sentiment has been observed in the largely institutionalized politics practiced by black leaders today, however, there are some hints in the popular culture of a shift toward more militant or nationalistic expressions. Before turning to analysis of these hints of change, it should be noted that unlike the adoption of *black* in the 1960s, adoption of *African-American* occasioned very little controversy and was almost immediately embraced by the black intelligentsia and white opinion-makers and politicians. However, as with the change from *Negro* to *black* in the 1960s mass opinion has not followed elite opinion. According to a 1990 Gallup survey commissioned by the Joint Center 72 percent of blacks say they preferred *black*; 15 percent, *African-American*, 3 percent *Negro*, with the rest giving no opinion or other responses.[91] Black men, the college-educated, and young people were more likely to favor the new name but even among these groups more than two-thirds continued to favor *black*. It took several years of struggle and controversy before *black* was embraced at the mass level. Yet unlike the 1960s the name *black* was not accepted in isolation, rather it was part of a mass movement of cultural revitalization. Such a movement may be on the horizon, but it has not yet reached this status, therefore the prospects for the rapid mass acceptance of *African-American* are not as good as was the 1960s name change.

In addition, it is likely that the term *black* has had greater resonance among ordinary blacks than does *African*. The tangible ties, cultural and otherwise, between Africans and African-Americans are not widespread. Certainly, they are not as strong as that of Polish, Italian, or other European groups to their native countries. Blacks in the United States have often rejected their African heritage, seeing Africa, as Rev. Leon Sullivan—a proponent of the African-American offensive and cultural linkage—put it, as "the dark continent, a place of crocodiles, jungles and Tarzan."[92] In addition, in the 1960s Africa was on the move as country after country achieved its independence and new world leaders of the stature of Kwame Nkrumah, Jomo Kenyatta, and Julius Nyerere served as sources of inspiration for the black freedom struggle in the United States. There was a sense then that Africa was about to reclaim the glories of its ancient past and establish itself as a major force in international politics. By contrast, the image and reality of Africa today is of a continent in decline, wracked by wars, famines, and dependency.[93] Indeed, in many ways the status of Africa in the post independence era is worse than the status of African-Americans in the post–civil rights era. It is likely therefore that *African-American* will remain the preferred name of the elite—black and white—while at the mass level *black* will remain the name of preference.

This does not mean, however, that the shift from *black* to *African-American* is merely symbolic and without political consequence. The intelligentsia—artists, students, intellectuals, clergy, and politicians—in their adoption of this new name may reflect an inchoate ferment, a nationalist sentiment at the grass roots level that is groping for a voice, culturally and politically. This incipient nationalist impulse has not yet found a clear-cut political expression, organizationally or in terms of new leadership. But hints of it maybe seen culturally in some of the new black music and other expressions of nationalistic ethos among young people. It is probably the case that, just as the civil rights protests and black power movements of the 1960s were sparked by young people who rebelled against the status quo gradualism of the established black leadership of that time, any renewal of militancy in the post–civil rights era will also come from this source. It is useful therefore to try to make sense of "What's Going On?" among the young and in popular culture.

One way to do this is through an examination of black popular culture. Music and other artistic expressions were an important part of the black power movement. In *The Death of Rhythm & Blues* George presents an analysis of the processes and consequences of the institutionalization of black music that occurred simultaneous with the movement's institutionalization. George's work is a learned, historically informed interdisciplinary treatise. At the outset he recalls the often-heard comment among blacks that "you can tell where black people are at any point in our history by our music."[94] George argues that in the 1960s and early 1970s the music of black people was both inspired by and gave inspiration to movement activism. In the 1970s, however, the integration or institutionalization of the black music industry (radio, nightclubs, concert halls, and recording labels) resulted in a compromise of its integrity and authenticity, as it was increasingly created not for blacks but for the multimillion-dollar nonblack crossover market. thus, "In the twenty years since the Great Society, which marked a high point in R & B music, the community that inspired both social change and artistic creativity has become a shell of itself; unhappily, while the drive behind the movement for social changes was the greatest inspiration for the music, the very success of the movement spelled the end of the R & B world."[95] If there is, as George suggests, a symbolic relationship between music and movement in black society then recent developments in the music of black America may indicate a nascent movement revitalization.

The clearest expression of this new authenticity is in the work of the rap groups that emerged in the 1980s. Unlike most post–civil rights era popular black music, rap emerged not out of the commercial minds of New York and Los Angeles producers and impresarios but from the streets of the ghettos, and to some extent it is still under the creative control of blacks. Several of these rap groups—Laquan, Movement EX, Paris, and Public Enemy—have been influenced by the Nation of Islam and its philosophy of black nationalism and by the new emphasis by some scholars on Afrocentricity, which sees Africa as the original center of philosophy, culture, and science.[96] Although they are not the dominant themes, some rap focuses on post–civil rights era race issues of racism, joblessness, drugs, crime, police brutality, and the irrelevance of inner-city education. There is also a militant spirit of rebellion and discontent, as in Public Enemy's "Fight the Power," the theme song of Spike Lee's influential film "Do the Right Thing."[97] Rap music also include nonpolitical themes, and it is often sexually explicit, sexist, homophobic, and in a few instances anti-Semitic. It is shortsighted, however, to view the music, as Juan William does, as simply the "public venting of racism, homophobia and woman hating" by "singing young multi millionaire bigots."[98] First, in addition to the rappers whose themes Williams makes the focus of his criticism, there are also rappers who use their music to attack racism, capitalist exploitation in consumerism, drugs, sexual permissiveness, gang violence, and other ills of young black America. Also, among its primary consumers—young people— the themes of race consciousness and activism may be more salient. Stanford, for example, in a survey of Howard University students found that rap music and other contemporary cultural emblems—t-shirts with African and black nationalist motifs, juju bags, African medallions, and kente cloths—represent and upsurge of black consciousness and solidarity.[99]

One should not, however, make too much of these new developments in black music and other aesthetic expressions of militancy and nationalism, including the change from *black* to *African-American*. They may be largely symbolic, reflecting passing trends and fads.[100] The relationship between music and movement is, after all, according to George and others who have posited such a nexus symbiotic.[101] This was clearly the case in the 1960s. As Walker's work shows, the peak of message music occurred simultaneously with the peak of movement activism. What is clear at this writing is that at the dawn of a new century among elements of the intelligentsia, the young, and ordinary men and women struggling to get by, there is a growing mood of discontent. A mood not easy for those who do not live and work in the community to see—a mood not captured in the national media's discussion of race. It is for this reason that the hints of rebellion in the music and other forms of popular culture may be well worth the attention of social scientists who would seek to understand what's going on in black America.

6

Racism in the Emergence and Persistence of the Black "Underclass": A Critique of the Wilson Paradigm*

A fundamental reason for the mood of discontent discussed near the end of Chapter 5 is the persistence and growth in the post–civil rights era of what is now called the black "underclass," especially the notion that it is a permanent phenomenon about which nothing can be done or, worse, even attempted. In the introduction I indicated that it was a principal thesis of this study that the so-called black underclass was a major manifestation of a racism in the post–civil rights era. Since this thesis is contrary to that of William Wilson—the leading authority on the black underclass—I elected to pursue its development through analysis and criticism of Wilson's definitive statement on the subject, *The Truly Disadvantaged: The Inner City, the Underclass and Public Policy.* In this influential treatise Wilson dismisses racism as an explanation of the "recent" rise of the ghetto underclass as "indiscriminate" and "worn-out" talk that "immediately suggests one has nothing to say."[1] In this rather facile rejection of racism as part of an explanation of the deterioration of inner-city black communities in the post–civil rights era Wilson does not present any empirical evidence or cite any empirical studies to support his judgment. His conclusions on the matter are therefore analytical rather than empirical. Given the centrality of racism in the discourse on the black predicament in the United States and the controversial nature of his position on the problem, Wilson and his legion of associates and graduate students at the University of Chicago might have conducted some empirical studies or analysis before so quickly and decisively rejecting racism and moving on to other explanatory devices. At a minimum, given the resources available to him a research design or model for the rigorous empirical testing of the effects of rac-

---

*This chapter was originally delivered as a paper at the 24th annual meeting of the National conference of Black Political Scientists, March 11-13, 1993, Oakland, California.

ism on the rise and persistence of the underclass might have been developed so that one could accept or reject his proposition on the basis of evidence rather than argument.[2] One gets the impression, as Clay Carson points out in his review of the book, that "Wilson's discounting of racism as a cause of urban poverty stems as much from political expediency as from empirical evidence. Emphasizing race as a cause would require programs designed especially to confront racial barriers as well as economic forces. But such racially targeted programs Wilson believes are unlikely to attract public support."[3] Thus, Wilson, like virtually all Western scholars who study poverty, allows ideological inclinations rather than, or perhaps in addition to, good theory and method to shape the outcomes of research.

To an extent, since Wilson does not present empirical studies to support his thesis, his thinking might be rebutted by simply referring the reader to the chapters in this book on racism where extensive data are presented on attitudinal, individual, and institutional racism in the post–civil rights era. These data—one might argue, following Wilson's approach —that show continuing individual prejudices against blacks as well as continuing discrimination in education, employment, housing, and consumer services are sufficient to make the case for the persistence of racism as *part* of an explanation of black poverty in the post–civil rights era. That is, these chapters might be cited to show that blacks are relegated to ghetto poverty not only by the present effects of historical racism but also by the effects of ongoing, contemporary racism. However, I would like to be more systematic than Wilson especially since the data discussed in the previous chapters are unsystematic and generally not longitudinal. Because racism is a causal factor in the persistence of black poverty, the data must be analyzed within a framework that is conceptually clear and that is specific in relationship to Wilson's modeling of the phenomenon.

The major difficulty with Wilson's analysis of racism is conceptual. Wilson does not define the concept of racism that he dismisses, and one almost gets the sense that he believes that no such concept can be unambiguous enough to capture the complexities of the post–civil rights era black predicament. In the immediately preceding chapters I employed a concept of racism that is historically informed, theoretically comprehensive, and empirically relevant. This multidimensional concept distinguishes between the historical subordination of blacks, the justificatory ideology of white supremacy and attitudinal, individual, and institutional modes of racism. It is this concept and its various modes that I use to examine Wilson's work.

Finally, it should be made clear at the outset that one's views on the explanation of poverty are largely a matter of intellectual taste, ideology, or policy preferences. For example, research on poverty in the Western world has produced two overreaching perspectives: a structural one that emphasizes enduring features of the economic and social systems (including racism) in explanation of persistent poverty and a culturalist one that emphasizes the values, beliefs, attitudes, and lifestyles (intergenerationally transmitted) of the poor themselves. In more than a century and a half of work it is difficult to identify a conservative scholar—no matter what his academic training, data, or method—who has embraced a structuralist explanation. Conservatives tend to look to changes in the individual psyche or the cultures of groups as solutions to the problems of poverty while liberals and socialists embrace changes in the social structure to deal with the problem. Similarly, whether one embraces racism to explain the black underclass in the United States is a function of one's policy preferences. For example, Wilson and I are both, broadly speaking, structuralists. However, he chooses to emphasize aspects of the economic structure while I choose to emphasize racism. In part this difference in tastes is a result of our respective policy and political perspectives. Wilson prefers non–race-specific programs and interracial coalitions to deal with the problem of black poverty, while my inclinations are more rooted in the philosophy of black nationalism in terms of race-and ghetto-specific solutions and in terms of the mobilization of an independent base of black power and pressure.

My procedure is first to briefly examine some of the seminal investigations of poverty in the United States generally and black poverty specifically, noting in particular the wealth of material generated by Lyndon Johnson's war on poverty and those studies in later years that emerged in reaction to the Great Society programs. I then examine the origins and evolution of the underclass concept as it relates to black poverty in urban America, focusing on its conceptual and statistical fuzziness, before briefly reviewing the underclass literature, popular and academic. This review is by no means comprehensive. The literature on the underclass generated in just the last decade is far too extensive for me to undertake here anything but an overview, whose purpose is to provide a context for the detailed assessment of Wilson's work.[4]

Studies in Black Poverty Before There Was an Underclass

Michael Harrington's *The Other America* is rightly credited with sparking widespread intellectual interest in the problems of poverty during the 1960s. "Widespread" is the key since black leadership had long been concerned with the problem of black poverty, giving it near equal priority with the problem of state-imposed segregation. Harrington's book, which focused more on the persistent poverty of Appalachian whites and the elderly than it did on black poverty, was more important politically than intellectually. This is because it is said to have sparked President Kennedy's interest in the problem, leading him to direct his staff to begin study of possible initiatives that might be undertaken by his administration as part of his overall economic policy. After the president's murder, Lyndon Johnson seized on the sketchy outlines of the Kennedy proposals and launched what he called an "unconditional war" on poverty. Johnson's Great Society included many programs designed, however haphazardly, to deal with the problem multidimensionally. One result of this was a substantial increase in government and foundation support for research on poverty, which quickly resulted in a small cottage industry, institutionalized at the University of Wisconsin's Institute for Research on Poverty established as the research and evaluation arm of the poverty war. The result was scores of monographs, books, articles, conference papers, and social experiments, mostly forgotten, dealing with the causes and consequences of poverty and evaluations of sundry welfare and job-training programs and Great Society projects.[5]

If Harrington's book was important politically, Oscar Lewis's studies were the seminal intellectual contribution to the renewal of interest in poverty. Unlike most students of poverty who have tended to be economists or sociologists, Lewis was an anthropologist who employed ethnographic methods in field studies in the Mexican and Puerto Rican communities. Lewis argued that a culture of poverty, passed down from one generation to the next, emerges in capitalist societies that exhibit high class stratification and few or none of the characteristics of a highly developed social welfare state. This kind of culture occurs among groups who, over time, experience high rates of unemployment or poorly paid under employment. Its characteristics include those things we have come to associate with the black underclass, such as female-headed households, a high incidence of substance abuse, communal violence, and an exaggerated masculinity.[6] Although Lewis's studies focused on Latinos, he explicitly formulated the culture of poverty concept in universalistic terms that cut across national, ethnic, and urban-rural differences.[7] The commonality was long-term, persistent unemployment in a society that did not provide alternatives to the market that would permit individuals (especially men) to sustain themselves and their families adequately. And since such individuals and families tend to be residentially concentrated the result is a community or neighborhood characterized by high levels of social disorganization.

Lewis's culture of poverty concept generated enormous controversy, largely because it was misunderstood. Although in the introduction to *La Vida* (pp. xiii–xiv) Lewis argues in a clear structuralist vein that the culture of poverty is both an adaptation and reaction of the poor to their marginal position in a class-stratified, highly individualistic, capitalist society, many of his critics overlooked this and instead focused on his portrayal of the pathological behavior of the poor. Thus, the culture of poverty concept was seen as an attack on the poor and their way of life rather than an attack on the structure that gave rise to it.[8] Lewis's structural-culturalist analysis contrasts with the psychological-culturalist perspective of Edward Banfield in *The Unheavenly City*, a book that briefly gained some currency among policymakers in the late 1960s and early 1970s. Banfield agrees with Lewis on the existence and properties of the culture of poverty but departs sharply in his explanation of its causes. Banfield argues that, rather than the economic and social structures, the culture of poverty is rooted in psychological processes, writing that "extreme present orientedness, not lack of income or wealth is the principal cause of poverty in the sense of the culture of poverty."[9] This is more nearly a "blame the victim" perspective since Banfield is unable to explain the sources of this psychological predisposition among poor people nor—and most interestingly, for my purposes—its disproportionate incidence among blacks and Latinos, although a genetic implication is evident.[10]

A review of poverty research before there was an underclass would not be complete without reference to the controversial report by Daniel Patrick Moynihan on the "Negro" family because it, like Lewis's work, was misinterpreted, and its misinterpretation distorted subsequent analysis and discussion of the structural bases of black poverty; its consequences in terms of the culture of poverty and its solution in terms of both structural *and* cultural changes. Wilson, for example, writes that the "virulent attacks against Moynihan" was one reason liberal intellectuals abandoned poverty research in the 1970s, leaving the field to right-wing scholars such as Banfield and Charles Murray.[11]

In the spring of 1965 Moynihan, then an assistant secretary of labor, wrote a report on the condition of blacks titled *The Negro Family: A Case for National Action*. The report focused on the deteriorating status of the family as a central barrier to black progress in the post–civil rights era and urged that dealing with its status become a priority on the agenda of national policymakers. The basis of Moynihan's notion of Negro family deterioration were data on the increasing number of out-of-wedlock births and male-absent households in the black community. At the time of the report roughly a third of black families were female-headed, compared with 10 percent among whites. Since family stability is the key to community well-being, Moynihan argued, the situation of the black family constituted a major crisis that, unless urgently dealt with, would become increasingly worse, with dire consequences for the well-being of the black community and the nation as a whole. As Rainwater and Yancey note in their excellent intellectual history of the report and ensuing controversy, there was nothing new in it.[12] Indeed, as Moynihan acknowledged in notes throughout, it was little more than a statistical and analytic update of work on the black family by the eminent black sociologist E. Franklin Frazier.[13] Yet the report generated much controversy and occasional bitter attacks on Moynihan, with some black scholars and civil rights leaders accusing him of racism and "blaming the victim." The report was not racist, and it *clearly* did not blame the victim. Like Frazier before him, Moynihan linked the condition of the black family historically to the effects of slavery and urbanization,[14] but his most basic explanation was structural in terms of unemployment and the low-wage ghetto economy. He wrote:

> The impact of unemployment on the Negro family, and particularly on the Negro male, is the least understood of all the developments that have contributed to the present crisis. There is little analysis because there has been almost no inquiry. Unemployment, for whites and nonwhites alike, has on the whole been treated as an economic phenomenon, with almost no attention paid for at least a quarter century to social and personal consequences.. . . . The fundamental overwhelming fact is that *Negro Unemployment* with the exception of a few years during the Korean War, *has continued at disastrous levels for 35 years.* Once again, this is particularly the case in the northern urban areas which the Negro population has been moving (emphasis in original).[15]

If the report so clearly "blames the system" with respect to inadequate employment and income for the plight of the black family and proposes national action in terms of employment and welfare reform, why was it so widely misinterpreted at the time?

First, the initial reporting, especially by Mary McGrory and Rowland Evans and Robert Novak, was distorted, and these reports did much to influence early academic and political commentators (who did not take the time, as usual, to withhold comment until they had read the document).[16] Second, some academic commentators deliberately distorted the report, even after a careful reading of it. Third, coming as it did at the peak of the civil rights movement and the dawn of black power, some black scholars rejected any criticism, however muted, of black people by whites. Related to this emerging race consciousness, some black scholars suggested that out-of-wedlock births and female-headed households were not problems at all. Rather, the problem was the illegitimacy of the notion of illegitimate children, as the view was advanced that the two-parent family was based on a "white middle class" norm. In this view what was seen by middle-class whites as deviancy was in fact normal in the context of black culture, with roots perhaps in the group's African heritage.[17] But the most basic explanation for the negative reception of Moynihan's report was a long-held concern of black leaders that to discuss openly the internal disabilities of blacks would simply reinforce racist stereotypes and encourage talk about "moral reform" in the black community rather than structural reform. In 1963 Whitney Young of the Urban League told Louis Lomax in private interviews:

> Why in the hell should we sit back and let reactionary magazines and newspapers expose the sad truth about the Negro crime rate and other social breakdowns? Why let them expose it and then place their interpretation of what has happened to our people? I say we should tell the truth about our own community. . . . We know about the family breakdown—why say it ain't so? We know about relief stealing—why say the white man is making the figures lie? Let's research and expose these things ourselves. That puts us in the driver's seat; we can say "Here's what has happened, here is why it has happened, let's all pull together to do something about it." The family is the primary rocket that thrusts the human into social orbit. . . . The Negro family unit must be strengthened. . . . The Negro family breaks down for two reasons: the lack of a consistent bread winner and the influence of, or apathy toward, community institutions designed to help the family in moments of crisis.[18]

Young's interest in 1963 in what is now called the problems of the black underclass as priority items on the black agenda was rejected by his colleagues in the movement, and after the Moynihan controversy arose it was effectively taken off the black agenda for twenty years.[19]

The emergence of the underclass concept has a lot to do with these changes. Except for terminology and new conceptual language, little in this vast new literature is radically at odds with the Moynihan report. And the popular and political discussion of the problems of the black underclass has had some of the effects Young's colleagues in the movement feared. It has fueled reactionary and racist discussion of the problem; shifted blame away from the system toward its most vulnerable victims; and encouraged discussion by conservative intellectuals and politicians of moral reform and black self-help as the only solution to the problem. This is because it is relatively easy to display in the popular press, especially on television the pathological dimensions of the underclass in terms of teenage sex, crime, drugs, and the "vanishing black male." The CBS television program "48 Hours" has made a specialty of this kind of sensation-seeking journalism, and even a somewhat thoughtful program such as Bill Moyers's "The Vanishing Black Family" broadcast on CBS suggested to the audience that the problems of the ghetto are the result of the irresponsible, immoral behavior of black men, women, and children. But the structural conditions that give rise to the "vanishing black family," such as long-term, depression-level joblessness, plant location decisions that remove jobs from the black community, and racism—individual and institutional—in housing, employment, and consumer services do not make for good visuals, assuming that network news executives had an inclination to present such "news" to the public.

This is why Wilson, who has done so much to popularize the term *underclass*, now wants to abandon it, at least temporarily. In his 1990 presidential address at the American Sociological Association, Wilson said the term ought to be rejected because it has become a "code word" for inner-city blacks, has enabled journalists to focus on unflattering behavior in the ghetto, and has little scientific usefulness. Wilson defended his earlier use of the term because it sparked much-needed research and because it "led to more precise specification . . . concerning life in the inner-city ghetto," but he now concludes that its stigmatizing consequences outweigh whatever other values its continued use might have, at least at present.[20] While the term certainly has been associated with greater research activity, it is not correct to say that it has led to more precise specification of the problem of black poverty in the United States. On the contrary, its use has contributed little beyond the 1960s' spate of research on black poverty, nor is it likely to, notwithstanding the huge ongoing investment in underclass research. This may be seen to some extent in Wilson's facile substitution of the term *ghetto poor* for underclass. It is estimated that the underclass, properly defined, includes about 2.5 million people of whom about two-thirds are black and less than that are in the inner-city ghettos. Yet, the population that constitutes the "ghetto poor" is at least three times as large as the estimated size of the entire underclass. So, by what logic or evidence may the terms be so easily substituted. They may not be, which points to the problem I turn to next—the fuzziness and imprecision of the idea of an underclass.

Origins and Meaning of the Underclass Concept

The term *underclass* in its modern usage has been traced by Ralison to Gunnar Myrdal's 1963 book *The Challenge of Affluence*, however, its operational content in terms of the intergenerational transmission of poverty has been around for more than a hundred years.[21] MacNicol, for example, after an extensive review of the history of the concept in the United States and Europe going back to the 1880's, writes, "The concept of an intergenerational underclass displaying a high concentration of social problems . . . has been reconstructed periodically over at least one hundred years, and while there have been important shifts of emphasis between each of these reconstructions there have also been striking continuities. Underclass stereotypes have always been part of the discourse on poverty in advanced industrial societies."[22] In fact, MacNicol suggests that, at least in the United States and Great Britain, "cycles of rediscovery" of the phenomenon—variously labeled as social problem groups, social outcasts, a residual stratum of the economically unproductive, or the underclass—have occurred over the last century. While the notion has been occasionally advanced by the left in critiques of capitalism, it has been most frequently propagated by right-wing intellectuals in periods of conservative political ascendancy. In such periods, as in the present one, the notion of an underclass is advanced as a means to define as a problem group individuals who are said to consume disproportionate public resources through welfare and therefore serve as impediments to capitalist productive relations.

In England the most recent cycle of attention to the underclass occurred, as in the United States, in the early 1970s at the nadir of liberal, Labor governments. According to MacNicol public interest was sparked in 1972 when Sir Keith Joseph, the health secretary, identified what he called a "cycle of deprivation," transmitted intergenerationally and nearly proposed the compulsory sterilization of the poor. Joseph's rhetorical excesses launched a public debate that led to an explosion of social science research, much of it funded by the government, on every conceivable aspect of poverty—family and childrearing, health, crime, mental illness, and so on—including detailed studies of the most intimate aspects of respondent families. The results were predictable. MacNicol comments, "In this painstaking and expensive research, surprisingly little new has been learned about the age old riddle of structural vs. culturalist explanations of underclass behavior or whether it's pathological or functional, raising questions about the possibility of meaningful analysis by the conventional tools of social science."[23]

At about the same time as this research was taking place in England, there was also a massive outpouring of work in this country. Before turning to the American case, it would be useful to discuss a brief historical and comparative perspective on the underclass since so little attention has been paid to the origins of the concept. Before reviewing some of the literature on the American underclass, I would like first to deal with some of the conceptual and methodological problems that muddle research on the underclass and its black variant.

In *The Challenge to Affluence* Myrdal defined underclass as the "unemployed and gradually unemployable and underemployed persons and families at the bottom of society."[24] For Myrdal, writing in 1963 this group had emerged in the United States because of the transformation in the economy that reduced the need for unskilled labor and therefore increased the pool of redundant, unemployed, and unemployable persons "who have happened to be born in regions, localities or economic and social strata where education and training for life and work in this new America are not provided as a normal thing."[25] This definition is somewhat akin to Marx's notion in *Capital* where he refers to a "part of the active labor army, with extremely irregular employment [which is the result] of decaying branches of industry where handcraft is yielding to manufacture, manufacture to machines."[26] Myrdal and Marx's notion of the centrality of unemployment in the development of this group of persons is central to most contemporary discussions, except for the notion that it is permanent in terms of intergenerational continuity. This is a major problem with the concept. Why is it permanent? Why is upward mobility blocked? The answer is not clear, but most scholars seem to suggest that its permanency is a function of attitudes and behavior in the group that maladapt it for the changing economy. That is, the underclass is to be defined in terms of attitudes as well as behavior, but it is not clear how this attitudinal component adds very much to the structural explanation of Marx and Myrdal or the 1960s' studies of poverty, or for that matter the centuries-long debate on poverty in industrial societies.

To some extent this problem is resolved by treating the group not as a group, stratum, or class, but as a statistical artifact in terms of certain behavioral characteristics of individuals and families—long-term unemployment, welfare dependency, female-headed households, drug addiction, crime, and violence. For example, one scholar defines the underclass as that portion of the nation's poor whose ability to dig their way out of poverty is blocked by "violence, drugs and despair."[27] Auletta, in a major journalistic study, used as data the results of interviews with four categories of people (in New York and Appalachia) enrolled in government manpower programs. They included long-term welfare mothers, ex-addicts, ex-criminal offenders, and "problem youth." On the basis of this "sample" he concluded that there exists a distinct black and white underclass that stands outside the "normative structure of society."[28] This formulation, akin to categories of Marx's lumpen proletariat rather than an actual class or even fraction of a class, makes little sense to me. It is like interviewing the young street people along Berkeley's Telegraph Avenue and then concluding that there is a class of young people who stand outside the societal normative structure.

In addition to its conceptual and methodological fuzziness this way of defining the underclass effectively ignores the character of poverty among Americans generally and black Americans particularly. For example, it is estimated that there are 30 million poor people in the United States, of whom 10 million are black. Yet the statistical artifact that is the underclass is estimated at about 2 million, of which about 60 percent are black.[29] Thus, even if the underclass were to disappear tomorrow this would do nothing in terms of the massive number of poor Americans. So, ironically, the recent academic and policy focus on the underclass deflects attention away from the millions of people who are poor but who attitudinally and behaviorally are within the society's "normative structure." Again, this breaks clearly with the broader notions advanced by Myrdal and Marx.

Conceptually, the underclass is universal, cutting across racial and regional lines; however, many scholars implicitly link the concept operationally to race and residence, so we refer to the black underclass in urban areas, as in the subtitle of the Wilson book *The Inner City, The Underclass and Public Policy* or in the 1989 collection of papers edited by Wilson titled *The Ghetto Underclass*.[30] This of course ignores the fact that among blacks poverty is greatest not in urban areas but in the rural south, and, as Nicholas Lemann shows in his valuable book *The Promised Land*, the culture of urban poverty has its roots in the rural south, where it still flourishes.[31] This urban bias in Wilson's and much work on the underclass is a function of Wilson's wish to argue that the underclass is a new phenomenon to be explained by such post–civil rights era factors as changes in the urban industrial economy and the flight of the black middle class from the ghettos, which together result in social isolation, his key explanatory construct. Obviously, these factors cannot explain the rural variant of the underclass.

The race bias in Wilson's construct is implicit in part because he wishes to propose non–race-specific public policies. Other scholars, not inhibited by the desire to influence policy and policymakers, are quite explicit in linking the American underclass to race and racism. Jones, for example, writes "the presence of the black underclass is a logical, perhaps even necessary, outgrowth of the American political economy conditioned by white racism."[32] Gidden incorporates an ethnic dimension in her definition, writing that the underclass is "a status group where ethnic difference serves as a disqualifying market capacity, such that those in the category in question are heavily concentrated in the lowest paid occupations, or are chronically unemployed or semi-employed."[33] Finally, Rogolin states that the underclass is that "subgroup of the propertyless engaged in capitalist social relations who are denied the exchange of their labor as an interactive function of their subordinate class position and racial membership. In short, it should be understood that the black underclass differs fundamentally from the white poor because of its exclusion from the labor market as a result of the cultural construction of racial membership as an axis of social closure.[34] These writers all see the black underclass as a function of the changing character of the economy, coupled with the continuing significance of racism as a market allocative mechanism. Thus, like me, they break fundamentally with Wilson in terms of the contemporary role played by racism in the disproportionate size of the black fraction of the underclass, or more generally American poor people. This argument is developed in more detail in the next part of this chapter. Rogolin's definition seems to suggest that there is not a white underclass but rather simply the "white poor" Mincey, in his unpublished Urban Institute paper, infers that while the black underclass dwarfs its white counterpart in proportion it nevertheless exists. Using data on "extreme poverty neighborhoods"—areas where at least two-fifths of the population live below the poverty line—in the nation's 100 largest cities he found that 10 percent of the residents are white, 68 percent black, and 21 percent Hispanic. Extreme poverty is not equivalent to underclass, and the nation's largest cities, where blacks are concentrated, may conceal the dimensions of white poverty or its proportion of the underclass. Thus, Mincy developed a database that included extreme poverty neighborhoods in all of the nation's metropolitan areas and added four criteria that are used to distinguish simple poverty from the underclass. These criteria are high percentages of female-headed households, households on welfare, adult males not in the labor force, and high school dropouts. Using this statistical definition of the underclass in cities of less than one million, whites represent 28 percent of the underclass and 20 percent of the urban underclass as a whole.[35] It is clear then from this analysis that whatever the underclass is in America it cuts across race and ethnic categories to include a category of poor people routinely produced in the American political economy. It is also clear that the role of race and racism cannot be dismissed in any complete analysis of the phenomenon.

The Emergence of the Underclass in the Post–Civil Rights Era

Douglas Glasgow's modest study of young people in Watts was the first to employ the term *underclass* to analyze the problem of inner-city poverty.[36] Since then there has been and continues to be a massive outpouring of research and publications on the underclass. As in England in the 1970s, in the United States this new interest in underclass research coincided with the election of Ronald Reagan and the consolidation of conservative power at the national level. Also as in England, this research has been very well funded by the government or quasi-public entities such as the Ford Foundation, and it has quickly gone beyond the narrow confines of academic discourse into the broader popular media.[37] And again as in England some of this work probes the most intimate details of the lives of poor black people.[38] Finally, in yet another parallel with the research in England, it is probable that when this new wave of underclass-oriented poverty research has run its course, the conclusion MacNicol reached about its English counterpart will be applicable. That is, we will conclude that after all this time-consuming and expensive research hardly anything new or meaningful will have been learned. This may seem harsh, but the history of poverty research and analysis of ongoing projects suggests it is nevertheless accurate. I have reviewed a bit of this research here, and before turning to a critique of Wilson, I would like to discuss briefly an ongoing project that further substantiates this conclusion.

At Princeton University's Woodrow Wilson School of Public Affairs a large-scale, multiyear, well-funded project has been set up in order to develop a design for "systematic long term research on the urban underclass."[39] The project, headed by Richard Nathan, includes interdisciplinary faculty, graduate students, and outside consultants. Despite more than a decade of academic research on the urban underclass, Nathan—astonishingly—writes in a discussion paper outlining the project, "beyond journalistic accounts relatively little is known abut its size, character and duration."[40] The basic questions for research during the project include a definition of the phenomenon, a delineation of its size, the characteristics of the people, its growth and decline, how people get out, and whether it is permanent. Nathan and his colleagues assume at the outset that the underclass is defined and studied along two dimensions, demographic and psychological. The demographic dimension includes long-term unemployment, low educational attainment, female-headed households, and so forth, while the psychological dimension includes attitudes and values as they relate to family, education, work, and the like. Given these two dimensions and the basic research questions, the project will develop and administer a longitudinal questionnaire because, Nathan writes, "There is no existing data set that can be used to answer the research questions proposed for attention here."[41] Yet there is a longitudinal data base on poverty in the United States, the University of Michigan's Panel Study on Income Dynamics (PSID) established in 1968. The results of these two decades of statistical analysis of correlates of poverty may be simply stated: none of the scores of behavioral or attitudinal measures affected economic status. Nathan cites this work, referring to James Morgan et al.'s *Five Thousand American Families: Patterns of Economic Progress* (1974):

> The results are clear: nothing individuals believe or do has an effect that persists consistently through the different statistical procedures and measures. In this same volume Duncan and Hill did not find evidence of a future orientation or culture of poverty affect; rather labor force experience and cognitive skills were more important determinants of income. Similarly, Frank Levy found no evidence to sustain the culture of poverty thesis.[41]

One would think this cumulation of evidence using the most sophisticated research techniques would settle the matter, but Nathan states, "There is reason to suspect PSID is not adequate for research on the underclass because of low attrition in the sample and a low attrition rate is inconsistent with the belief that the underclass is transient and difficult to locate, which would explain the failure to find any evidence of the culture of poverty."[43] In other words, the consistent failure to find evidence to confirm the thesis is evidence not that the thesis is valid but rather that the evidence is inadequate. This shows the project's culturalist bias and makes the case for funding yet another large-scale research project on the poor. As I first write this in the summer of 1991 no results of this project are available. But I am prepared to say now that the results will not differ substantially from what we already know, and if it does it will be meaningless, contributing only to more scientific debate about sample design, t-statistics, beta and gamma coefficients, and on and on ad nauseam. One seriously wishes that the millions of dollars used to fund these middle-class students of the poor could be used simply to draw a random sample of poor people in nearby Newark, New Jersey, and send them the project grant (including overhead), equally divided. Doubtless, what they would do with the money would serve the public good as much as does this academic boondoggle.

The Wilson Paradigm and the Continuing Significance of Racism

Of the vast literature on the underclass, Wilson's work is generally conceded to be the most interesting and significant. More than any other scholar, Wilson in the last decade had made research on the urban underclass respectable. Through his books, papers, edited works, and articles in many journals and books; public lectures, radio and television appearances, op-ed essays, and countless interviews with journalists; and congressional testimony; and as a consultant to government, business, and foundations; and professor at the University of Chicago, with its distinguished tradition of research on urbanism, Wilson has undoubtedly become the single most influential commentator on the subject of the black underclass. *The Truly Disadvantaged* is his definitive statement to date on subject; indeed it may be *the* definitive statement on the subject. A well-crafted work, it has much in it that is of value in terms of analysis and policy. This is why I find it useful for critical analysis; although it is a significant work, it is flawed in two important ways. The first is analytical: Wilson's off-hand dismissal of racism as an explanatory factor in the rise and persistence of the underclass. The second is in terms of policy: not so much substantive policy, which as far as he goes is largely on target, but rather in terms of strategic policy calculations, where he seriously misreads post–civil rights era black politics and the limits of interracial coalition politics.

I wish to critique Wilson's theory of the underclass from the perspective of the concept of racism that I have employed in this study. The concept is multidimensional, focusing on historical, individual, and institutional modes of racism. In his dismissal of racism as a "worn out," uninteresting explanation of the ghetto underclass, Wilson refers only to the latter two modes—individual and institutional—which he lumps together in a category called "contemporary racism." With regard to the historical mode, Wilson writes, "I should like to emphasize that no serious student of American race relations can deny the relationship between the disproportionate concentration of blacks in impoverished urban ghettos and historic racial subjugation in American society."[44] Thus, the burden of my critique is to try to show a relationship between the urban underclass and "contemporary racism." Before turning to this task, I would like to develop a bit more of the analysis of the role of historical racism in the "disproportionate concentration" of blacks in the underclass by drawing on an elegant case study of Philadelphia.

Although Wilson acknowledges the role of historical racism, that is all he does in *The Truly Disadvantaged*, although in an earlier book he develops a multistage model of historical racism and its decline in the United States.[45] The thesis in the earlier work—that racism's effects on black life chances had declined significantly in the post–civil rights era—is essentially carried to its logical conclusion in *The Truly Disadvantaged*. Nevertheless, it might have been useful to revise and extend his historical model to make it specifically applicable to his analysis of the underclass. This would have provided much-needed historical context and perspective, particularly if the historical model had been developed with specific reference to Chicago, the city on which he bases his theoretical arguments. Therefore, this critique provides this perspective by tracing the underclass to its historical roots in racism.

Historical Racism and the Origins of the Black Underclass

In a study that is a model of historically informed social science scholarship, Theodore Hershberg and his colleagues at the Philadelphia Social History Project at the University of Pennsylvania innovatively demonstrate the role of racism in the formation of the black underclass.[46] The study employs what is called a "structural perspective" to analyze the experience of separate waves of immigrants to Philadelphia during three historical periods: the Irish and Germans who settled in the "industrializing city" of the mid-to late nineteenth century; the Italians, Poles, and Russian Jews who arrived in the "industrial city" at the turn of the century; and blacks who, although present throughout, arrived in their greatest numbers in the "post industrial city" after World War II. The structural perspective employed combines in a single explanatory framework (1) a city's "opportunity structure"— the vertical distribution of jobs—with (2) it's "ecological structure"— the distribution in space of people, housing, transportation, and jobs, and (3) racism as a mechanism for the allocation of jobs and housing. The principal conclusion that flows from application of this framework is that an ethnic group's economic status is a result less of what it brought with it to the city in terms of culture and more the result of the structural conditions that awaited each wave of immigrants as they arrived in the city at a given point in history.

For example, it is often argued that immigrant ghettos formed as a result of the cultural inclinations of ethnic groups who wished to live among their own kind. Yet in nineteenth-century Philadelphia immigrant ghettos did not form because industry was more important than ethnicity in organizing the city's residential patterns. Hershberg states that "workers of different ethnic groups employed in the same industry had residential characteristics . . . more in common with each other than with members of their own ethnic group."[47] Except, that is, African-Americans, who although relatively few in number were almost totally excluded from nineteenth-century Philadelphia's opportunity structure. Hershberg and his colleagues write:

> The only major exception to the above generalizations were blacks. They were marginal to the rapidly industrializing urban economy of this period, and were considerably more segregated than white immigrants. They had few manufacturing jobs, even though they lived within easy access to more jobs of this type than any other ethnic group. . . . Racism proved more powerful than the rules that normally governed spatially conditioned job access. In the few instances when blacks did obtain manufacturing jobs, they did not live close to their white co-workers. Rather, they tended to live close to one another regardless of industrial affiliation.[48]

Further, "during the antebellum years, blacks were not only excluded from the new and well paying positions, they were uprooted as well from many of their traditional unskilled jobs, denied apprenticeships for their sons, and prevented from practicing the skills they already possessed."[49] During this period, the authors also note, blacks were denied the right to vote and were the victims of frequent race riots in which their homes, churches, and schools were destroyed over and over again, experiences unlike those of any other ethnic group.

Thus, we see in the nineteenth century the historical roots of the disproportionate location of blacks in the late twentieth-century underclass. While the Irish, WASPs, and Jews were laying the groundwork for the middle-class status of their grandsons and daughters in the twentieth century, African-American parents could do little more than struggle to avoid downward mobility for themselves. That the underclass has its origins here maybe seen in another study based on the Philadelphia project, a study dealing with female-headed households, which for many students is perhaps the single most remarked about characteristic of the urban underclass today. In nineteenth-century Philadelphia, Furstenberg, Hershberg, and Model write, "Blacks occupied the worst housing in the Moyamensing slums and suffered from the greatest degree of impoverishment. Their mortality rate was roughly twice that of whites, and the death of black men early in their adult lives was the major reason that blacks were forced to raise their children in fatherless families."[50] This of course reads like a report on the status of blacks in Chicago or Philadelphia today, which again suggests that the notion that there is something new about the black underclass should be embraced with caution.

Turning from the nineteenth-century "industrializing" city to the twentieth-century "industrial" city, hardly anything changes. While Italians, Irish, Jews, Germans, and the English continued to find good jobs in the trades and manufacturing, blacks were still relegated to the low-paying domestic and laborer jobs at the bottom of the occupational structure. Hershberg writes, "Although they continued to live in and near areas characterized by high industrial concentration, blacks were excluded from industrial work. Although 80 percent of the blacks lived in the city within one mile of 5,000 industrial jobs, less than 13 percent of the black work force fund gainful employment in manufacturing."[51] In the final period, the post–World War II "industrial city," one observes a clear reversal of this pattern. Although compared with whites, blacks were still disproportionately concentrated in low-skill, low-wage jobs, they for the first time in the city's history penetrated the relatively high-wage manufacturing sector. Yet, to anticipate a key component of Wilson's theory of the "recent rise of the underclass," just as blacks were allowed access to these jobs in the manufacturing sector they began disappearing. Between 1930 and 1970 Philadelphia lost 75,000 manufacturing jobs, and of every ten manufacturing jobs in the city, the three-mile ring from downtown had nine jobs in 1930 but only four in 1970. The result, as Hershberg notes, is that

> Today's blacks inherit the oldest stock of deteriorated housing once inhabited by two earlier waves of immigrants, but the jobs which once were located nearby and provided previous newcomers with avenues for upward mobility are gone. Precisely at the moment when the worst of the racist hiring practices in industry appear to have abated, the most recent immigrants find themselves at considerable remove from the industrial jobs that remain and thus are unable to repeat the essential experience of earlier white immigrants.[52]

This essentially brings us to the present situation and Wilson since a principal burden of his analysis of the emergence of the post–civil rights era black underclass is the decline of inner-city manufacturing employment, which results in the deterioration of the neighborhood and community. On this Wilson is quite consistent with Hershberg, who writes "the stability of neighborhoods results from the continued presence of industrial employment opportunities."[53] I have relied on and quoted generously from the fine work of the Philadelphia Social History Project in order to detail the role of historical racism in understanding the origins of the black underclass. The reason for this historical detour is stated well by Hershberg, so it is perhaps fitting that I close this discussion with one final quotation from his work: "Since our sense of history—conscious or not—exercises a real power in the present, it should sensitize us to the dangers of ahistorical social science."[54] Since so much of the discourse, scientific and journalistic, about the underclass is ahistorical, the foregoing historical sketch, although perhaps well known, as Wilson puts it, to "serious students of American history," nevertheless should be included in any comprehensive analysis of and proposed solutions to the problems of the underclass.[55]

Individual and Institutional Racism in the Persistence of the Black Underclass

Wilson   states that the purpose of *The Truly Disadvantaged* is to address the problems of the ghetto underclass in a comprehensive analysis and spell out the policy implications of his work in response to the reaction to his book *The Declining Significance of Race*, which led critics to label him a neoconservative. Although Wilson writes that he is a social democrat, he avers that the title of the book lent itself to the assumption of conservatism and that his failure to spell out its policy implications and a selective reading of some of his arguments might have reinforced these conclusions.[56] Wilson now wishes to distinguish and disassociate himself from conservatism and neoconservatism but even more so from liberalism and the ideas of traditional black leadership in the post–civil rights era. This ideological animus is probably the underlying rationale for his refusal to embrace racism as part of his analytical framework.

Wilson writes that the "liberal perspective has become less persuasive and convincing in public discourse" because liberals are reluctant to discuss "the sharp increase in social pathologies in ghetto communities" because of a fear of providing fuel for racist arguments or because of a concern of being charged with racism or "blaming the victim.'"[57] Ironically, given his own disavowal of the term just four years after the publication of this book, Wilson also criticizes liberals for refusing to use the term *underclass* because they argue it is misleading and stigmatizing (these, of course, are among the reasons he cited in 1991 for abandoning the term). He comments, "However, the real problem is not the term underclass or some similar designation but the fact that the term has received more systematic treatment from conservatives who tend to focus almost exclusively on individual characteristics, than from liberals who would more likely relate these characteristics to the broader problems of society."[58] It is the embrace of racism as an explanatory device by liberals and black leadership that seems to bother Wilson the most. Liberals, he claims, are unpersuasive when they focus on racism as an explanation. While conceding the role of historical racism in the disproportionate location of blacks in the underclass, Wilson states, "But to suggest that the recent rise of social dislocation among the ghetto underclass is due mainly to contemporary racism, which in this context refers to the 'conscious' refusal of whites to accept as equal human beings and their willful, systematic effort to deny blacks equal opportunity, is to ignore a set of complex issues that are difficult to explain with a race specific thesis."[59] This is the crux of the problem with Wilson's work as it relates to racism—his conceptualization and operationalization of the concept are simply inadequate.

For example, the definition of racism that he uses in the above quotation is drawn not from the extensive academic literature on the subject but from a polemical essay written by Carl Gresham in a debate with Kenneth Clark.[60] Gresham's definition is not comprehensive but rather deals with only one type of racism—individual. Wilson therefore dismisses racism as an explanatory factor here because his concept is too narrow, ignoring altogether the rich literature on institutional racism. For example, he writes, "However, some liberals know that racism is too easy an explanation" because in the words of Michael Harrington, it implies that the social and economic disorganization faced by black Americans was the result of the psychological state of mind of white America, a kind of deliberate—and racist—ill will."[61] Again, the problem here is conceptual and typological, focusing only on the individual, overt type of racism and linking it to attitudes rather than behavior. (I should note here that Harrington is, as Wilson knows, not a liberal but a democratic socialist. Indeed, he was until his death perhaps the leading democratic socialist spokesperson in the United States. In view of his attack on liberals, his own embrace of democratic socialism, and his own distemper about being mislabeled, Wilson ought to have labeled Harrington correctly.) In another jab at liberals that betrays his conceptual confusion, Wilson states:

> Indeed, because the term has so many different definitions and is often relied on to cover up a lack of information or knowledge of complex issues, it frequently weakens rather than enhances arguments concerning race. Indiscriminate use of this term in any analysis of contemporary racial problems immediately signals that the

arguments typify worn-out themes and makes conservative writers more interesting in comparison because they seem, on the surface at least, to have some fresh ideas.[63]

In some ways this is a silly observation. First, the mere fact that a concept has many definitions does not mean it necessarily is used to "cover up a lack of knowledge on complex issues." In fact, as I pointed out earlier, virtually all the major social science concepts—class, culture, power, and ideology—and many minor ones (underclass, for example) have many definitions, but this has not prevented their effective use by the scientific community. Nor does it mean that simply because conservative writers ignore racism their ideas are somehow fresh. At a minimum, rather than engage in this kind of polemic Wilson should have carefully reviewed the literature on racism, especially the scientific work and the legal scholarship on disparate impact, before dismissing the concept as worn-out. Such a review might have made the discussion below conceptually and operationally richer:

> Thus, instead of talking vaguely about an economic structure of racism, it would be less ambiguous and more effective to state simply that a racial division of labor has been created due to decades, even centuries, of discrimination and prejudice; and that because those in the low-wage sector of the economy are more adversely affected by impersonal economic shifts in advanced industrial society, the racial division is reinforced. One does not have to "trot out" the concept of racism to demonstrate for example, that blacks have been severely hurt because of their heavy concentration in the automobile, rubber, steel, and other smokestack industries.[64]

In one broad concept of the phenomenon (one that I do not share) of institutional racism and in legal reasoning in disparate impact cases one might conclude that the disproportionate effects of deindustrialization on blacks is at least partly an effect of institutional racism. However, the more intriguing question is how one knows *empirically* that the joblessness observed in the black communities of Chicago compared to the white areas are not in face partly the result of racism, both individual and institutional. It may very well be the case that plant location and hiring decisions in Chicago and elsewhere are based on explicit and implicit racist criteria that have an effect independent of "impersonal economic shifts" in relegating blacks disproportionately to the underclass. I do not know (although I will note some suggestive evidence to this effect below), but neither does Wilson, and simply saying that racism has no explanatory power does not make it so. Research and analysis are needed here, not polemics.

Thus, the major problem with Wilson, racism, and the underclass is that he does not use the concept but simply dismisses it as part of rhetorical flourishes against liberals and the black leadership. This maybe seen once again in his attacks on black leaders: "the deteriorating social and economic conditions of the ghetto underclass were not addressed by the liberal community as scholars backed away from research on the topic, policy makers were silent and civil rights leaders were preoccupied with the affirmative action agenda of the black middle class."[65] At least with respect to black leaders, this is simply not correct. Although liberal academics and policymakers may have been silent on the problems of the ghetto, black leaders (as I will discuss briefly in the conclusion to this chapter) have had the problems of poverty, joblessness, and the income needs of the black poor at the centerpiece of their agendas throughout the 1970s and 1980s. On affirmative action Wilson embraces the neoconservative canard about its being a program that benefits only the black middle class. This is simply not the case, as can be learned, for example, by analysis of the major affirmative action cases of the 1970s and 1980s. Of scores of such cases only two (*Bakke* and *Wygant*, the latter, dealing with schoolteachers, is arguable) have dealt with middle-class economic opportunities. The remainder have dealt with technical issues of judicial standards and administrative implementation and minority business set-asides; but the vast majority have clearly involved jobs—cannery workers, firefighters, sheet metal workers, police officers, and manufacturing and construction jobs—accessible to poor and working-class blacks.[66]

Turning from Wilson's polemics to the specifics of his explanatory model, with a few wrinkles it is quite compatible with Hershberg's structural perspective. The key variables in both Hershberg's and Wilson's work are the decline of low-skill, high-wage manufacturing jobs in and around inner-city black neighborhoods and the resulting decline in family and community in those neighborhoods. Wilson adds a third explanatory variable the out-migration from those neighborhoods of the black middle class. Wilson paints a picture of inner-city black communities as late as the 1960s as vertically integrated areas with poor, working-class, and middle-class blacks living in close proximity. This vertical integration is very important to Wilson because working-class and middle-class blacks living in the community provided the neighborhoods with organization, leadership, and social and economic stability, or, in the much-abused phrase, "role models for the poor." Today this is not the case, Wilson argues, as the black middle class has moved out of the ghettos, and the result is a significant increase in poverty concentration, which in turn leads to the formation and perpetuation of an underclass culture of joblessness, welfare dependency, female-headed households, and crime.[67] In this formulation the culture of poverty as a principal explanation of the rise of the underclass is rejected, as is Nicholas Lemann's notion that the underclass has its origins in the culture of rural southern blacks. In rejecting this explanation Wilson cites studies showing that southern migrants to northern cities were, despite lower levels of education, less likely to receive welfare and tend to have higher labor force participation rates and lower unemployment rates.[68] This does not, however, suffice to invalidate the notion of the southern roots of underclass culture since the thesis of Lemann and others is not that southern migrants are more likely to exhibit underclass behavioral characteristics, but rather, that the culture pre-existed the urban experience of blacks. Lemann in both his *Atlantic* articles and *The Promised Land* seems to have adequately documented this proposition and it is consistent with anthropological field studies, and, I might add, with my own personal experience growing up in rural Louisiana, where there was always an "underclass" population of 15–25 percent characterized by frequent joblessness or low-wage, occasional employment, welfare dependency, alcohol abuse, high school dropouts, and intermittent violence. And on my frequent return visits home I have observed that not only does the rural underclass exist but that since the 1960s it has grown both in its size and the acuteness of its disabilities. Wilson has difficulty in accepting the notion of the rural origins of the underclass because it does not fit his explanatory model of the urban phenomenon in terms of the decline of manufacturing employment, the flight of the middle class, and the resulting poverty concentration and social isolation. This is a general problem with poverty research in the United States, which since the 1960s ghetto rebellions has overlooked the massive and debilitating poverty of the rural south, although it is the home of more than one-fourth of the black population.

The key theoretical construct for Wilson is "not the culture of poverty but social isolation. Culture of poverty implies that basic values and attitudes of the ghetto subculture have been internalized and thereby influence behavior. . . . Social isolation does not mean that cultural traits are irrelevant in understanding behavior in highly concentrated areas, rather it highlights the fact that culture is a response to social structural constraints and opportunities.[69] For Wilson the concentration and social isolation of the black urban poor is the characteristic that distinguishes it from the white poor and makes it (or at least significant parts of it) not just poor blacks but an underclass of poor blacks. Wilson writes, "whereas poor blacks are frequently found in isolated urban neighborhoods, poor whites rarely live in such neighborhoods . . . whereas 68 percent of all poor whites lived in nonpoverty neighborhoods in the five large central cities in 1980 only 15 percent of poor blacks . . . lived in such areas.[70]

Wilson does not raise the obvious question of why poor blacks are more isolated than are poor whites (and Hispanics). The answer in part would surely point to the "worn-out" explanation of racism in the sale and rental of housing in metropolitan areas, as has been amply documented in HUD housing audits and in the social science literature (see Chapters 3 and 4). Racism in the housing market also calls into question the central component of Wilson's overall theoretical framework, which links the rise of the underclass since the 1960s to out-migration of middle-class blacks from the ghetto. A recent study of race, income, and residence in the nation's sixty largest metropolitan areas in the decade 1970 to 1980 found that black middle-class families have not been able to move out of inner-city neighborhoods. Massey and Denton conclude that in cities with large black populations affluent blacks tend to live in neighborhoods with poor blacks, in significant contrast to whites in these cities.[71] Thus, while middle-class blacks may not reside in "extreme poverty" neighborhoods, they may not be as isolated from the ghetto poor as Wilson's theory implies. And this is partly because of the continuing significance of   racism.

But for purposes of understanding the underclass this is a rather minor point since the flight of the black middle class is really not as central to the phenomenon as Wilson's theory would have it. The central variable in explanation of the black underclass, the culture of poverty, or ghetto poverty, is joblessness; long-term persistent unemployment or employment at wages that do not provide income sufficient to sustain families above the poverty level. Virtually all students of the phenomenon—from Moyniham to Oscar Lewis—agree on the centrality of unemployment in the dislocation of poor communities, whether urban or rural, black or white. Thus, if one is to explain the causes of the black underclass one must explain the cause of the disproportionately high black unemployment rate, especially among males.

Before I critique Wilson's explanation of ghetto joblessness in terms of his notion of impersonal nonracist economic forces, I should point out that Wilson's essentially structuralist perspective allows him to avoid the kind of simple-minded moralisms and moralizing that so often accompany analysis of the lives of poor people. This focus on the allegedly amoral or immoral attitudes and behavior of poor blacks became particularly fashionable in the 1980s, especially among conservative intellectuals and politicians. It is easy for middle-class intellectuals studying the most intimate aspects of the lives of the poor—especially sex and family life—to get into a "more moral than thou" attitude with regard to the motivations of the poor. It is also easy for embarrassed and, to a degree, guilt-ridden black intellectuals to get into the mindless drivel that suggests that the ghetto poor need role models, specifically male role models (presumably like themselves) to teach young blacks how to live with proper middle-class attitudes and values.[72] To his credit Wilson avoids this, although he spends too much time peering into the data on the sex lives of black teenagers.[73] Indeed, Wilson observes, "It is an intellectual paradox that living in a society that has a sea of unemployment, American poverty researchers have concentrated their interests on the motivations of the poor."[74] Thus, from a public policy perspective, Wilson concludes that "programs . . . should place primary focus on changing the social and economic situations, not cultural traits of the ghetto underclass."[75] This is not to argue that there is not in the ghetto some of what blacks call "sorriness" that takes the form of the avoidance of hard work, sexual promiscuity and irresponsibility, and substance abuse; simply that it is not limited to poor blacks, but instead is widespread in American society, cutting across lines of race and social class.[76] However, because of their poverty and dependency and color it *appears* to be a problem of the ghetto poor. I have known persons black and white from the "highest" (at least in terms of education, since most of my friends are Ph.D.s) to the "lowest" (high school dropouts and the unemployed), and I have not observed any consistent differences between the two in terms of ethics and morality and life styles (except for the styles of life that money buys). I should also note the "sorriness" of those who are neither poor nor black that is now routinely reported in the press (the Kennedy boy who died of a heroin overdose, the Palm Beach debauchery of the young Kennedy having sex on the lawn beneath his mother's window, the sexual irresponsibility of President Kennedy; I could go on and on) or the unseemly popularity of such exaggerated portrayals of the rich, famous, and white in the 1980s like "Dallas," "Falcon Crest," and "Dynasty." The point is that the ghetto poor may need moral reform, but in America today so do the nonpoor, nonghettoized, and the nonblack. Indeed, Martin Kilson is correct in his notion that effective reconstruction and integration of the ghetto into the mainstream will require strategies that deal *simultaneously* with cultural and structural changes, but the former must occur in both mainstream and ghetto.[77] Certainly the vacuous preaching about the "moral quandaries" of black America by those who themselves are morally suspect will only reinforce the cynicism about America and its leadership that is already widespread among the ghetto poor. All who write of poverty and morality should remember the biblical injunction "Let he without sin cast the first stone. "The paradigmatic case for this injunction is Glenn Loury, former professor of political economy at Harvard's Kennedy School of Government. Loury, a leading black neoconservative analyst of the black underclass, has written and lectured extensively on the immorality of underclass blacks.[78] In 1986 President Reagan nominated Loury to be assistant secretary of education. In poetic and biblical justice, a routine FBI background check disclosed that Loury, married, had a secret lover that he maintained in a Boston apartment. When this was revealed, Loury apparently tried to get the young woman to agree to a concocted story that she was only a poor student that he was helping to get through school (as a role model, I assume). She claimed that when she refused, he beat and threatened to kill her. After this became public knowledge, Loury withdrew his nomination and was later arrested for possession of marijuana and cocaine. Yet, now on the faculty of Boston University, he continues to prattle on about the moral irresponsibility of poor and dispossessed young black people.[79] Another example of this kind of hypocrisy is the shameless behavior of former District of Columbia Mayor Marion Barry, who as mayor constantly lectured young people on irresponsible drug use and sexual behavior while he engaged in such acts himself. Yet when he was caught in an FBI sting operation, he was embraced as a "brother" by elements of the black leadership including the NAACP's Benjamin Hooks and the Nation of Islam's Minister Louis Farrakhan.[80] Similarly, when the boxer Mike Tyson was accused of raping a young black woman he was also defended as a "brother" by some black leaders including Rev. T. J. Jamison, the head of the Nation's largest black church organization.[81]

Black Unemployment in the Post–Civil Rights Era and the Racist Residual

Black joblessness is not a recent or post–civil rights era problem. Table 6.1 displays data on black—white unemployment rates for selected years between 1948 and 1987.

If one takes a rate of unemployment of 4 percent as full employment, then in no year during this forty-year period did black males experience full employment (the nearest was 4.8 percent in 1953), while white males experienced this rate of unemployment during several periods, falling to as low as 2.5 percent in 1953. Looked at another way, if

TABLE 6.1

Black and White Unemployment Rates Selected Years, 1948–87*

Year	Black males	White males	Black females	White females
1948	5.8	3.4	6.1	3.4
1953	4.8	2.5	4.1	3.1
1958	13.8	6.1	10.8	6.2
1963	20.5	4.7	11.2	5.8
1968	5.6	2.6	8.3	4.3
1973	7.7	3.8	10.6	5.3
1978	11.0	4.6	13.0	6.2
1983	20.3	8.8	18.6	7.9
1986	14.8	6.0	14.2	6.1
1987	12.7	5.4	13.2	5.2

Source: U.S. Department of Labor, Bureau of Labor Statistics, *Employment and Earnings Annual Averages* (1987).

*1948–78 figures includes blacks and other races, 1983–87 figures are for blacks only.

one takes an unemployment rate of 5 percent as an indicator of a recession then in every selected year save one (1953) the black male community has been in recession, while for white males recessions were experienced in only four of the ten selected years. The black-white unemployment gap for females is similar during this period. Therefore, it is clear that whatever the causal nexus between joblessness and the underclass, unemployment has dogged the black community for a long time. In six of the ten years in the forty-year cycle black male unemployment reached double digits (seven for black females), while in no year did this occur for white males or females. In two years—1963 and 1983—the black unemployment rate reached depression levels. Thus, while social isolation and poverty concentration *may* be helpful in explaining certain aspects of the underclass in the post civil rights era, this long-term persistent joblessness is a central explanation of the disabilities of black people in the United States. Indeed, it is only a slight exaggeration to say, as Jesse Jackson quipped, "Blacks have only had full employment during slavery."

The effects of long-term unemployment on the social and psychological well-being of a people are also well known. Harvey Brenner estimated in a study prepared for the Joint Economic Committee of Congress that for every 1 percent increase in the rate of unemployment there is an associated increase of 5.7 percent in murders, 4.1 percent in suicides, 1.9 percent in mortality, 3.3 percent in mental institutionalization, and a 4.4 percent increase in divorce and separations.[82] Other studies have found correlations between unemployment and child abuse, alcoholism, wife battering, and other individual and social pathologies.[83]

But poverty consists not only of joblessness but also low-wage employment. A relative concept, poverty is simply not having enough money to sustain one's self and family. What is enough is relative, but since 1964 poverty researchers have used the government's official definition of poverty, which is based on the minimum food budget thought sufficient to sustain individuals and families. While this figure, adjusted for inflation since 1964, understates the amount of money needed for a family of four to support itself (about $12,000 in 1991 for an urban family of four), it is useful as a benchmark measure. Using it shows that poverty in black America is not only a function of unemployment but more frequently of low-wage work: full-time jobs that do not provide enough income to raise the worker above the poverty level. The image of ghetto poverty is often of idle men and women on welfare or engaged in selling drugs or other criminal behavior, as seen in the view of a majority of whites (58.9 percent) and a substantial minority of blacks (38.6 percent) in the 1991 General Social Survey that blacks "tend to prefer to live on welfare rather than be self supporting" (see Chapter 3). This is an illusion. Most poor blacks work. Indeed, it is an irony and a lingering effect of white supremacist doctrine that while many whites think most blacks are lazy or prefer not to work, blacks, far more than whites, work at the hardest jobs for the least pay and benefits. Blacks are disproportionately involved in the nation's most menial labor, literally in some cases society's scut work. In 1980 although only 12 percent of the population black workers constituted 37 percent of housekeepers, 53 percent of private house cleaners and servants, 22 percent of janitors and cleaners, and 27 percent of nurse aides, orderlies, and attendants.[84] It may seem strange that so many whites could think that blacks are indolent when they must daily confront blacks doing this kind of work. This is but another example of the tenacity of white supremacist thinking.

These jobs not only pay wages at or below the poverty line but typically do not include health benefits, vacation time, or the other benefits associated with decent working conditions. Data on wage poverty clearly show the disproportionate burden that black workers carry. In 1987 of those working twenty-seven hours or more per week, but still below the poverty line, blacks constituted 24.4 percent of the total, 18.5 percent of males and 30 percent of females.[85] Thus, while joblessness in the black community is an important aspect of black poverty, wage-based poverty, especially among women, which Wilson like most poverty researchers ignores, must also be included in explanation of and solutions to black poverty.[86]

Wilson's focus is the jobless problem, which he seeks to explain almost wholly in terms of nonracial, large-scale impersonal economic changes. These changes basically fall into two analytical categories, the jobs/skills mismatch that Myrdal referred to in his definition of the underclass in *The Challenge of Affluence* and the spatial mismatch on which Wilson relies. Wilson does not reject the jobs/skills mismatch explanation, however, he attaches less significance to it than he does to the spatial mismatch hypothesis. That is, while there may be a gap between the skills required of the new knowledge-intensive jobs in the city and the educational and skill attainments of inner-city blacks, Wilson believes the more important explanation for inner-city joblessness is not the absence of skills but the absence of jobs.[87] Paralleling Hershberg's analysis of "postindustrial" Philadelphia, Wilson observes that between 1947 and 1972 the central cities of the nation's thirty-two major cities lost more than 800,000 manufacturing jobs while the suburbs gained 2.5 million. Similarly, in retail and wholesale trade the cities lost 867,000 jobs while the suburbs gained a million such jobs.[88] Two issues related to racism are suggested by this movement of jobs from city to suburb. First, might the movement of jobs from areas where blacks are concentrated be a result at lease in part of racism, individual and institutional, in addition to the large-scale impersonal forces to which Wilson refers? Second, why have whites but not blacks been able to move in large numbers to the suburbs where the jobs are? Might this be at least in part a function of contemporary racism, individual and institutional? The answer to the second question is straightforward. The evidence reviewed in Chapters 3 and 4 on racism in the housing market is clear and convincing: widespread racial discrimination continues in the sale and rental of housing in the United States, which has the effect of depriving blacks not only of the access to decent and affordable housing, neighborhoods, and schools but also the opportunity to compete for the good jobs that are increasingly being located in the suburban fringes.

The evidence on the second question is not clear. Relatively little research has been conducted on plant location decisions, and it is unlikely that if racism is one of the motives in decisions to locate firms away from black areas (where the need is greatest) to largely white suburban areas (where the need is not so great) that it would be easily discovered, given the standard focus of research of this kind on impersonal factors such as the cost of land, the quality and cost of labor, transportation linkages, and the "business climate." Yet because we do not know in terms of available research does not mean that racism is not a factor.

Rather than ignore this hypothesis as Wilson does, one should follow the typical injunction of social scientists (nowhere better illustrated than among poverty researchers) to call for more research, further study. For example, a study of the location decisions of Japanese firms in the United States and of American auto companies found a fairly consistent pattern of location in rural and suburban areas about thirty miles from the nearest concentration of blacks, a distance that is thought to be about the limits of worker commuter time.[89] This study does not point to racism directly in such decisions, however, taken together with the more extensive research on racism in housing it does suggest that a fully developed explanation of the persistence of the black underclass should include in addition to the jobs/skills mismatch and the spatial mismatch also racism, individual and institutional.

Some research points directly to racism as a factor in black joblessness, holding constant both skills and spatial mismatches. In Chapter 3 I reviewed the findings of the Urban Institute's 1991 hiring audit study in Chicago and Washington that showed that young black job seekers with the same skills and demeanor as their white counterparts faced what the authors called "entrenched and widespread" racism. The authors of this Urban Institute report note that their work is preliminary and that "there is little empirical investigation of discrimination in hiring."[90] There is also little research on racism in plant and firm location decisions. But given the limited state of empirical research and knowledge on these questions it is probably best to pursue research on its effects on inner-city joblessness rather than facilely dismiss it as "worn out" and "uninteresting." My view here is confirmed by a recent research paper that emerges from Wilson's own poverty research project at the University of Chicago.

In a paper entitled "We'd Love to Hire Them But . . . " Kirschenman and Neckerman explore the meaning of race and racism for a sample of Chicago area employers. Their project, a part of Wilson's Urban Poverty and Family Project, was conducted in 1988–89, a year after the publication of *The Truly Disadvantaged*. It involved face-to-face interviews with a sample of 185 Chicago area employers concerning the role of race in hiring decisions for the typical entry-level employee. At the outset they note (in an ironic twist, given Wilson's dismissal of racism) that "analyses of inner city joblessness seldom consider racism or discrimination as a significant cause."[91] Although Kirschenman and Neckerman report that they were "overwhelmed" by the reluctance of employers to talk about the subject of race in their personnel decisions, the results of the interviews reveal a complex pattern of attitudes and actions that point to racism as an important factor in black joblessness in Chicago. They write, "Our interviews at Chicago area businesses show that employers view inner city workers, especially black men, as unstable, uncooperative, dishonest and uneducated. Race is an important factor in hiring decisions. But it is not race along; rather it is a complex interaction with employers' perception of class and space, or inner city residence. *Our findings suggest that racial discrimination deserves an important place in analysis of the underclass"* (emphasis added).[92] Their findings show elements of both individual and institutional racism as well residues of white supremacist thinking. Employers repeatedly invoked white supremacist stereotypes about blacks with remarks such as "They don't want to work"; "They are lazy"; "They steal"; "They lack motivation"; "They don't have a work ethic."[93] Others commented, "I need someone who will fit in"; "my customers are 95 percent white . . . I wouldn't last very long if I had some black"; "my guys don't want to work with blacks." These comments indicate employer racism in the individual sense in attitudes and behavior, but the data also contain evidence of institutional racism in both Anthony Downs's concept and my own. In the Downs sense many employers use race as a proxy, or what Downs calls an "indirect mechanism" for lower-class, low-quality labor; a "ghetto black." Other indirect indicator of the lower-class, ghetto black is the individual's place of residence and his or her speech or dress.[94] But there is also some evidence of institutional racism in the sense that I define it, in which the effects of social class are held constant. For example, Kirschenman and Neckerman write, "This negative opinion of blacks sometimes cuts across class lines . . . a personnel officer in the suburbs said with the professional staff, black males that we've had . . . they're not oriented to details. They lack some of the leadership skills."[95] As a preliminary effort, the work of Kirschenman and Neckerman is useful if only to show empirically that those who talk of racism as one causal element in explaining the black underclass should not be dismissed. "immediately" as "having nothing to say."[96]

Similarly, a study by the Wall Street Journal of job looses during the 1990–91 recession suggests a possible role for racism in explaining black unemployment, although the data here (as in the mortgage loan and certain health procedure cases discussed in Chapter 4) are ambiguous, with the now familiar "now you see it, now you don't" quality. The Journal analyzed the reports filed with the Equal Employment Opportunity Commission (EEOC) of 35,242 companies, covering more than 40 million workers. It found that African-Americans were the only group to experience a net loss of jobs during the recession, losing 59,470 com-

TABLE 6.2

Estimated Percentage Change in Employment at Companies Reporting
to the EEOC by Ethnicity and Job Category, 1990–91

	Blacks	Whites	Hispanics	Asians
Laborers	-5.2%	4.5%	-.5%	.5%
Skilled workers	-2.0	0	2.3	5.0
Semi-skilled	-2.0	0	-1.8	2.3
Service	-1.8	1.7	4.1	6.2
Clerks	-1.6	0	1.8	3.9
Sales	-1.6	1.5	5.7	5.1
Managers	1.1	0	2.1	2.2
Technicians	4.2	2.3	4.2	6.9
Professionals	5.9	2.2	5.0	8.0

Source: Calculated from data in Rochelle Sharp, "Losing Ground: In Latest
Recession Only Blacks Suffered Net Employment Loss," Wall Street Journal,
September 14, 1993, p. A14.

pared with gains by Asians of 55,104, by Hispanics of 60,060, and by
whites of 71,144.[97] As the data displayed in Table 6.2 show, blacks lost
jobs in precisely those categories—laborer, service, sales, clerks, and
semi-skilled—that one would expect to be available to inner-city workers with relatively low skills and training. By contrast, blacks gained
disproportionately in the white-collar categories of managers, professionals, and technicians, but the Journal reports, "they held such a small
percentage of these jobs before the recession began that their actual gains
were meager."[98]

Why this huge racial disparity (the Journal calculates that this loss
of jobs by blacks wiped out three years of employment gains)? Did
employers—as the numbers might suggest—deliberately use race as a
criteria to reduce their labor force? Or are there nonracist institutional
mechanisms at work here that render black labor expendable, compared
to Hispanic, Asian, and white. The answer is we do not know. Employers interviewed by the Journal denied that race and racism were involved, citing such other factors as the low seniority of blacks; their
concentration in job categories where companies decided to cut back;
the location of company operations in states—Arizona and New Mexico,
for example—where the black population is small; and decisions by
firms to close operations in the inner city and move them to predominantly white suburban areas. These explanations are plausible, and one
would not expect employers to admit to racial animus in their decision-
making. But, given the starkness of the disparity—blacks lost fully one-

third of all blue-collar jobs lost during the recession—and the kind of animus expressed by Chicago area employers toward black labor in the Kirschenman and Neckerman study, racism as a factor among many cannot be dismissed.

The Black Underclass and Public Policy:
A Note on Wilson's "Hidden Agenda"

Unlike his first book on race in the post–civil rights era, Wilson's *The Truly Disadvantaged* painstakingly spells out the policy implications of his analysis of the black underclass. While generally an informed and useful contribution to the policy and political debate on race and class, it is marred by his insistence on discounting the effects of racism on the problem and consequently on the necessity, at least in part, of race-specific policies. Related to this, as Clay Carson points out in his review of the book, Wilson, like most liberal reformers, "ignores the mobilization of the poor as a necessary component of social change. Like liberals of the past he disapproves of political strategies and intellectual arguments that might alienate whites who are needed for interracial coalitions."[99] Finally, Wilson writes as if he is ignorant of the entire post–civil rights era agenda of "universalist" policies and a "deracialized" strategic approach that has been the approach of black leadership since the early 1970s.

Wilson rejects the notion of race-or ghetto-specific reforms in favor of class-based programs that would target the poor of all races with programs of preferential treatment designed to "equalize the life chances" of all Americans who are disadvantaged on the basis of present class status.[100] While such universalist policies (full employment, national health insurance, child care, educational equity) ought to be pursued and indeed have been pursued by black leadership since the early 1970s,[101] with respect to the ghetto underclass such policies are probably necessary but not sufficient to deal with its deep-rooted problems. This is so first because, as Wilson's analysis shows, poor whites are not as disadvantaged as poor blacks (not "the truly disadvantaged"); white poverty, for example, is not as concentrated, and the white poor are not as isolated as poor blacks, and as a consequence these universalist policies are likely to be much more effective in dealing with their problems. Second, the magnitude of the problem of poverty is much greater in the black community (more than one-third of blacks are poor compared with about 10 percent of whites, and in the statistical artifact that is the American underclass blacks constitute 60 percent because of, as even Wilson concedes, historical racism). And because of their concentration and isolation, the black ghetto poor constitute more of a societal problem than do the white poor. Thus, in addition to the universalist, class-based programs effective actions to a meliorate the problems of the ghetto underclass will require race-specific government programs as well as programs of internal community mobilization and self-help initiatives. What I have in mind is something like a revised, well-funded, long-term set of experimental new Great Society programs to attack the *structure* of poverty, linked to black initiatives to mobilize the institutions of the black community in a sustained movement of community revitalization.[102] Wilson rejects this race-specific approach for political reasons, writing, "In the final analysis the question of reform is a political one. Accordingly, if the essential political message underscores the need for economic and social programs that benefits all groups in society, not just minorities, a basis for generating a broad based coalition would be created."[103] His political calculus may be correct, but the history of post–civil rights era black politics, Wilson's view to the contrary, suggests that this approach alone is not enough to create such broad-based coalitions.[104]

Wilson writes that full employment is central to his reform agenda in terms of "a general economic policy that would increase long term planning to promote both economic growth and sustained full employment, not only in higher income areas but in areas where the poor are concentrated as well."[105] Full employment at adequate wages is central to the problems of the underclass. This hardly anyone should doubt, although given the history of the Humphrey-Hawkins bill one might doubt its political, if not economic feasibility.[106] The problem with Wilson's analysis is that he suggests that what he proposes is something new; that black leadership has ignored full employment in favor of a myopic pursuit of race preference policies. He writes that "minority leaders could play an important role in this coalition once they fully recognized the need to shift or expand their definition of racial problems in America and broaden the scope of suggested programs to address them." What Wilson ignores is that full employment was a priority item on the agenda of the civil rights movement itself and since the late 1960s it has been the top priority of black leadership; indeed one can trace the centrality of unemployment in the black leadership's definition of the race problem as far back as Ralph Bunche's critique of the New Deal.[107] And the strategy that Wilson proposes in *The Truly Disadvantaged* was proposed by Charles Hamilton in a paper called "Full Employment as a Viable Strategy," presented at a 1973 conference called by the National Urban League to consider the post–civil rights era agenda. Hamilton even used the term *deracialization* to emphasize that blacks should turn to an issue that would cut across race lines and thus facilitate the creation of a broad-based multiracial coalition.[108] This strategy became the basis for the black leadership's development of the Humphrey-Hawkins Act and the coalition that secured its enactment. This bill, although fatally flawed, bears the exact language that Wilson now proposes: "The Full Employment and Balanced Growth Act." If Wilson had considered in his analysis the origins and evolution of the Humphrey-Hawkins Act his condemnation of black leadership myopia probably would have been less harsh.[109] That is, while there maybe much to criticize in the behavior of black leaders in the post–civil rights era, the notion that they have not recognized the imperative of full employment and the need for deracialized or universalist issues and multiracial coalition is without merit. Recognition of this is an important first step in any serious effort to develop a realistic strategy to deal with the problems of race, class, and politics in the United States in the next century.

Epilogue

I end this book on a rather pessimistic note. In his most recent book, *Faces at the Bottom of the Well*, Derrick Bell argues that racism is an immutable feature of American society.[1] This study suggests that he is probably correct.

While there is an ambiguous, "now you see it, now you don't" quality to the evidence, both the individual and institutional levels demonstrate that race is still from time to time and place to place taken into consideration in a manner that denies blacks equal access to societal values and resources. While the doctrine of white supremacy or black inferiority is rarely articulated in public places today, its lingering effects or residues are occasionally expressed by public figures, and at least one-fourth of white Americans are still willing to tell survey researchers that they believe blacks in a variety of ways are an inferior people. Evidence of individual racist behavior is largely anecdotal and scattered, but at the institutional level there is systematic evidence of racism—the differential treatment in an adverse or negative way of blacks on the basis of race—even after controlling for the effects of social class and other relevant variables. In education, in the sale and rental of housing, in access to mortgage loans, in employment, in access to health care (including certain surgical procedures), in the purchase of an automobile or in the punishment for the use of illegal drugs, American institutions continue to operate so as to produce racially disparate outcomes. And despite some progress during the last twenty-five years, the evidence is also clear that a significant minority of blacks continue to internalize negative images and stereotypes about the race.

Social scientists, no matter how bleak their findings, are inclined to end their studies on a favorable note with recommendations to improve the situation. My inclination, however, is to refrain from proposing broad solutions or strategies to deal with post–civil rights era racism. This is because I do not see any realistic or politically feasible strategies or policies to deal with the problem. When I was growing up in the rural south in the late 1950s and 1960s, racism was easy to see. Even in the cities of the north during this period, racism was relatively easy for both scholar and citizen to see. The civil rights revolution changed all this, making virtually all forms of racism illegal and therefore less visible and more intractable. As Dr. King said shortly before his death, the civil rights revolution represented a frontal attack on the doctrine and practice of white supremacy, but it did not destroy what he called the "monster" of racism itself. He was, of course, correct. But racism today has an ambiguous character. This is the central dilemma in dealing with it. How can one propose specific policies or programs to deal with what cannot be seen or what one refuses to see or acknowledge even when it is seen.[2] The consequence of this is that Congress, the courts, and the civil rights enforcement bureaucracies are not likely to be able to muster the will or capabilities to ensure that blacks have equal access and fair treatment, whatever their social class, to the nation's values and resources.

Among the many useful comments of the three anonymous reviewers selected by SUNY to review this manuscript, none was more insistent and consistent than the suggestion that I spell out the policy and political implications of the findings. One reviewer wrote, "Rather than end the book on a pessimistic note, the author might point to specific policies that could work—at least to diminish racism—if tried and the way to mobilize coalitions in support of these policies." And another wrote, "Has Mr. Smith just thrown up his hands, given up and in essence accepted the fact blacks will always be victims of racism, or can he offer a few ideas or suggestions about changing the status quo?" It is not that I wish to "throw up my hands" (although I do believe that racism can be reduced but is likely to remain a characteristic of American society), but rather that I do not envision any realistic strategies or policies to deal with the problem, and as a social scientist I feel it is my responsibility to state my honest conclusion. This is not to say that I cannot conceive of policies and programs that would ameliorate racism's effects. On the contrary, several might be suggested—modification of the seniority rule in layoffs, enforceable goals or quotas in hiring and firing, universal, comprehensive national health insurance, a renewed war on poverty, a government role in plant location decisions. The problem is that—at least for the foreseeable future—such programs lack public, congressional, presidential, or judicial support.

Perhaps such support might develop if the leadership of black America would recognize that mobilization of the ghetto poor is a necessary part of social change in the post–civil rights era. But this does not seem likely either.[3] In the last twenty-five years virtually all the talent and resources of the leadership of black America have been devoted to integration or incorporation into the institutions of the American polity, while the core community it purports to lead has become increasingly segregated, and its society, economy, culture, and institutions of internal governance and communal uplift have decayed. Simultaneously, this leadership is engaged in forms of politics that are incapable of producing public policies that effectively deal with the problems of racism and poverty and is increasingly irrelevant in terms of programs of action that would deal with the internal disabilities of the black community. Thus, realistically there is little prospect—at least in the near term—for the development of a politics or for the adoption of policies that effectively deal with the interrelated problems of racism and poverty in the United States.

Notes

Introduction

1. Although these problems are not unique to the scientific study of racism, they are probably more acute in this area of inquiry because social scientists have paid very little attention to problems of concept formation, indicator construction, measurement, and systematic data collection. Yet these problems bedevil even the most advanced area of scientific research on politics. Asher, for example, writes, "The field of voting behavior is often viewed as the area within political science that has made the greatest progress in the generation of an empirically based cumulative body of knowledge . . . when one asks where is the 'science' in political science, a common reply is to point the questioner to the field of voting behavior." Yet Asher quotes a leading voting behavior specialist, Warren Miller, as arguing that "in many respects the field of voting behavior does not merit the label of science." He attributes this to the fact that scholars in the field often treat questions of measurement, design, methodology, and substantive theory in a disjointed fashion. Such practices yield a portrait of confusion and the apparent noncumulativity of research findings in the field even when results may actually be complementary. See Herbert Asher, "Voting Behavior Research in the 1980s: An Examination of Some Old and New Problem Areas," in A. Finifter (ed.) *The State of the Discipline* (Washington: American Political Science Association, 1983): 339, 377.

2. Ruth Benedict, *Race: Science and Politics* (New York: Modern Age Books, 1940).

3. An emergent alternative to the difficulties involved in the empirical study of racism is postmodernism. Using analytical instruments derived from philosophy and literary criticism, postmodernists seek to "dissect the textual basis" of racist discourse and specify its historical and contemporary modes as expressed in literature, philosophy, science, and popular discourses in music, sports, politics, and the law. David Theo Goldberg presents a good collection of postmodernist writings on race and racism in his edited collection of papers *Anatomy of Racism* (Minneapolis: University of Minnesota Press, 1990).

4. Cornell West argues for a somewhat similar multidimensional approach to the analysis of racism. He suggests "three methodological steps in inquiry into racism" including the "genealogical" (focusing on predominant European supremacist thought in Judeo-Christian, scientific, and psychosexual discourses), the "microinstitutional," and the "macrostructural." See "Toward a Socialist Theory of Racism," Institute for Democratic Socialism (n.d.): 4. Al-

though there are semantic differences and I add the dimension of internal inferiorization, my analysis parallels West's conceptual and methodological approach to the study of racism as a historical and empirical problem. See also Matthew Holden, Jr., *The White Man's Burden* (New York: Chandler, 1973): 20–39 for a typology of racism similar to that employed here.

5. Stokely Carmichael and Charles Hamilton, *Black Power* (New York: Vintage Books, 1967): 3–4.

Chapter 1. Historical Considerations on the Doctrine of White Supremacy and Its Status in the Post–Civil Rights Era

1. Mack Jones, "A Frame of Reference for Black Politics," in L. Henderson (ed.), *Black Political Life in the United States* (San Francisco: Chandler, 1972):8.

2. Ibid., p. 9.

3. Ibid.

4. Jones does not focus explicitly on the third component—violence—essential to understanding of black politics. Racism—the subordination of blacks to whites—was justified on the basis of the doctrine of black inferiority, but it was accomplished through violence, extraordinary violence.

Frantz Fanon's work provides the most theoretically sophisticated treatment of the integral role of violence in black society and politics. He discusses not only the role of white violence in black subordination but also the role of internal or communal violence (what he calls the phenomenon of "niggers killing niggers on Saturday night," which he argues explains the extremely high rate of black-on-black murders, robberies, and rapes) and revolutionary violence, or that violence employed to end racial subordination. See his *Black Skin, White Masks: The Experiences of a Black Man in a White World* (New York: Grove Press, 1967) and *The Wretched of the Earth* (New York: Grove Press, 1968); see also Robert Staples, "Violence in Black America: The Political Implications," *Black World* 23 (May 1974):17–32, and my "Beyond Marx: Fanon and the Concept of Colonial Violence," *Black World* 27(May 1973): 23–33.

5. Joel Kovel, *White Racism: A Psychohistory* (New York: Vintage Books, 1971):3.

6. Charles Lawrence, "The Id, the Ego and Equal Protection: Reckoning with Unconscious Racism," *Stanford Law Review* 39(1987): 338.

7. West, "Toward a Socialist Theory of Racism," p. 3.

8. Among the better studies of this sort are Winthrop Jordan, *White Over Black: American Attitudes Toward the Negro, 1550–1812* (Baltimore: Penguin Books, 1968); Kovel's *White Racism*; and George Frederickson, *The Black Image in the White Mind* (New York: Harper & Row, 1971) and *White Supremacy: A Compara-*

tive Study in American and South African History (New York: Oxford University Press, 1981).

9. Jordan, *White Over Black*, pp. 3–43.

10. Fredrickson citing David Brion Davis's *Slavery in Western Culture* (pp. 48–49) in *White Supremacy* (p. 74) writes, "However unflattering the usual African stereotype may have been, it was probably less derogatory and venomous than that applied at this time to the Irish, who were undoubtedly white." This is a point that perhaps African-and Irish-Americans today find difficult to accept, but there is considerable evidence to support it. Michael Hechter, for example, quotes a nineteenth-century Cambridge University historian describing a visit to Ireland: "But I am haunted by the human chimpanzees I saw along that hundred miles of horrible country. I don't believe they are our fault. I believe there are not only many more of them than of old, but they are happier, better, more comfortably fed and lodged under our rule than they ever were. But to see white chimpanzees is dreadful; if they were black, one would not feel it so much, but their skins, except tanned by exposure, are as white as ours." See *Internal Colonialism: The Celtic Fringe in British National Development, 1536–1966* (Berkeley: University of California Press, 1975): xvi–xvii.

11. Karen Fields, "Ideology and Race in American History, unpublished manuscript (n.d.):6, 8.

12. On South Africa see Frederickson, *White Supremacy*, and on the Latin American case, see H. Hoetink, *Caribbean Race Relations: A Study of Two Variants* (New York: Oxford University Press, 1967).

13. Thomas Jefferson is the paradigmatic figure here—author of the Declaration of Independence, pre-eminent intellectual, acquaintance through correspondence with eminent black intellectual Benjamin Banneker and a man who perhaps had a genuine love relationship with a black woman. In his first draft of the Declaration he had included a clause condemning the British monarch for his sanctioning the slave trade (dropped as a result of the protests of the southern slaveholders), yet he was a slaveholder and steadfastly asserted the doctrine of African inferiority. On Jefferson's ambivalence on race and equality, see Jordan *White Over Black*, pp. 429–81 and Jean Yarbrough, "Race and the Moral Foundation of the American Republic: Another Look at the Declaration and the Notes on Virginia," *Journal of Politics* 53(1991): 91–104.

14. Rudyard Kipling, "The White Man's Burden," in *Collected Verses* (New York: Doubleday, 1907): Stanza 1, p. 215.

15. Forrest Wood, *The Arrogance of Faith: Christianity and Race in America from the Colonial Era to the Twentieth Century* (New York: Knopf) 1990: 22.

16. Jordan, *White Over Black*, p. 23.

17. Ibid., p. 24. Jordan notes that Aristotle and other classical Greek philosophers had argued that a people without God, law, or state were without

humanity and thus fit only for slavery.

18. Ibid.

19. Ibid., p. 33.

20. Even today there is still not yet a good and comprehensive historical or social scientific study of the relationship between race and sexuality. Calvin Hernton's little book *Sex and Racism in America* (New York: Grove Press, 1965) has some insights, but perhaps the best treatment is in Fanon's chap. 2, "The Woman of Color and the White Man," and chap. 3, "The Man of Color and the White Woman," in *Black Skin, White Mask*. The matter is also treated sensitively in black literature, as for example, in Leroi Jones's *The Dutchman* (New York: William Morrow, 1964) and James Baldwin's *Another Country* (New York: Dial, 1962). And although it is profoundly distasteful, Eldridge Cleaver's chapter "White Woman, Black Man" in *Soul on Ice* (New York: McGraw–Hill, 1968) is also insightful.

21. Jordan, *White Over Black*, pp.28–29.

22. Ibid.

23. Ibid.

24. Wood, *The Arrogance of Faith*, p. 38.

25. Ibid.

26. See Jordan, *White Over Black*, pp. 17–20; Wood, *The Arrogance of Faith*, chap. 3; Edith R. Sanders, "The Hamitic Hypothesis: Its Origins and Functions in Time Perspective," *Journal of African History* 4(1969): 521–32; and St. Clair Drake, *Black Folk Here and There* (Los Angeles: University of California, Center for Afro-American Studies, 1990): 17–23.

27. In this respect, Jordan writes, "the English experience was markedly different from that of the Spanish and Portuguese who for centuries had been in close contact with North Africa and had actually been invaded and subjected by people both darker and more highly civilized than themselves. The impact of the Negro's color was the more powerful upon Englishmen, moreover, because England's principal contact with Africans came in West Africa and the Congo where men were not merely dark but almost literally black: one of the fairest-skinned nations suddenly came face to face with one of the darkest people on earth," *White Over Black*, p. 6.

28. Ibid., p. 7. There are parallels to these negative meanings of black in contemporary English dictionaries. It should also be noted that the definition of white then and now has exactly the opposite meaning, indicating that this attitude toward color reflects a high degree of race chauvinism. While Jordon does not note African attitudes toward the English it is possible that they had similar negative, chauvinistic attitudes with respect to the color white.

29. Jordan notes that the term Ham originally connoted both dark and hot and that given the association of heat with sensuality (and the sexual nature of Ham's offense) a logical connection might have been drawn in this way. Yet, he suggests very few thinkers seized on this as a possible explanation (*White Over Black*, p. 18).

30. Sanders, "The Hamitic Hypothesis," p. 522.

31. John David Smith of North Carolina State University has collected post–Civil War era white supremacist writings—from popular magazines, newspapers, scholarly journals, scientific monographs, and polemical tracts—in a massive multivolume anthology. See *Anti-Black Thought 1863–1925: A Eleven Volume Anthology of Racist Writings in Facsimile* (Hamden, CT: Garland Publishing, 1992).

32. Rhett Jones, "Proving Blacks Inferior: The Sociology of Knowledge," *Black World* 21(July 1967).

33. Ibid., p. 8. This is akin to the notion advanced by some commentators today on the so-called black underclass who argue that a relative absence of morality among blacks is an important explanation for such things as the high incidence of joblessness, welfare dependency, female-headed households, crime, and drug abuse. See, for example, Glen Loury, "The Moral Quandary of the Black Community," *The Public Interest* 79(spring 185): 9–22.

34. Jones, "Proving Blacks Inferior," p. 9.

35. Ibid., p. 15. It was occasionally argued that the brain of a black person resembled in size that of a chimpanzee rather than a European. I recall reading somewhere—I have not been able to locate the source—that when the NAACP was founded a press conference was held with several Columbia University biologists who brought along the preserved brains of a black man, a white man, and a chimpanzee in order to prove to a doubting public that the black man's brain was more akin to that of the European than to that of the chimpanzee.

36. Ibid., p. 15.

37. There is a voluminous literature on the IQ test and the controversy surrounding its use and abuse. Although as I shall argue here the IQ test as a valid instrument to establish race group differences in intelligence is now largely discredited, this argument even today is itself controversial. For views similar to mine (indeed on which I base my argument) see Stephen Gould, *The Mismeasure of Man* (New York: W.W. Norton, 1981); Leon Kamin, *The Science and Politics of IQ* (Potomac, MD: Lawrence Erlbaum, 1974); and David Gersh, "The Corporate Elite and the Introduction of IQ Testing in American Schools," in M. Schwarz (ed.), *The Structure of Power in America* (New York: Holmes & Meier, 1987): 163–84. The alternative view is advanced in R. J. Herrenstein, *IQ in the Meritocracy* (Boston: Little, Brown, 1973); and Daniel Seligman, *A Ques-*

tion of Intelligence: The IQ Debate in America (New Brunswick, NQ.: Transaction 1992).

38. Larry P. v. Riles, 495 F. Supp. (1979), p. 935. This opinion, holding that use of the IQ test to place black children in classes for the educable retarded was a violation of Title VI of the Civil Rights Act of 1964, the Rehabilitation Act of 1973, the Education for All Handicapped Children Act of 1975, and the equal protection clause of the Fourteenth Amendment, provides a thorough history and overview of the IQ test based on a fairly extensive review of the literature, expert testimony, and an analysis of its use in placing white and minority children in classes for the educable mentally retarded in California from 1968 to 1977. I draw on it in part here for this discussion and later in Chapter 5 in my discussion of the persistence of racism in the post–civil rights era.

39. Ibid., p. 953.

40. Fields, "Ideology and Race in American History," p. 8. On these points see generally Gould, *The Mismeasure of Man*, and Alice Littlefield, Leonard Liberman, and Larry Reynolds, "Redefining Race: The Political Demise of a Concept in Physical Anthropology," *Current Anthropology* 23(1982):640–47. On the racial heterogeneity of the American population, it has been estimated that about 20 to 31 percent of the genes of the black population are from white ancestors and about 1 percent of the genes of whites are from blacks. See F. James Davis, *Who Is Black?* (University Park, PA: Pennsylvania State University Press, 1991):21.

41. Quoted in Gersh, "The Corporate Elite and the Introduction of the IQ Test," p. 167.

42. Cited in Larry P. v. Riles, p. 957. Under political pressure in the early 1970s the Stanford-Binet was restandardized to include a proportional number of black children and the WISC was revised later in the decade.

43. Ibid., p. 955.

44. Kamin, *The Science and Politics of IQ*. Although the fraudulent character of Burt's work has been noted by a number of respected commentators in addition to Kamin, including his official biographer (see Leslie Hearnshaw, *Cyril Burt, Psychologist* [Ithaca: Cornell University Press, 1979]), Burt continues to have his apologists who would like to see his reputation restored. See Ronald Fletcher, *Science, Ideology and the Media: The Cyril Burt Scandal* (New Brunswick, NJ: Transaction, 1990).

45. Among blacks it was found that lighter-skinned persons tended to score higher, which led the testers to conclude that this simply confirmed their white supremacist view that the relative success of blacks in this country was in direct proportion to their genetic makeup, i.e., the amount of "white blood." The real explanation of course has nothing to do with blood but with the environment; the fact that historically and even today light-skinned persons tend to have higher social class standing and the results of the tests are highly cor-

related with class. On the social class advantages of light-skinned blacks historically, see Gunnar Myrdal, *An American Dilemma: The Negro Problem and American Democracy* (New York: Harper Torchbooks, 1944): 695–700, and E. Franklin Frazier, *Black Bourgoisie* (New York: Conllier, 1957): passim. On the social class advantages of lighter-skinned blacks today, see Richard Seltzer and Robert C. Smith, "Skin Color Differences in the Afro-American Community and the Differences They Make," *Journal of Black Studies* 21(1991): 279–86. I discuss the material and psychological basis of this skin color difference in class and status in the chapter on internal inferiorization.

46. Quoted from Kamin, *The Science and Politics of IQ*, pp. 850–51. "Evidence" and argument of this sort was used to justify the continued subordination of blacks but also to help to make the case for the immigration act of 1924, which virtually excluded from entry into the country persons of southern and eastern European origins. This ethnic bias in immigration law was not corrected by law until 1965.

47. On the white supremacist propaganda in the leading literary magazines—*Harper's Atlantic* and *Scribner's*—see chap. 13 in Rayford Logan, *The Betrayal of the Negro* (New York: Collier, 1965).

48. The work of a small band of black scholars led by W. E. B. DuBois in countering the intellectual claims of white supremacists in science should also not be overlooked. During the 1920s and 1930s the NAACP's *Crisis* magazine, edited by DuBois, was filled with articles and notes countering the claims of the geneticists and making the case for environmentalism.

49. See Elazar Barkan, *The Retreat of Scientific Racism* (New York: Cambridge University Press, 1992).

50. On the choice of Myrdal, Ralph Ellison wrote, it "aroused a sense of alienation and embarrassment . . . by reminding [him] that it was necessary in our democracy for a European scientist to affirm the Negro's humanity"; see "An American Dilemma: A Review," pp. 80–81 in Joyce Ladner (ed.), *The Death of White Sociology* (New York: Random House, 1973). One aspect of Myrdal's background was overlooked—that he was a socialist—which was later used, especially in the southern press after the *Brown* decision, to discredit the study. (In its famous footnote 11 the *Brown* opinion cited Myrdal's work to sustain its proposition that, contrary to what may have been thought in 1896 at the time of the *Plessy* decision, there was now no scientific basis for the notion of black inferiority.)

51. Myrdal, *An American Dilemma*, p. lxxv.

52. John Ehrlichman notes that President Nixon constantly made racist remarks indicating a belief in black inferiority. See *Witness to Power* (New York: Auburn House, 1982):222–23.

53. Earl Butz, among other things, made a scatological remark in terms of sexual stereotypes (President Ford fired him); Howard Cosell, the ABC televi-

sion sportscaster, referring to a black football player remarked, "look at the monkey run" (he first denied saying it but when the audio tape showed the contrary he apologized, saying the remark was not racial); Jimmy "the Greek" Snyder, the CBS sports commentator, remarked that black athletes were superior to whites because they were "bred to be that way" since slavery (he was fired); and Los Angeles Dodgers Vice President Al Campanis was fired after he declared in a television interview that blacks lacked the "necessities" to work in the front offices of baseball. It is worth pointing out that many of these incidents dealt with sports and black athletes, a point I return to later in this chapter.

54. Lawrence Hafastad, Marianne Mele Hall and John Morse, *Foundations of Sand: A Hard Look at the Social Sciences* (Centerville, MD: Distributed by Corsica Books, 1982):59 Hall repudiated the quote suggesting it was an editorial error but subsequently withdrew her nomination.

55. Goodwin later apologized for his statement saying, it was made without "malice" but was insensitive; and finally under pressure from the Congressional Black Caucus he resigned. See Michael Iskoff, "HHS Official Apologizes for `Male Monkey' Remarks," *Washington Post*, February 22, 1992; "Black Caucus Seeks Review of U.S. Health Official," *New York Times*, February 28, 1992; and "Health Official Quits After Harsh Criticism," *New York Times*, February 29, 1992. It was later learned that Goodwin, with the support of the National Institutes of Health, was in charge of a so-called Violence Initiative, designed to identify potentially violent inner-city black children based on genetic and biological factors. It included studies of rhesus monkeys, violent behavior, and the testing of psychiatric drugs as a possible means of violence prevention. Under pressure from blacks and others, the government withdrew support for the initiative. See "Faced with Complaints, the National Institutes of Health Withdraws Support of Violence Project," *New York Times*, September 18, 1992.

56. Whites frequently express their opposition to neighborhood school integration because of the high black crime rate, the number of blacks on welfare, or the loss of property values, but sometimes the deep-seated, tenacious hatred of blacks is verbalized in situations of intense conflict. For example, residents of a working-class white neighborhood in Queens, New York, in early 1970s waged a year-long struggle to force a black doctor and his wife from a house they had recently purchased. When interviewed by Bill Moyers on PBS, the neighbors said they were opposed to having blacks (even those of manifestly higher social class status) move into the neighborhood because blacks were sexually aggressive and would endanger their daughters; because they would not work; that their women had too many men; and because they did not have the same standards (civilization) as whites. Similar sentiments were expressed by persons interviewed in the Bensonhurst and Howard Beach communities in New York City in the wake of the murders of black men who happened to be in the wrong place at the wrong time.

57. See "A Few Words with Willie Horton," an interview by Dr. Jeffrey M. Elliot, *Playboy*, December, 1989, pp. 166, 218–23.

58. Martin Schram, "The Making of Willie Horton," *The New Republic*, May 28, 1990, pp. 17–19; and Kathleen Hall Jamieson, *Dirty Politics: Deception, Distraction and Democracy* (New York, Oxford University Press 1992): 131–35.

59. Schneider is quoted in Anthony Lewis, "The Dirty Little Secret," *New York Times*, October 20, 1988. As usual in the post–civil rights era, when the ad was attacked as racist Bush disavowed it and after twenty-eight days ordered it withdrawn. And Lee Atwater, Bush's campaign manager, two years later terminally ill with cancer, apologized for the ad because of its racist implications. See "Lee Atwater's Last Campaign," *Life*, February 1991, p. 61. Appeals to such psychosexual racist stereotypes are not limited to white candidates and campaigns. In the 1989 Atlanta mayoral campaign Michael Lomax, black and a leading contender, ran an ad showing a white woman executive talking about her fears of rape while in downtown Atlanta. After widespread condemnation by the city's black clergy as "the Willie Horton thing" and the Atlanta *Journal-Constitution* as "blatantly racist," Lomax withdrew the ad and subsequently withdrew from the race. On the ads and the response, see Ronald Smothers, "Styles Conflict in Mayoral Campaign," *New York Times*, July 24, 1989.

60. Patrick Buchanan, "The Barbarians Are at the Gates," *Houston Chronicle*, April 30, 1989. It is difficult for me to believe that Buchanan would have written a column so rich in imagery of savagery and the beneficent effects of horse whipping, and conversion to Christianity if the victim had been black or the perpetrators white. Indeed, he did not when a young woman was gang raped in a New Bedford, Massachusetts, poolhall by several white men, or when a group of Long Island "All American" white boys raped a young retarded girl or when a group of St. John's University white students over several hours raped and sodomized a young black coed.

61. The Forrest City story was reported in Barbara McIntosh, "The Class That Crossed the Great Divide," *Washington Post*, May 2, 1988. Another example of the persistence of this psychosexual racist sterotype is revealed in a book by Stacy Koon, the officer in charge at the scene of the Rodney King beating. Koon wrote that one factor in King's beating was the fear he generated in a white female officer. Koon wrote, "He [King] grabbed his butt with both hands and began to shake and gyrate his fanny in a sexually suggestive fashion. As King sexually gyrated, a mixture of fear overcame Melanie [the white female officer]. The fear was of a Mandingo sexual encounter." See Richard Serrano, "Officer in King Case Writes Blunt Memoir," *West County Times*, May 17, 1992.

62. These "first impressions" are also reinforced by the media's commonly distorted coverage of the admittedly terrible conditions of postindependence Africa. Africa usually does not appear in the media unless it is to depict starv-

ing, near-nude women and children, tribal wars, coups and countercoups, and most recently stories about a continent dying of AIDS. The discussion of AIDS in Western medical research and in the press often traces its origins to Africa and its pervasiveness there to sexual license. While I do not suggest any kind of conspiracy or overt ill will in this research and reporting, it may reflect the deeply embedded association in the white psyche of Africa and blackness with disease, dirt, and sexual promiscuity. On this aspect of racism's psychodynamic, see Kovel's interesting analysis in Chap. 4, "The Fantasies of Race," in *White Racism: A Psychohistory*. On how these attitudes may influence research on AIDS in Africa, see Richard and Rosalind Chirimula, *AIDS, Africa and Racism* (North Derby on Trent, England: Richard Chirimula, 1987). Interestingly, in the American context, Pat Robertson, the television evangelist and one-time presidential candidate, on his television program "The 700 Club"—I did not record the date of the broadcast but soon after the recognition of the disease—resurrected one of the worst of the fantasies of the white man's burden by suggesting that AIDS may have its origins in sexual relations between humans and apes in Africa.

63. Although there are relatively few (less than 3 percent) black athletic directors, coaches, managers, umpires, announcers, league executives, or owners, black athletes dominate both Division I collegiate and professional basketball and football. In Division I college basketball 65 percent of the players in 1990 were black but only 10 percent of the coaches. In football the figures were 55 percent and less than 10 percent while blacks constituted only 4 percent of the student body of these institutions. By contrast in baseball only 7.2 percent of Division I baseball players were black. Professionally, 74 percent of NBA players are black but only 10 percent of the coaches, in the NFL 62 percent of the players are black, but only one black head coach and in baseball 18 percent of the players and two black managers. These figures are from Charles Farrell, "In Sports Race Still Calls the Plays," *New York Times*, June 22, 1991. See also John Underwood, "On the Playground," *Life*, spring 1988, pp. 102–08; and William Rhoden, "Many Black College Athletes Express Feelings of Isolation," *New York Times*, April 6, 1990. The reasons for the relatively small number of blacks in baseball are said to include the lack of youth baseball programs in urban areas, the steering and gravitation of blacks to football and basketball, the scarcity of full scholarships, and recruiting bias at the collegiate and minor league levels. See "College Baseball Has Become Lily White," *New York Times*, June 11, 1990.

64. Especially given the well-known failure of these Division I institutions to graduate these young men, the refusal of the NCAA to allow them to be financially compensated in spite of their near full-time workloads. The NCAA reported in 1991 that the average Division I athlete practiced twenty-eight hours per week but spent only eleven hours preparing for class.

65. Richard Lapchick, "Pseudo-Scientific Prattle About Athletes," *New York*

Times, April 29, 1989.

66. Ibid.

67. Underwood, "On the Playing Ground," p. 104.

68. Ibid., p. 109. Georgetown University basketball coach John Thomas called Proposition 42/48 "institutional racism" because of its disparate impact on blacks. Given the way institutional racism is defined and operationalized by some scholars, Thomas's conclusion cannot be discounted. However, as tennis player and sports historian Arthur Ashe noted, while it is conceivable that some may see Proposition 42/48 as a convenient cover for reducing the number of blacks in sports, the requirements are relatively low and "The rule still contains the most powerful inducement yet for high school athletes to abandon their cynical belief that they will get scholarships even if they don't bother to study. . . . It is no secret that 75 percent of black football and basketball players never graduate college. . . . We should either get serious about academic standards or cut out the hypocrisy and pay college athletes as professionals." See "Coddling Black Athletes," *New York Times*, February 10, 1989.

69. Ira Berkow, "Black Quarterbacks Bloom," *New York Times*, January 5, 1989.

70. Ibid. In comments that echo these sentiments regarding black capabilities, General Carl Mundy, commandant of the Marine Corps, remarked that black officers were not promoted as rapidly as whites because " [It] has to do with performance. In the military skills, we find that the minority officers do not shoot as well as the non-minorities. . . . They don't swim as well. And when you give them a compass and send them across the terrain at night they don't do as well at that sort of thing." Surprisingly, there was not the usual uproar or protest about the general's remarks although they were said on the widely viewed CBS "60 Minutes" broadcast (October 31, 1993) and the general was not asked to apologize and was not reprimanded.

71. I should emphasize in the public media since the doctrine may still be articulated in the segregated white fundamentalist churches, especially in the south, of which I don't have firsthand knowledge. However, in their radio and television sermons (which I frequently monitor) I have not heard the doctrine preached since the late 1960s.

72. Quoted in Walt Harrington, "Well Wrought," *Washington Post Magazine*, July 29, 1988, p. 24.

73. See Bob Jones v. United States v. Goldsboro Christian Schools v. United States , United States Supreme Court, 103, S.CT. 2017 (1983). Although Bob Jones University is clearly an isolated case at the college level, at the elementary and secondary levels there are probably a large number of Christian "segregation academies" established in the south after the implementation of the

Brown decree that continue to teach a religious basis for racism.

74. Carlos Byars, "Paper on Evolution Ignites Controversy," *Houston Chronicle*, January 20, 1989. Professor Rushlon has expanded his paper into a book. See *Race, Evolution and Behavior: A Life History Perspective* (New Brunswick, NJ: Transaction, forthcoming). Professor Vincent Sarich at the University of California, Berkeley, has been the focus of faculty and student protests because of his work on brain size and human intelligence and behavior.

75. Arthur Jensen, "How Much Can We Boost IQ and Scholastic Achievement," *Harvard Educational Review* 39(winter 1969): 1–123.

76. *Harvard Educational Review* 39(spring–summer 1969). See especially the paper by Professor Jerome Kagan.

77. Jerry Hirsch, "To Unfrock the Charlatans," *Sage Race Relations Abstracts* 6(May 1981): 1–66. Hirsch, a professor of psychology and ecology at the University of Illinois, Urbana, has done yeoman's work in tracing the origins of the post–civil rights era resurgence of interest in IQ to racist and segregationist groups, in refuting its theoretical and methodological underpinnings, and in trying to inform the public and policy makers about the dishonest, pseudoscientific character of this latest eugenics movement. I appreciate his sharing selected papers and correspondence with me as well as taking the time to explore the matter with me in a couple of conversations.

78. Wychliffe Draper, a New York millionaire, funded the establishment of the Pioneer Fund with the avowed aim of getting "some solid evidence that Negroes are congenitally inferior to whites." This organization provided substantial financial support to both Jensen and Shockley, according to a *New York Times* report of December 11, 1977, giving at least $179,000 to Shockley alone in the ten-year period 1967–77. See Hirsch, "To Unfrock the Charlatans," p. 13.

79. Ibid., pp. 11–12.

80. Cited in Ibid., p. 7.

81. Cited in Ibid., p. 8.

82. Ibid., p. 8.

83. See "Some Biology Teachers See Link Between Race, Intellect," *Houston Chronicle*, September 11, 1992.

84. Jason DeParle, "Architect of Reagan Vision Looks at Race and IQ," *New York Times*, November 30, 1990. In spite of his long-time association with New York's conservative Manhattan Institute, Murray left it (with a $100,000 grant) to conduct the study at the American Enterprise Institute because his Manhattan Institute colleagues were reluctant to give their imprimatur to the project.

Chapter 2. Racism: Toward Conceptual Clarification of the Institutional Mode

1. In many parts of the world, racism in the sense understood here is practiced without any explicit rationale or ideology while elsewhere it is practiced on the basis of a belief in the superiority of the group that is subordinated. This latter is the case to an extent for the Jews in Europe, the Ibos in Nigeria, or the East Asians in Kenya. In these cases these groups were or are subordinated because it is alleged that because of some superior social, economic, or cultural characteristics if they are not held in a subordinate position they will "take over." I should note that a few commentators on racism in the United States argue, the ideology of white supremacy notwithstanding, that racism is the result of some inchoate sense of black superiority. An unconvincing version of this notion is advanced by Frances Cress Welsing in *The Iris Papers: The Keys to the Colors* (Chicago: Third World Press, 1991), where she contends that whites fear and subordinate blacks because blacks are genetically superior to them in terms of their capacity to produce melanin, which, without racism, would result overtime in the dominant black genes, overwhelming the recessive white ones and thereby destroying the European group as a distinct entity. Although Welsing's theory is without scientific merit, in racism's long history in this country it has played a role in the thinking of some white supremacists in terms of their alleged fear of "mongrelization" and their advocacy of antimiscegnation laws.

2. C. Wright Mills, *The Power Elite* (New York: Oxford University Press 1956): 9.

3. Quoted from Earl Caldwell, "Risked Debate—and Her Job," *New York Daily News*, June 10, 1989.

4. "Disciplinary Reprimand, Carolyn Pitts," issued by Arnold Kickecked, n.d. On this controversy, see also Ester Iverem, "Racist Remarks Force Recall of Manual," *New York Times*, April 4, 1987; Mario Desmond, "Cuomo Has Racist Manual Barred," *The Chief-Leaders*, May 15, 1987; and the editorial "Racism Is Wrong—Period," *New York Post*, May 5, 1987.

5. In her statement of regret Pitts indicated that the document did not reflect her personal views and was "intended to stimulate discussion . . . and provide a foundation from which participants could exchange thoughts, views and ideas on racism." Statement of Carolyn Pitts to Board of Commissioners of the New York State Insurance Fund, May 28, 1987.

6. To take a couple of such isolated cases, at Howard University where power is both individually and institutionally in the hands of blacks a number of whites have charged racism in tenure and promotion decisions. Almost invariably when these charges were heard in the federal district court at Wash-

ington (an institution dominated by whites) the white plaintiffs have prevailed. Thus, even if the allegations were, as the court found, valid blacks even at an institution where they are in power could not be effective racists. Similarly, in her opinion invalidating the City of Richmond's minority contract setaside program Justice O'Connor argued that since the city had a black-dominated government special scrutiny had to be given to its race-based programs because blacks might use their power to discriminate against whites. This prompted Justice Marshall to retort angrily that no such special scrutiny was given when white-dominated governments routinely make policies that might harm blacks, writing that "such insulting judgments have no place in constitutional jurisprudence." See City of Richmond v. J. A. Croson, U.S. Supreme Court, #87–998 (1989): 28.

7. "Racism Is Wrong—Period," *New York Post.*

8. The *Bakke* case is the Supreme Court's seminal attempt to come to grips in its jurisprudence with the use of race not as a means to subordinate but rather as a means to overcome the historic pattern of race subordination or to deal effectively with ongoing patterns or practices of institutional racism.

9. The frequent refrain of conservative judges and scholars is that the "Constitution should be color blind." In response to this notion Justice Marshall wrote in *Bakke,* "While I applaud the judgment of the Court that a university may consider race in its admission process, it is more than a little ironic that after several hundred years of class-based discrimination against Negroes, the Court is unwilling to hold that a class-based remedy for that discrimination is permissible. In declining to so hold, today's judgment ignores the fact that for several hundred years Negroes have been discriminated against not as individuals, but rather solely because of the color of their skins," Regents of the University of California v. Bakke, 98 S.CT 2733 (1978): 869.

10. This is not to in any way detract from the value of the book. On the contrary it made a signal contribution to the literature of black politics both academically in terms of the institutional racism concept, but also to post–civil rights era policy debate on race; the book also articulated a new strategy and new institutional forms that fundamentally shaped the nature and practice of post–civil rights era black politics.

11. Carmichael and Hamilton, *Black Power,* p. 4. As an example of the book's conceptual confusion the authors write, "Institutional racism has another name: colonialism" (p. 5). Although there are some similarities between a fully specified internal colonialism model and institutional racism, they are really quite distinct in terms of basic theoretical properties.

12. Ibid.

13. This distinction is not clear to Louis Knowles and Kenneth Prewitt, who prepared the first academic work on the concept after the Carmichael and Hamilton book. They write, "The difference, then, between individual and in-

stitutional racism is not a difference in intent or visibility. Both the individual act of racism and the racist institutional policy may occur without the presence of conscious bigotry and both may be masked intentionally or innocently." See *Institutional Racism in America* (New York: Prentice-Hall, 1969): 5. I think this is a misreading of both Carmichael and Hamilton's language and the logic of institutional processes that normally operate independently of individual motivations. This is the inference to be drawn from Carmichael and Hamilton's observation that institutional racism is "far more subtle, less identifiable in terms of specific individuals committing acts [because] it originates in the operation of established and respected forces in society" (p. 4).

14. This perspective has been haltingly adopted by the Supreme Court in its post–civil rights era jurisprudence on employment discrimination (see Chapter 5).

15. Jenny Williams, "Redefining Institutional Racism," *Ethnic and Racial Studies* 8(1985): 323. Williams goes on to suggest that this "theoretical imprecision" means the concept "does not provide a guide to empirical research" or the development of policy. For a critique that reaches similar conclusions, see David Mason, "After Scarman: A Note on the Concept of Institutional Racism," *New Community* 10(1982): 169–75. (I am grateful to Sadu Sowa, my graduate research assistant at Howard, for sharing his copy of this useful paper with me.) Although the Williams and Mason papers were useful in helping me to understand the inherent limits of the concept, I am not as pessimistic as they are about its ultimate utility. Indeed, a principal burden of this and Chapter 6 is to show the concept's theoretical but especially empirical usefulness in the analysis of racism in the post–civil rights era.

16. See, for example, Adolph Reed's review of Wilson's *The Truly Disadvantaged*, where he praises Wilson for dismissing the utility of the concept of institutional racism in explaining the persistence of the underclass, but then in the next paragraph employs the concept to explain the persistence of the phenomenon. See "The Technocratic Liberal," *The Nation*, February 6, 1988, pp. 167–70.

17. Williams, "Redefining Institutional Racism," p. 330. See also Joe Feagin, "Indirect Institutional Discrimination: A Typological and Policy Analysis," *American Politics Quarterly* 5(April 1977): 177–99; Feagin and N. Bencksrits, "Institutional Racism: A Critical Review of the Literature" in Charles Willie (ed.), *Institutional Racism: In Search of a Perspective* (New Brunswick, NJ: Transaction, 1974); Charles Bullock and Harrell Rogers, "Institutional Racism: Prerequisites, Freezing and Mapping," *Phylon* 37(1976): 212–23; Anthony Downs, *Urban Problems and Prospects* (Chicago: Markham, 1970): 79. Even Knowles and Prewitt, their conceptual confusion notwithstanding, write that "in pragmatic terms we ask not what the motives of the individuals might be, rather we look at the consequences of institutions they have created," *Institutional Racism in America*, p. 4.

18. Feagin, "Indirect Institutionalized Discrimination," p. 183. Feagin notes that "Representatives" would include "subordinate group members . . . acting routinely under the guidance of organizational norms and regulations."

19. This is perhaps the critical element in Thomas Sowell's theory of race and ethnic inequalities in the United States and elsewhere. See his *Race and Economics* (New York: Longman, 1975) and *Preferential Policies: An International Perspective* (New York: William Morrow, 1989).

20. This is the view advanced by Wilson in *The Truly Disadvantaged* in explaining the origins and persistence of the black underclass. One could make the argument that society's failure to undertake affirmative action to overcome the historically structured present-day pattern of racial inequality is itself racist. This is one part of the justification for one version of affirmative action, whose origin in race policy can be traced to Lyndon Johnson's famous 1965 Howard University commencement address: "You do not take a person who for years has been hobbled by chains and liberate him, bring him up to the starting line of a race and then say `you are free to compete with all others' and justly believe you have been completely fair. [This] . . . is the next and most profound stage of the battle for civil rights. We seek not just freedom but opportunity—not just legal equity but human ability—not just equality as a right and a theory but equality as a fact and as a result." Quoted in Hugh Davis Graham, *The Civil Rights Era: Origins and Development of National Policy* (New York: Oxford University Press, 1990): 174. Although I share this view philosopically, to embrace it conceptually in terms of institutional racism would be a mistake.

21. Again, one might argue that the fact that blacks are disproportionately lower class is itself a result of racism, and I would agree, but I contend that conceptually it is a consequence of the historical mode unless one can show empirically the operation of the individual or institutional modes.

22. This would be especially the case since the SAT and related tests—unlike many employment examinations—have to some extent been validated in that it can be shown that there is a relationship between performance on the tests and subsequent performance in college and graduate and professional schools. However, to continue the discussion of the close nexus between the historical and institutional modes, one might argue that blacks of all classes perform less well on the SAT than whites because historically they have been denied equal educational opportunities, which results in the denial of opportunities for advanced study, which in turn results in comparatively lower occupational and income attainments for the group. This is Myrdal's familar principle of the cumulative nature of discrimination, where direct discrimination in one area (education) can result in discrimination in another (employment) and then another and another in what he referred to as "the theory of the vicious cycle as a main explanatory scheme for this inquiry into the Negro problem." See *An American Dilemma*, vol. 2, appendix 3. Early in its post–civil rights era jurisprudence the Supreme Court adopted this view of cumulativeness in

deciding cases of discrimination in education, employment, and voting. I discuss these cases in Chapter 4 dealing with empirical indicators of institutional racism.

23. This is one of the limitations of Downs's definition of the phenomenon. He defines institutional "subordination" as "placing or keeping persons in a position or status of inferiority by means of attitudes, actions or institutional structures which do not use color itself as the subordinating mechanism, but instead use other mechanisms indirectly related to color," *Urban Problem and Prospects*, p. 79. The problem with this formulation is that the most socially decisive indirect mechanism related to color in the United States is class, thus the empirical referants for race subordination become difficult to disentangle from class subordination. Other mechanisms indirectly related to race in the United States—crime, welfare dependency, lower educational attainments—that might be used institutionally to subordinate blacks are also ultimately rooted in the class disparity between the races. These other mechanisms result in subtle forms of both individual and institutional racism as when, in the former case, a cab driver refuses to pick up a black because of fear of crime, or in the latter when a firm refuses to locate in a black neighborhood for the same reason. These subtle mechanisms are discussed in detail in the several chapters that follow.

Chapter 3. Individual Racism in the Post–Civil Rights Era

1. Examples include Angus Campbell and Howard Schuman, *Racial Attitudes in Fifteen American Cities* (Ann Arbor: Institute for Social Research, University of Michigan, 1970); J. Condran, "Changes in White Attitudes Toward Blacks, 1963–67," *Public Opinion Quarterly* 43(1979):463–76; J. McConahay et al., "Has Racism Declined in America?: Depends on Who Is Asking and What is Asked," *Journal of Conflict Resolution* 25(1981): 563–79. See also the two landmark surveys of white and black attitudes toward race and racism conducted by Louis Harris for *Newsweek*, which are reported in the issues of July 29, 1963, and October 21, 1963, and Louis Harris, *A Study of Attitudes Toward Racial and Religious Minorities and Women* (New York: National Conference of Christians and Jews, 1978); and Howard Schuman, Carlotta Steeth, and Lawrence Bobo, *Racial Attitudes in America: Trends and Interpretations* (Cambridge: Harvard University Press, 1985). The Schuman, Steeth, and Bobo volume is the most comprehensive compilation and analysis of postwar survey data on racial attitudes.

2. Barry Sussman and Herbert Denton, "Lingering Racial Stereotypes Still Damage Blacks," *Washington Post*, March 26, 1981.

3. The "hidden" racist vote is thought to have been a factor in Thomas Bradley's narrow loss of the California governorship in 1982 and Virginia Governor Douglas Wilder's narrow victory in 1989. In both cases pre-election surveys and election-day exit polls indicated a higher degree of white voter sup-

port than was the case in the final election tabulations. On the Bradley race and this factor, see Thomas Pettigrew and Denise Alston, *Tom Bradley's Campaign for Governor: The Dilemmas of Race and Political Strategy* (Washington: Joint Center for Political Studies, 1988), and Charles Henry, "Racial Factors in the 1982 California Gubernatorial Campaign: Why Bradley Lost?" in M. Preston, P. Puryear and L. Henderson (eds.), *The New Black Politics* (New York: Longman, 1987): 76–94, and on the Wilder election, see Joseph McCormick, "The November Elections: The Politics of Deracialization," *New Directions* 17(1990): 22–27 and Charles Jones, "Deracialization and the Election of Governor Douglas Wilder," paper presented at 1990 annual meeting of the National Conference of Black Political Scientists, Atlanta.

4. The Harris surveys for *Newsweek* and the National Conference of Christians and Jews may have created a response-set bias in favor of the expression of less racist attitudes since respondents were told that the purpose of the survey was to study attitudes toward minorities. This may have created a predisposition toward less racist responses while the General Social Survey is a general survey of attitudes with only a small number of items on racial attitudes embedded in a survey of more than two hundred items.

5. On the notion that the Reagan administration at least implicitly encouraged an increase in racist sentiments, see Ronald Walters, *White Racial Nationalism in the United States* (Washington: Eaford, 1987), and W. Farrell and C. Jones, "Recent Racial Incidents in Higher Education: A Preliminary Perspective," *Urban Review* 20(1988): 211–16.

6. These data are taken from Schuman, Steeth, and Bobo, *Racial Attitudes in America*.

7. Sussman and Denton, "Lingering Racial Stereotypes Damage Blacks."

8. Mary Jackman and Robert Jackman, *Class Awareness in the United States* (Berkeley: University of California Press, 1983): 96. On the class distribution of racist attitudes generally, see Schuman, Steeth, and Bobo, *Racial Attitudes in America,* and Sussman and Denton, "Lingering Racial Stereotypes Damage Blacks."

9. Harris, *A Study of Attitudes Toward Racial and Religious Minorities*, p. 15.

10. For example, only 27 percent of whites in 1978 said they would be concerned if a black family moved next door, compared with 51 percent in 1963. Ibid. Of all the areas of controversy with respect to racial integration—schools, public accommodations, employment, voting—during the civil rights era opposition is greatest in housing and virtually nonexistent in the other areas.

11. See Thomas Cavanagh, *Inside Black America: The Message of the Black Vote in the 1984 Elections* (Washington: Joint Center for Political Studies, 1985): 64, and Linda Williams, "White/Black Perceptions of the Electability of Black Political Candidates," *National Political Science Review* 2(1990): 53.

12. Williams, "White/Black Perceptions," p. 53. It also should be noted that in 1988 when whites were asked whether there were any black persons currently on the scene that they personally considered qualified to be president only 25 percent of whites said yes while 56 percent said no black was qualified and 18 percent had no opinion. As William writes (p. 53), "In short, slightly more than three quarters of the white electorate might automatically oppose a black candidate for president or, even in the best possible scenario, take a lot of convincing. A black candidate for higher office begins with a bias among many (and in the case of the presidency, most) whites that he or she is not qualified."

13. This literature is thoroughly reviewed in A. Liska, *The Consistency of Controversy* (New York: John Wiley, 1975), and Howard Schuman and Michael Johnson, "Attitudes and Behavior," *Annual Review of Sociology* 2(1976): 161–207.

14. Schuman, Steeth, and Bobo, *Racial Attitudes in America*, pp. 135–36.

15. Mary Jackman and Marie Crane, "Some of My Best friends Are Black... Interracial Friendship and Whites' Racial Attitudes," *Public Opinion Quarterly* 50(1985): 481.

16. U.S. Department of Health, Education, and Welfare, *Toward A Social Report* (Washington: Government Printing Office, 1969): xi.

17. Ibid.

18. Walters, *White Racial Nationalism*, pp. 12–13.

19. Isabel Wilkerson, "Campus Blacks Feel Racism's Nuances," *New York Times*, April 17, 1988, and W. Farrell and C. Jones, "Recent Racial Incidents in Higher Education"

20. See Farrell and Jones, "Recent Racial Incidents in Higher Education," and Walters, *White Racial Nationalism*.

21. Daniel Coleman, "As Bias Crimes Seems to Rise, Scientists Study Roots of Racism," *New York Times*, May 29, 1990.

22. Congress recognized this need when it enacted the National Hate Crime Statistics Act of 1990, which directed the Justice Department to develop a national statistical system to monitor incidents of bias crimes, defined as acts of violence inspired by racism and other forms of prejudice. The Department directed the FBI to include this statistical data in its annual uniform crime report.

23. Randal Samborn, "Many Americans Find Bias at Work, But According to Poll Few Have Taken Formal Action," *National Law Journal*, July 16, 1990, p. 47.

24. Ibid.

25. Roy Brooks, *Rethinking the American Race Problem* (Berkeley: Univer-

sity of California Press, 1990): 187. Brooks also writes (p. 187), "Personal perceptions of discrimination cannot be ignored. Even if they are `wrong' or exaggerated they are real to the perceiver. More important, these perceptions affect an African American individual's behavior and chances for success."

26. Ibid., p. 45.

27. Ibid.

28. Phillip Shenon, "Black FBI Agent Talks of Years of Racial Harassment on Job," *New York Times*, August 12, 1990.

29. Craig Wolff, "New York Sues 4 Job Firms in a Case of Discrimination," *New York Times*, September 29, 1989.

30. Brooks, *Rethinking the Race Problem*, p. 187.

31. Margery Austin Turner et al., *Opportunities Denied, Opportunities Diminished: Discrimination in Hiring* (Washington: The Urban Institute, 1991): 31. Overall, in 15 percent of the audits whites were offered jobs compared with 5 percent of blacks.

32. Compared to other cities that have elected black mayors, the Los Angeles police are unique and, at least administratively, out of control. First, given the relatively small size of the black population the election of Tom Bradley did not result in the coming to power of an effective black regime, as is the case with most black-led cities. In addition, Los Angeles' reform government means that whatever the mayor's inclinations, administrative control of the police department and its chief rests with an independent commission who may only remove the chief for cause under civil service procedures.

33. While the actions of the officers who beat King may be described as individual racism, the independent commission appointed to investigate the department after the King incident concluded that it represented a systemic or institutional pattern that tolerated "excessive force and overt racism" because officers repeatedly accused of such offenses were seldom punished and often given glowing evaluations. See Robert Reinhold, "Study of Los Angeles Police Finds Violence and Racism Are Routine," *New York Times*, July 10, 1991.

34. I recall an incident in Brooklyn on Thanksgiving day around 1979 or 1980, when a white police officer for no reason whatsoever walked up with his partner and shot an eleven-year-old black boy point blank in the head. The officer was found not guilty by reason of insanity. He was then committed to a mental institution. After six months or so of confinement, he was released on a finding by the institution's staff that he was not mentally impaired. Upon his release the officer sought back pay and reinstatement, both of which were denied. And several days after the Rodney King verdict two unarmed blacks, one mentally retarded, were killed by the police in Baton Rouge, Louisiana. In both instances the police claimed that the killings were "accidents" because

they thought the men were armed. See "Farrakhan Says Blacks Suffer Injustices in Every City," *New York Times*, May 12, 1992.

35. Richard Pryor, "That Nigger Is Crazy" (Warner Brothers, Black Rain, Inc., 1974).

36. *Ebony*, "Black on Black Crime," March 1981, p. 47.

37. Walters, *White Racial Nationalism*, p. 14.

38. Ibid.

39. Kim Lersch, "Current Trends in Police Brutality: An Analysis of Recent Newspaper Accounts" (master's thesis, University of Florida, 1993):34. I thank Professor Joe Feagin for calling this study, done under his supervision, to my attention.

40. Harold Rose and Paula McClain, *Race Place and Risk: Black Homicide in Urban America* (Albany: SUNY Press, 1990).

41. On the Los Angeles videotapes see the dispatches by Seth Mydans for the *New York Times*, "Tape of Beating by Police Revives Charges of Racism," March 7, 1991; "A Videotape of a Police Beating Puts National Glare on Issue of Brutality," March 18, 1991; and "Officers in LA Joked About Beating Blacks," March 19, 1991.

42. Perhaps the best way in this age of technology to document individual racism is for each black person to equip him or herself with audio and video recorders. This is not so far-fetched. For example, in 1989 a black police officer seeking to document what he thought to be widespread brutality by the police against blacks in the Los Angeles suburb of Long Beach equipped himself with a video recorder and simply drove around late at night until he was eventually stopped by police and, as he anticipated, recorded for the record evidence of verbal and physical harassment. See William Raspberry, "He Knew Where to Find Trouble," *Houston Chronicle*, August 25, 1989. Two years later a jury deadlocked in an 11–1 vote to acquit, and a mistrial was declared. Unlike the Rodney King jury, this jury had one black member, and he alone voted to convict. See *West County Times*, "Police Brutality Case Ends after Mistrial," May 14, 1991.

43. Lawrence Thomas, a black professor of philosophy at Syracuse University, discusses such minor irritants in his essay, "Next Life, I'll Be White," *New York Times*, August 13, 1990. He writes, for example, that "my 40 year journey through life has revealed to me that more often than not, I need only be in the presence of a white woman and she will begin clutching her pocketbook." Other irritants of this sort cited by Thomas include being reported to the police as a suspicious person as he stood dressed in shirt and tie reading the bulletin board outside a university conference room; and being watched suspiciously as he engaged in routine shopping. Thomas's general point in the column is that blacks do not enjoy the trust of whites, writing "If we well-

groomed and mannered blacks do not enjoy the public trust, it is discomfort-
ing to think how less well off blacks fare." (Joe Feagin documents systematically this kind of "public place" racial discrimination against middle-class blacks
in "The Continuing Significance of Race: Anti-Black Discrimination in Public
Places," *American Sociological Review* 56[1991]: 101–16.) Since I am not usually
well groomed—I wear a coat and tie only for church, formal lectures, television appearances, and other formal occasions and rarely comb my hair except
for such occasions and even when I do I am sometimes told it does not appear
that I have, I am quite familiar with how less well-off blacks fare because in
dress and demeanor I look like one. Thus, I encounter experiences of the sort
described by Thomas on an almost daily basis and now accept them with a bit
of humor and with no more discomfort than mosquitos during the summer.
After all, as Leroi Jones says, "It's hard to be black in a society controlled by
whites," and given the really disabling hardships many blacks in this country
face those described by Thomas are trivial.

44. The government's suit involving this incident was United States v
Seymour Orlofsky et.al., Southern District of New York, 79. C.A. 4798 (1981).
We also filed a separate action against the agency Lashley, Rose and Smith v.
Orlofsky, 82 Civ. 0892 (1982) but the case was dismissed on the grounds that
the three-year stature of limitations for filing such claims had lapsed.

45. Hanes Walton, Jr., "Foreword," Jeffrey Elliot (ed.), *Black Voices in American Politics* (New York: Harcourt Brace 1986): xi.

46. Even when the white academy deals with race, it is frequently by scholars who dabble in the field rather than by those with a sustained and substantial interest in it. There is also a tendency for white institutions doing work on
race to ignore the contributions of black scholarship and academic organizations, as was the case with the organization and staffing of the National Research Council's recent study of the status of blacks America in the post–civil
rights era. On this point with respect to the National Research Council's study,
see the several articles in the symposium "Controversies: American Dilemmas
and Black Responses," *Transaction/Society* 24(1987): 3–38.

Chapter 4. Institutional Racism in the Post–Civil Rights Era

1. Bullock and Rogers, "Institutional Racism;" p 213.

2. These examples and others are catalogued in Joe Feagin, "A Slavery
Unwilling to Die," *Journal of Black Studies* 18(1988): 451–69, and Mark Green,
"How Minorities Are Sold Short," *New York Times*, June 18, 1990.

3. See *National Assessment of Education Progress* (Princeton: Educational
Testing Service, 1986); D. Bock and R. Mislevy, *Profiles of American Youth* (Washington: U.S. Department of Defense, 1980); and College Entrance Examination
Board, *Equality and Excellence in Education: The Educational Status of Black Americans* (New York: College Entrance Examination Board, 1985).

4. The miseducation of inner-city black youth really is scandalous and various post–civil rights era educational reforms, from school desegregation to community control to magnet schools, have largely failed to improve the condition. It may be that educational reforms, absent changes in the socioeconomic conditions of the families and the communities, can be only palliatives for the few. Yet, traditionally the schools have been the mechanisms for transforming the children from impoverished families and communities into upwardly mobile persons. That this does not appear to be occurring with black kids, as it did for example with Jewish kids in the ghettos of New York's lower east side earlier, suggests to some that the problem is race, not class. Race in the sense that the curriculum is Eurocentric—geared to the education of middle-class whites—and the personnel is largely white while the students are black and poor. Consequently, unlike in the pre-*Brown* era of segregated schools, in the post–civil rights era, the schools are largely segregated but the personnel and curriculum are "integrated," that is largely white. Thus, increasingly in the third decade of the post civil rights era black educational reformers are calling for a radical "resegregation" of the schools in terms of faculty and staff and in terms of what is called an "Afrocentric" curriculum. While there are difficulties in this project, it probably should be attempted since hardly anything else appears to be working. On this reform idea, see Derrick Bell, "The Case for a Separate Black School System," and Asa Hillard, "Reintegration for Education: Black Community Involvement with Black Students in Schools," in Willy Smith and Eva Chunn (eds.), *Black Education: A Quest for Equity and Excellence* (New Brunswick, NJ: Transaction, 1989): 136–45, 201–08.

5. See L. Feinberg, "Study Rejects Bias Charge in Tests," *Washington Post*, February 3, 1982.

6. This point is forcefully made by Donald Stewart, the black president of the Educational Testing Service, in a letter to the *New York Times*. See "SAT Scores Are Valid, Reliable and Consistent," February 16, 1989.

7. See A. Wells, "Teachers Tests Assailed as Biased and Vague," *New York Times*, March 16, 1988. Minority group teachers in California have filed suit, charging that the state's teacher qualification test is racially discriminatory and unrelated to teaching skills. Since 1983 when the test was first required, of more than 350,000 people who have been examined, whites passed at an 80 percent rate, Latinos at 51 percent, Asian Americans 59 percent, and blacks 35 percent. One consequence is that while the state's student population is 55 percent minority, its teachers are 82 percent white. See "Minority Teachers Sue Over State's Skill Test," *West County Times*, September 24, 1992.

8. Mary Dilworth, "Black Teachers: A Vanishing Tradition," in Smith and Chunn, *Black Education*.

9. Ibid.

10. Eva Chunn, "Sorting Black Students for Success and Failure: The Inequity of Ability Grouping and Tracking," in Smith and Chunn, *Black Education*,

p. 161.

11. Ibid., p. 102.

12. Larry P. v. Riles. The Court held that its decision could rest on federal statutory claims but it elected to use the Fourteenth Amendment because of the ambiguity of the Supreme Court's interpretation of Title VII in the *Bakke* and related cases.

13. Ibid.

14. Ibid.

15. Ibid.

16. California elected not to appeal the decision, thus the matter of the institutionally racist character of the IQ test was never presented to the Supreme Court for a judgment that might have invalidated its use throughout the country. During the period of the trial the Court put a moratorium on the use of the test to identify learning-disabled black kids or to assess their performance in special education classes. During the moratorium the Court concluded, "School psychologists, teachers and others involved in the process are now making decisions based on a wide number of factors, and the evidence suggests that the results are less discriminatory than they were under the IQ test." The state subsequently completely eliminated the EMR classification, and the court later permanently banned the use of the tests to test or place blacks.

17. In 1989 the Court expanded its 1986 injuction to prohibit the use of the IQ tests in the placement of black children in all special education classes, not just those for the retarded. In an interesting twist this 1989 order was challenged by a group of black parents who claimed that without use of the IQ test they were denied the option of having their children in special education classes, which they argued violated their due process and equal protection rights under the Constitution. The Court agreed and in 1992 vacated the 1989 injunction. See *Crawford, et. al. v. Honig, Larry P. v. Riles*, United States District Court, Northern District of California, memorandum and order (#C-89-0014).

18. The 1989 decisions of the Court were to *some* extent reversed by the Civil Rights Act of 1991. See Steven Holmes, "Lawyers Expect Ambiguities in New Rights Laws to Bring Years of Lawsuits," *New York Times*, December 12, 1991.

19. These specific distinctions were initially used in employment cases and subsequently in voting rights litigation in terms of the intent versus effects standard developed in *Mobile v. Bolden* but rejected by the Congress in its 1982 amendments to the Voting Rights Act. In *Bolden* the Court held that only intent to discriminate was actionable under the Voting Rights Act, but in its amendments Congress rejected the Court's intent standard in favor of an effects test. For an analysis of these standards in voting rights cases, see Abigail

Thernstrom, *Whose Votes Count: Affirmative Action and Minority Voting Rights* (Cambridge: Harvard University Press, 1987, and Frank Parker, *Black Votes Count* (Chapel Hill: University of North Carolina Press, 1990). See also my "Liberal Jurisprudence and the Quest for Racial Representation," *Southern University Law Review* 15(1988): 1–51. On the use of these distinctions in employment cases, see Barbara Schlei and Paul Grossman, *Employment Discrimination Law* (Washington: Bureau of National Affairs, 1976).

20. Gaston County v. United States, 395 U.S. 285(1969).

21. In his typology of institutional discrimination Feagin identifies the type of racism recognized by the Court in *Gaston* as "side effects" discrimination where direct or overt racism in one area (education) may result in indirect or institutional racism in other areas, such as employment and voting. See his "Indirect Institutionalized Discrimination: A Topological Analysis." Feagin's side effects notion is akin to Myrdal's principle of cumulativeness in racial discrimination discussed in Chapter 3.

22. Griggs v. Duke Power Company, 401 U.S. 424(1971).

23. Washington, Mayor of Washington, D.C. et al v. Davis et.al, Syllabus # 74 1492, (1976).

24. American Tobacco Company et al v. Patterson et al, Syllabus #80–1199 (1982): 69.

25. The city ultimately laid off twenty-four firefighters, three of whom were black. Had the seniority system been followed six blacks would have been dismissed. Thus, three white firemen lost their jobs as a result of the consent decree. It should be noted that while Memphis was about 50 percent black, in 1980 only 11.5 percent of its firefighters were black, most of them hired since 1974. Firefighters Local Union #1784 v. Stotts. et al, Syllabus (107 S.CT. 1756, 1987) #82–206 (1984).

26. This kind of reasoning recalls Justice Powell's opinion in McClesky v. Kemp (107S. CT. 1756, 1987), where he suggested that while the evidence might support a claim of racism in implementation of the death penalty, to remedy it would require not only abolition of the death penalty for blacks but a radical restructuring of the entire criminal justice system since racial disparities probably exist throughout the sentencing process.

27. Brooks, *Rethinking the American Race Problem*, p. 187.

28. Luevano v. Campbell, Civil Action #79–0271, U.S. District Court, Washington (1979).

29. J. Haveman, "Civil Service to Revise Hiring," *Washington Post*, June 23, 1988. In 1992 the Office of Personnel Management implemented a revised PACE—six broad-based tests, each covering a range of related occupations— which it claims was validated and nondiscriminatory. This new series of tests are to be monitored by the Court for a five-year period to ensure that actual

hiring is free of bias. See Haveman, "Revised at Behest of Minorities, New Civil Service Exams Ready," *Los Angeles Times*, April 22, 1990.

30. Quoted in Peter Kilborn, "Race Norming Test Becomes a Fiery Issue," *New York Times*, May 19, 1991. Until a more valid test was devised the Academy recommended continued use of race norming (the Academy undertook its study at the request of the Justice Department, which in the mid-1980s challenged the Labor Department's position on race norming as illegal). The National Academy's conclusions about the validity of employment tests are ambivalent. On the one hand, the evidence is clear that blacks do less well on the test, even when social class is controlled. What is less clear is whether the test actually predicts job performance for blacks as well as it does for whites. See its two massive, technical reports Alexander Wigdor and Wendell Ganner (eds.), *Ability Testing: Uses,Consequences and Controversies,* 2 vols. (Washington: National Academy Press, 1982), and John Hartigan and A. Wigdor (eds.), *Fairness in Employment Testing* (Washington: National Academy Press, 1989).

31. The most comprehensive overview of the methodology and findings of these audit or site surveys is Department of Housing and Urban Development, *Fair Housing Enforcement Demonstrations* (Washington: Office of Policy Development and Research, 1983): 23–28, 37–44.

32. Douglas Massey and Nancy Denton, "Trends in the Residential Segregation of Blacks, Hispanics and Asians: 1970–80," *American Sociological Review* 52(1987): 802–25.

33. In 1980, for example, the black suburbanization rate was 28 percent compared to 48 percent for Hispanics and 53 for Asians. Ibid.

34. In 1980, 62 percent of white households held equity in their homes compared with 48 percent of blacks. The average value of black household equity was $25,589, compared with $35,599 for whites. See William O'Hare, *Wealth and Economic Status: A Perspective on Racial Equality* (Washington: Joint Center for Political Studies, 1983): 6.

35. "Study Finds Bias in House Hunting," *New York Times*, September 1, 1991.

36. On the Atlanta *Journal-Constitution* story by Bill Dedman, "Race Gap in Loans Uncovered," see the *Houston Chronicle*, January 22, 1989. See also "Home Mortgage Disclosure Act: Expanded Data on Residential Lending," *Federal Reserve Bulletin*, November 1991.

37. Ibid.

38. Ibid.

39. "Home Mortage Disclosure Act," p. 864.

40. Ibid.

41. Ibid., p. 873. The data also indicate that applicants seeking loans in

low-or moderate-income neighborhoods (regardless of race) are denied credit more frequently than persons in upper-income areas.

42. Ibid., p. 875.

43. In order to remedy this problem, fair housing advocates have long proposed a modification of the housing audit surveys to test for mortgage loan discrimination in the same way as discrimination in the sale or rental of housing is audited. Bankers have strongly opposed this approach, and it was rejected by the Bush administration. However, the HUD secretary and the Comptroller of the Currency in the Clinton administration have both indicated that they plan to begin the use of undercover testers in the mortage loan area. However, given the range of possible variables involved, the methodology is not likely to be as reliable in mortgage loans cases as it is in the sale or rental of housing. See Steven Holmes "US Is Asked to Expand Undercover Bias Testing," *New York Times*, September 26, 1991, and John Cushman, "Undercover Mortgage Agents Will Probe for Bias," *West County Times*, May 6, 1983.

44. Late in the Bush administration the Justice Department for the first time legally or formally observed racism in mortgage loans, charging a suburban Atlanta savings and loan with systematically favoring white over black applicants. The Department and the Decatur Federal Savings and Loan agreed to an out-of-court settlement involving a range of remedial actions including more than a million dollars to rejected black applicants. See "US Charges Mortgage Bias," *New York Times*, September 18, 1992.

45. The race gap in assets is enormous. In 1980 only 3.9 percent of black households had assets in excess of $100,000 compared with 23 percent of white households. Of the total net worth of U.S. households (estimated at $6.8 trillion) blacks' share was 2.8 percent. See U.S. Bureau of Census, Current Population Report, *Household Wealth and Asset Ownership* (Washington: Government Printing Office, 1984).

46. For a good overview of the contemporary health status of black Americans, see the collection of articles edited by Mitchell Rice, "Black American Health," *Urban League Review* 9(1985–86).

47. Dorothy Howze, "The Black Infant Mortality Rate: An Unequal Chance for Life," *Urban League Review* 9(1985–86): 20–25.

48. Phillip Hiets, "Black Life Expectancy Declines," *West County Times*, November 29, 1990.

49. Twenty percent of blacks in the United States are uninsured compared with 12 percent of whites. Dr. George Landberg, editor of the *Journal of the American Medical Association*, argues that the lack of national health insurance may itself be an indicator of racism, arguing that it was "no coincidence that the United States and South Africa were the only developed countries that lack a national health policy insuring access to basic care for all." Overall, Lundberg concluded that racial inequality in access to health care was in part

due to "long standing institutionalized racial discrimination." See "National Health Care Reform," *Journal of the American Medical Association* 265(May 1991): 2566.

50. David McBride, *From TB to AIDS: Sociomedical Reactions to Epidemics Among Urban Blacks, 1900–Present* (Albany: SUNY Press, 1991): 9.

51. Eugene Schwarz et.al., "Black/White Comparisons of Deaths Preventable by Medical Intervention: United States and District of Columbia 1980–1986," *International Journal of Epidemiology* 19 (1990): 591–98.

52. Ibid. The authors did not control for social class but note, "A similar trend is observed among low income individuals irrespective of race" (p. 596).

53. Claudia Baquet, "Socioeconomic Factors and Cancer Incidence Among Blacks," *Journal of the National Cancer Institute* 83(1991): 551–56. See also Harold Freeman, "Race, Poverty and Cancer," *Journal of National Cancer Institute* 83(1991): 526–27.

54. Baquet, "Socioeconomic Factors and Cancer Incidence Among Blacks."

55. Paul Eggers, "Effect of Transplantation on the Medicare End-Stage of Renal Disease Program," *New England Journal of Medicine* 318(1988): 223–29; Mark Wenneker and Arnold Epstein, "Racial Inequalities in the Use of Procedures for Patients with Ischemic Heart Disease in Massachusetts," *Journal of American Medical Association* 260(January 1989): 253–57; Phillip Held et.al., "Access to Kidney Transplantation: Has the United States Eliminated Income and Racial Differences?" *Archives of Internal Medicine* 148(December 1988): 2594–2600; and Carl Kjellstrand, "Age, Sex and Race Inequality in Renal Transplantation," *Archives of Internal Medicine* 148(June 1988): 1305–9.

56. Held et.al., "Access to Kidney Transplantation," p. 2599.

57. Kjellstrand, "Age, Sex and Race Inequality in Renal Transplantation," p. 1309. Kjellstrand seems to prefer a "cultural" explanation, citing a study by Cleveland Callendar, a black physician at Howard University, showing that blacks are less likely than whites to want transplants and are less likely to be kidney donors. Thus, he concludes, "Lack of awareness of transplantation, fear, religious beliefs, distrust of the white medical establishment and racism (blacks want to give only to blacks) are thought to be responsible for this disparity," p. 1309.

58. Wenneker and Epstein, "Racial Inequalities in the Use of Procedures for Patients with Ischemic Disease."

59. Ibid., p. 257. The authors here also stress a "cultural" explanation, suggesting that blacks are less likely to accept surgery and other technological interventions when offered.

60. Letter From Michelle Holmes, David Hodges, and John Rich, *Journal of the American Medical Association* 261(June 1989). In their rejoinder Wenneker

and Epstein write:

> Our findings raise serious questions about the equity of the health care system in this country. Despite the civil rights movement in the 1960s, racial prejudice persists, and there is no reason to believe that the health care system is immune. A critical issue is the relative contribution of race, per se, vs social class in accounting for these differences. Depending on the answer, the solutions might be different.

> As indicated by the order of our discussion, we hypothesize that underlying and subtle differences in socioeconomic status that cut across racial boundaries contribute most to the observed inequalities. These may be manifest by differences in social support, differences in the sorts of physicians who provide services, and problems in communication patterns when physicians communicate with patients from a lower social class. Unfortunately, our data do not allow us to verify the extent to which either racial bias or socioeconomic differences account for these findings.

61. Craig Svenson, "Representation of Blacks in Clinical Drug Trials," *Journal of the American Medical Association* 261(January 1989): 263–65.

62. Ibid.

63. Ron Harris, "Blacks Feel Brunt of Drug War," *Los Angeles Times*, April 22, 1990, and "The Bias in Drug Laws," *California Lawyer*, May 1992, p. 19.

64. Minnesota v. Russell (1991) 477 NW2d 866. Most state courts and the federal courts have not accepted the reasoning of the Minnesota court, finding that its racial impact notwithstanding Congress could find a rational basis for treating crack and cocaine differentially. See U.S. v. Holt (9th Cir 1989) 879F2d 505 and U.S. v Thomas (4th Cir. 1990) 900 F2d 505.

65. See "A Law Distinguishing Crack from Cocaine Is Upset," *New York Times*, December 29, 1990.

66. Strictly speaking, the law may not be institutionally racist since we do not know whether powdered cocaine is also the drug of choice of middle-class blacks or whether crack is the drug of choice of poor whites. Thus, what appears to be a racist bias may conceal a class bias against lower-class drug users of whatever race.

67. In part as a result of Cohen's column, some blacks in Washington boycotted the *Post* for its alleged racial bias in coverage of the black community.

68. See Lena Williams, "When Blacks Shop, Bias Often Accompanies Sale," *New York Times*, April 30, 1991, and Feagin, "The Continuing Significance of Race."

69. Brooks, *Rethinking the American Race Problem*, p. 203.

70. Stephen LaBarton, "Benefits Are Refused More Often to Disabled Blacks," *New York Times*, May 11, 1992. I categorize this as a case of institutional racism, however, the GAO report also found that the greatest race disparity was at the administrative law judge level, the first time that the race of applicants is directly known, which suggests there also may be an element of individual racism.

71. Ian Ayres, "Fair Driving: Gender, and Race Discrimination in Retail Car Negotiations," *Harvard Law Review* 104(February 1991): 817.

72. Ibid.

73. Ibid., pp. 841–42. Testers were systematically steered to salespeople of their own race and gender, who gave them the worst treatment. All salespeople discriminated against black males, but blacks gave them the worst treatment. Ayres speculates that black salespeople might discriminate against blacks "if white consumers are reluctant to buy from black salesmen, to make their profit quota, black salesmen may be forced to earn higher profits from sales to blacks" (p. 849).

74. Ibid., p. 810.

75. Ayres calculates if the amount of racism found in this study holds for all sales blacks would pay $150 million more for new cars than white men (p. 823).

Chapter 5. Internal Inferiorization in the Post–Civil Rights Era

1. Joel Kovel, *White Racism;* pp. 249–89.

2. W. E. B. DuBois, *The Souls of Black Folk* (New York: Fawcett Books, 1903): 3.

3. Claud Anderson and Rue Cromwell, "Black Is Beautiful and the Color Preferences of Afro-American Youth," *Journal of Negro Education* 46(1977): 76.

4. Ibid.

5. John Dollard, *Caste and Class in a Southern Town*, (New Haven: Yale University Press, 1937): 89.

6. Ibid., p. 182.

7. Ibid.

8. A. Kardiner and L. Ovesey, *The Mark of Oppression: A Psychosocial Study of the American Negro* (New York: Norton, 1951).

9. Fanon, *Black Skin, White Masks*, p. 14.

10. Ibid., p. 33.

11. Ibid., p. 139.

12. Ibid.

13. The first study using the doll experiments to study racial group identity in children was conducted by Ruth Horowitz, "Racial Aspects of Self-Identification in Nursery School Children," *Journal of Psychology* 7 (1939): 91–99.

14. The results of the Clarks' work was initially published in "Segregation as a Factor in the Racial Identification of Negro School Children: A Preliminary Report," *Journal of Experimental Education* 8(1939): 161–63 and "Emotional Factors in Racial Identification and Preference in Negro Children," *Journal of Negro Education* 19(1941): 341–50. In addition to the doll test, the Clarks also used a test where the children were asked to color the pictures of boys and girls "the color you are" or the "color you like little girls to be." The results were essentially the same as those of the doll experiments.

15. In a similar doll experiment using both black and white children, Marian Radke and Helen Trager found the same kind of color preference. See "Children's Perception of the Social Roles of Negroes and Whites," *Journal of Psychology* 29(1950): 3-33.

16. The Supreme court in the *Brown* school desegregation decision, used the work of Clark to draw the even more tenuous inference that not racism in general but school segregation specifically generated a "feeling of inferiority" among black school children.

17. Gary Marx, *Protest and Prejudice* (New York: Harper & Row, 1967), pp. 88–89.

18. Quoted in various recordings of Malcolm's speeches including "Message to the Grass Roots."

19. Fanon, in his writings and in his leadership role of the Algerian revolution, consistently called for a struggle for political as well as psychological and cultural liberation, arguing that the first would be meaningless without the latter two.

20. David Lewis, "Parallels and Divergencies: Assimilationist Strategies of Afro-American and Jewish Elites from 1910 to the Early 1930s," *Journal of American History* 71(1984): 543–64.

21. Robert C. Smith, "Black Power and the Transformation From Protest to Politics," *Political Science Quarterly* 96(1981): 431–43.

22. Carmichael and Hamilton, *Black Power*, p. viii.

23. Ibid, pp. 38–39.

24. Ibid., p. 37.

25. Martin Luther King, Jr., on the 1966 Meredith March in Mississippi

expressed reservations of this sort, arguing that a new slogan for the movement might be necessary but that "The words `black' and `power' together give the impression we are talking about black domination rather than black equality." See King's account in *Where Do We Go from Here: Chaos or Community* (New York: Bantam Books 1968): 36.

26. See Lerone Bennett, "What's in a Name?" *Ebony*, November 1967, and Ben L. Martin, "From Negro to Black to African American: The Power of Names and Naming," *Political Science Quarterly* 106(1991): 83–107, and Robert C. Smith, "Renaming Old Realities," *San Francisco Review of Books* 15(1990): 16–19.

27. W. E. B. DuBois, "The Name Negro," *The Crisis*, March 1928.

28. John Leo, "Militants Object to Negro," *New York Times*, February 26, 1968.

29. I recall as a student activist in California in the late 1960s angry confrontations with students and faculty over the issue of *Negro* and *black*. Many white students and faculty who opposed black student demands for black studies and other race conscious campus reforms would often insist on use of the term *Negro* as a signal of their opposition. Thus, the names controversy early on took on a political and ideological connotation.

30. Martin, "From Negro to Black to African American, p. 94.

31. Although blacks were less than 6 percent of college students they were involved in more than half the campus protests in the years 1968–69, the peak year of student protests during the decade. In all of these protests the demand for black studies was the central item on the student agenda, unlike white students, whose protests tended to involve the Vietnam War or issues of campus governance. See "Student Strikes," *Black Scholar* (special issue) 1 (1970): 65–75, Harry Edwards, *Black Students* (New York: The Free Press 1970), and Ronald Walters and Robert C. Smith, "The Black Education Strategy," *Journal of Negro Education* 48(1979): 156–73. On the importance of black studies for the black political movement, see the two-part special series in *Black World*, "Toward A Black Unviersity," 23(February and March 1969).

32. Larry Neal, "The Black Arts Movement," *Tulane Drama Review* 23(1968): 29. Before his death in 1981 Neal began to turn away from a black aesthetic linked directly to politics, although his early death left his new direction here incomplete. See Michael Schwartz (ed.), *Visions of a Liberated Future: Black Arts Movement Writings by Larry Neal* (New York: Thunder's Mouth Press, 1969).

33. Nelson George writes, "Mayfield utilized a more personal voice that made him black music's most unflagging civil rights champion. . . . Starting in 1964 he composed an ongoing series of sermon songs that preached a commitment to social change." See *The Death of Rhythm and Blues* (New York: E. P. Dutton 1988): 84. Mayfield's 1968 song "We're a Winner" was thought to be so politically inflammatory that some black-oriented radio stations were pressed

not to play it for fear that it might inspire young people to rebellion during the so-called "long, hot summer." For discussion of this point by Mayfield see his album "Curtis Live" (Buddha Records). This double album, recorded at New York's Bitter End, is a good source of the political and cultural ferment of black power era popular music.

34. See Robert Walker, "Soul and Society" (Ph.D. dissertation, Stanford University, 1976). In a less sophistcated analysis I examined a randomly selected sample from Jet magazine's weekly "Soul Brothers Top 20" listing of the most popular songs from 1965 to 1972. Using this more restrictive data source I was unable to replicate Walker's findings of an inordinate increase in message music for this period. In no year during this period did message songs exceed 30 percent for any week. The difference here is probably a result of Walker's use of the more inclusive *Billboard* listing and perhaps his reliance on expert coders. On the increase in message music in the 1960s see also George, *The Death of Rhythm and Blues*, pp. 95–110.

35. William Cross, "The Negro to Black Conversion Process," *Black World* 20(July 1971):13–27.

36. Ibid.

37. J. Aberbach and J. Walker, "The Meaning of Black Power: A Comparison of White and Black Interpretations of a Political Slogan," *American Political Science Review* 64(1970): 364–72.

38. Quoted in P. Hagner and J. Pierce, "Racial Differences in Political Conceptualization," *Western Political Quarterly* 37(1984): 215.

39. Ibid.

40. Joesph Baldwin, "Theory and Research Concerning the Notion of Black Self-hatred: A Review and Reinterpretation," *Journal of Black Psychology* 5(1979): 68.

41. William Cross, *Shades of Black: Diversity in African American Identity* (Philadelphia: Temple University Press, 1991). Cross modifies his developmental model in light of the findings and interpretations of the new black psychology in his chapter "Rethinking Nigrescene."

42. Bruce Hare, "Children and Race: When Is a Doll Just a Doll," *Newsday*, October 10, 1987. See also his "Stability and Change in Self Perceptions and Achievement Among Black Adolescents," *Journal of Black Psychology* 11(1985): 29–42.

43. Although Professor Hare and I disagree on interpretation of the literature of black identity, he has been quite generous in a series of lively discussions that helped to clarify my own thinking on the problem. I also thank Professor James Jackson at the University of Michigan for similar assistance.

44. There is a fairly extensive literature that challenges the black self-ha-

tred paradigm. Examples include J. Heiss and S. Owens, "Self-evaluation of Black and Whites," *American Journal of Sociology* 78(1972): 360–70; J. McCarthy and W. Yancey, "Uncle Tom and Mr. Charlie: Metaphysical Pathos in the Study of Racism and Personal Disorganization," *American Journal of Sociology* 76(1971): 648–72; J. Porter and R. Washington, "Black Identity and Self-esteem: A Review of Studies," in M. Rosenberg and H. B. Kaplan (eds.), *Social Psychology of the Self Concept* (Arlington Heights, ILL,: H. H. Davidson 1982); W. Nobles, "Psychological Research and the Black Self-concept: A Critical Review," *Journal of Social Issues* 29(1978): 11–29; W. Banks, "White Preference in Blacks: A Paradigm in Search of a Phenomenon," *Psychology Bulletin* 83(1978): 1120–56; and J. Jackson, W. McCulloch, and G. Gurin, "Group Identity Development Within Black Families," in H. McAdoo (ed.), *Black Families* (Beverly Hills, CA.: Sage, 1981).

45. Jackson, McCulloch, and Gurin, "Group Identity Development in Black Families," p. 253.

46. See the studies by Heiss and Owens, McCarthy and Yancey and Rosenberg and Simmons cited above in note 44.

47. Hare, "Children and Race," and Cross, *Shades of Black*, chap. 3.

48. Cross, *Shades of Black*, pp. 16–38. In defense of the Clarks it should be noted that they did not explicitly draw a self-hatred conclusion in their work although they imply that such an inference might be appropriate.

49. Baldwin, "Theory and Research Concerning Self-hatred."

50. Banks, "White Preference in Blacks."

51. Ibid., p. 1185.

52. I think that Baldwin overstates the weaknesses of the substantive knowledge in this area when he writes (pp. 69–70), "Given, then, that no definitive data have been generated to support such a thesis, we have no clear-cut evidence from which to conclude that Black people either hate or reject themselves now or at any time previously." See "Theory and Research Concerning Self Hatred." Although in a narrow technical sense he may be correct, there is simply too much historical, theoretical, and empirical work, as well anecdotal material, to suggest we should conclude that there is not reason to believe that some degree of self-hatred and internal inferiorization has not existed in the Afro-American experience.

53. Robert C. Smith and Richard Seltzer, *Race, Class and Culture: A Study in Afro American Mass Opinion* (Albany; SUNY Press, 1992), chaps. 4–5.

54. Kenneth and Maime Clark, "What Do Blacks Think of Themselves," *Ebony*, November 1980, p. 176.

55. *Ebony* and the other mass circulation black magazines rarely publish serious, critical articles; rather they tend to emphasize celebrities, consumer-

ism, and the achievement of status by possession; they serve mainly as show-cases for the black middle class rather than as vehicles for hard news or controversial ideas.

56. Note here that the Clarks continued in 1980 to embrace the notion that a *majority* of black children preferred white dolls, rejected brown dolls, and embraced notions of black inferiority. This in spite of the fact that a re-examination of his published papers by the new black psychologists challenges the conclusion that black children expressed a preference for white dolls. Either they were unaware of the critics (which is doubtful) or simply chose to ignore the important methodological problems in their work revealed by the new black psychology. I should also note that Cross in his work ignores the Clarks' *Ebony* article. It is neither discussed in the text nor listed among the nearly 100 entries in the bibliography.

57. Ibid., p. 177.

58. Ibid., p. 178.

59. Ibid. The most likely explanation for the relatively higher degree of positive race group identification of blacks in the West (80 percent of whom live in California) is that they have higher education and income than blacks in other regions, which might have been ascertained by the introduction of controls for region by class.

60. J. Hraba and J. Grant, "Black Is Beautiful: A Reexamination of Racial Preferences and Identification," *Journal of Personality and Social Psychology* 16(1970): 398–402.

61. Cross, *Shades of Black*, p. 53.

62. Ibid.

63. B. Sussman and H. Denton, "Lingering Racial Stereotypes Damage Blacks," *Washington Post*, March 26, 1991. On the question about less inborn ability to learn, more blacks (25 percent) than whites (23 percent) agreed that this was true although the difference is probably not statistically significant.

64. Ibid. For example, a third of the *Post* sample were not high school graduates but among those with the most antiblack attitudes fully 80 percent were not high school graduates.

65. In their survey of the national black population, Jackman and Jackman also found that middle-class blacks were more likely to embrace notions of genetic reasons for racial differences than were poor blacks, 12.3 percent compared with 6.3 percent respectively. See *Class Awareness in the United States*, p. 56.

66. J. Howard and R. Hammond, "Rumors of Inferiority," *New Republic*, September 9, 1985.

67. Having been around higher education all my life, observing black and white kids at all kinds of institutions, I have no doubt that if blacks were given the same opportunity to compete on the level playing field that they have in competitive sport, they would do just as well. One should recall that it was said that blacks could never play baseball because they lacked the hand-eye coordination necessary to hit the ball.

68. A personal aside that shows how media images or reports about black inferiority may affect young children is the case of my eight-year-old daughter Jessica's initial reaction to radio and television reports of the NORC survey that said whites thought blacks were less intelligent. Jessica—who attends a mostly white school—is quite smart and knows it, often bragging "aren't I smart" as she effectively competes on some school competition. She initially, therefore, was dumbfounded that whites could think that blacks could be less intelligent, and for a moment one could see what Dr. King called "clouds of mental anxiety" growing as a result of this "rumor of black inferiority." My wife and I explained as best we could the racist nature of the "rumor" and assured her it had nothing to do with her or any other black person but that she should understand, which she did not, that this is an attitude held by many whites, including some of her teachers and that as a young black person it was something she would have to deal with for the rest of her life. I guess one point here is that no white parent will ever have to offer such racial reassurances to their children; it represents a kind of day-to-day assault on one's self that white people rarely encounter.

69. Signitha Fordham and John Ogbu, "Black Students' School Success: Coping with the `Burden' of `Acting White,' " *Urban Review* 18(1986): 181.

70. Not all black students are in schools where this is a predominant ethos. See, for example, James Banks study of black students from middle-and upper-class backgrounds in white suburban schools, "Black Youths in Predominantly White Suburbs: An Exploratory Study of Their Attitudes and Self-Concepts," *Journal of Negro Education* 53(1984): 3–17.

71. See Myrdal, *An American Dilemma*, p. 697. On this point also see Frazier, *Black Bourgoisie*, passim.

72. Holden, *The Politics of the Black "Nation,"* p. 27.

73. D. Forsythe, "A Functional Definition of Black Leadership," *Black Scholar* 3(1972): 19.

74. Leronne Bennett, *The Negro Mood* (New York: Ballantine, 1964): 40.

75. E. I. Mullins and P. Sites, "The Origins of Contemporary Eminent Black Americans: A Three Generation Analysis of Social Origins," *American Sociological Review* 49(1984): 672–85.

76. H. E. Ransford, "Skin Color, Life Chances and Anti White Attitudes," *Social Problems* 18(1970): 164.

77. The sample included the following skin color distribution: 21 percent light, 52 percent medium, and 27 percent dark.

78. Ibid. Ransford found that the occupational disparity between light and dark respondents disappeared for those persons with a college education, but for all levels less than college the lighter skinned persons were in higher-status occupations.

79. M. Seeman, "Skin Color Values in Three All-Negro School Classes," *American Sociological Review* 11(1946): 315–21; H. Butts, "Skin Color Perception and Self-esteem," *Journal of Negro Education* 32(1963): 122–28; and R. Udry, "Skin Color, Status and Mate Selection," *American Journal of Sociology* 76(1971): 722–23.

80. See Stuart Micher, "Spike Lee's Gotta Have It," *New York Times Magazine*, August 9, 1987. Orginally Morehouse had granted Lee the right to film the movie on its campus, however, once its direction became clear he was asked to leave, with the University President Hugh Gloster claiming that Lee's portrayal of color cleavages on campus ." just isn't true, and it's never been true."

81. Feagin in "A Slavery Unwilling to Die" (p. 12) cites one 1978 study at IBM that found that lighter skinned blacks were promoted at faster rates than were darker persons. And an interesting study of hypertension among blacks contains inferential data suggesting that there is more discrimination against darker than lighter blacks. The study was designed to see if there was a relationship between skin color and incidence of hypertension. It was found that individuals with the darkest skin have the highest incidence of the disease, and since they also have the highest percentage of black ancestors if a genetic factor was at work for blacks as a whole subsceptibility to hypertension should increase continously with darker skin. However, it was found that darker skin was a predictor of the disease among lower-class blacks but not for blacks of any shade who were well educated and employed. The authors speculated that these results suggest that darker blacks faced greater discrimination and psychosocial stress than those with lighter skins. See Michael Klug et.al. "The Association of Skin Color with Blood Pressure in U.S. Blacks with Low Socioeconomic Status," *Journal of American Medical Association* 265(February 1991): 599–602.

82. Richard Seltzer and Robert C. Smith, "Skin Color Differences in the Afro-American Community and the Differences They Make," *Journal of Black Studies* 21(1991): 279–86. Beyond liberalism—conservatism, however, several studies show that skin color is related to the nationalism—integrationism cleavage in black politics, with darker skinned blacks being decidedly more nationalistic. See Ransford, "Skin Color, Life Chances and Anti-White Attitudes," and Anderson and Cromwell, "Black Is Beautiful."

83. See Robert C. Smith, *Black Leadership: A Survey of Theory and Research* (Washington: Howard University, Institute for Urban Affairs and Research, 1982).

84. Clark and Clark, "What Do Blacks Think of Themselves," p. 178.

85. Anderson and Cromwell, "Black Is Beautiful;" J. Goering, "Changing Perceptions and Evaluations of Physical Characteristics Among Blacks, 1950–70," *Phylon* 33(1972): 231–41; and J. Hotzman, "Color and Caste Changes Among Black College Students," *Journal of Black Studies* 4(1973): 92–101.

86. It is still not uncommon to hear in the black community remarks such as "She is dark but she is pretty" (as if the two are somehow contradictory) or talk about bad hair (naturally black hair), and one should also note the insidious rise of the geri curl as the 1990s version of processed hair. Sometimes this reaches silly proportions. For example, a relative of mine recently raised objections to the possible marriage of her daughter to a young man who was otherwise eligible because she said, "he was too dark."

87. Cross, *Shades of Black*, p. 64.

88. Quoted in Martin, "From Negro to Black to African American," p. 83.

89. Ibid., p. 91. This observation overlooks the fact that in the 1960s black power activists initially rejected *Negro* in favor of *Afro-American* or *black*. So even at that time there was a conscious effort to identify with the African heritage; however, *black* came to be preferred because it was argued that it was a necessary antidote to the stigma that had attached to the color black by white supremacists. It also was a means to transcend the color differences and conflicts within the black community that Jackson refers to in terms of his household.

90. This is the view, for example, of Martin in "From Negro to Black to African American" and of two leading black columnists. See Carl Rowan, "Another New Label Won't Help," *Washington Post*, January 18, 1989; and William Raspberry, "Another Name for Black Is Despair," *Houston Chronicle*, January 6, 1989.

91. *New York Times*, "Poll Says Most Blacks Prefer `Black' to African American," November 29, 1991.

92. Sullivan made these remarks at a conference of African and African-American leaders held in the Ivory Coast in early 1991. The conference was designed to forge economic, political, and cultural links between the two groups. See Kenneth Noble, "A Conference in Africa to Stir U.S. Black Pride," *New York Times*, April 18, 1991.

93. Nelson Mandela's triumphant tour of the United States in 1990 certainly did much to revitalize interest and identification with Africa in the U.S. black community. However, the euphoria generated by the visit turned to disillusion as a result of the internecine squabble between Mandela and his principal black rival, Chief Mangosuthu Gatsha Buthelezi, which resulted in the near-indiscriminate killing of Africans by Africans.

94. George, *The Death of Rhythm and Blues*, p. xiv.

95. Ibid., p. xvii.

96. Afrocentricity itself may be interpreted as a part of this nationalistic cultural offensive. It is a growing force in some of the nation's black studies programs, has been proposed and in some places adopted as an alternative inner-city school curriculum, and has some influence on fashion and aesthetics among students and elements of the intelligentsia. For a good statement of Afrocentricity, see Molefi Kete Asante, *Kemet, Afro-Centricity and Knowledge* (Trenton: Africa World Press, 1992). On the controversy that has accompanied the emergence of Afrocentricity, see Joyce Mercer, "Nile Valley Scholars Bring Light and Controversy to African Studies," *Black Issues in Higher Education*, February 28, 1991, pp. 1, 12–16.

97. Representatives of this theme in rap, in addition to Public Enemy, include Movement EX, Laguan, and Paris.

98. Juan Williams, "Fighting Words–Music's Ugly New Trend: Racism, Sexism and Gay Bashing," *Washington Post*, October 15, 1989. For a more informed and balanced assessment, see Nelson George, *Buppies, B-Boys; Baps & Bohos: Notes on The Post Soul Black Culture* (New York: Harper Collins, 1992), and Houston Baker, *Black Studies, Rap and the Academy* (Chicago: University of Chicago Press, 1993).

99. See Karin Stanford, "Political Communications: Expressions by Today's Black Youth" (manuscript, Department of Political Science, Howard University, 1989). On the role of clothing and fashions during the period of black power activism, see J. E. Erly, "Clothing Symbolism: A Study of Afro Fashions and Their Relationship to Black Identity Among University Students" (Ph.D.) dissertation, Pennsylvania State University, 1979.

100. Stanford found that female students at Howard were more likely than males to view the new trends in black music and Afrocentric clothing as personal expressions of taste or passing fads.

101. Others who have attempted to show a relationship between black music and politics include Leroi Jones, *Blues People* (New York: William Morrow, 1963), Frank Kofsky, *Black Nationalism and the Revolution in Music* (New York: Pathfinder Press, 1970), and generally Charles Henry, *Culture and African American Politics* (Bloomington: Indiana University Press, 1990).

Chapter 6. Racism in the Emergence and Persistence of theBlack "Underclass": A Critique of the Wilson Paradigm

1. William Wilson, *The Truly Disadvantaged: The Inner-city, the Underclass and Public Policy* (Chicago: University of Chicago Press, 1987): 11–12.

2. For example, a forthcoming study by Wilson's associates at the University of Chicago, which included, among other things, detailed interviews with Chicago employers on their attitudes toward hiring persons of various

races, apparently has caused Wilson to reconsider his position on the irrel-evance of racism in explaining the situation of the underclass. Early in 1993 he reportedly said, "I would even go so far as to argue that for some black males, those with little education and few skills, race has become even more impor-tant in the past two decades." See Jason DeParle, "Responding to Urban Alarm Bells At Scholarship's Glacial Pace," *New York Times*, July 19, 1993.

3. Claybourne Carson, "Why the Poor Stay Poor," *Tikkun* 3(1990): 69.

4. Two very good assessments of the literature are David Lang, "Poverty Literature and the `Underclass Concept' " (Princeton University, School of Public Affairs, (n.d.) and Richard Nathan and Kenneth Clark, "The Urban Underclass" in *National Urban Policy: A Reconnaissance and Agenda for Further Study* (Washington: National Academy of Science, 1982).

5. Typical of titles in the 1960s genre of poverty research was Leonard Goodwin's *Do the Poor Want to Work?: A Social-Psychological Study of Work Ori-entations* (Washington: Brookings, 1972). Funded by the Labor Department's Manpower Administration, the study measured the attitudes, goals, and aspi-rations of more than 4,000 respondents, poor and nonpoor, black and white, urban and suburban in order to answer the question posed in the title. His conclusion:

> Evidence from this study unambiguously supports the following con-clusion: poor people—males and females, blacks and whites, youths and adults—identify their self esteem with work as strongly as do the nonpoor. They express as much willingness to take job training if unable to earn a living and to work even if they were to have an adequate in-come. They have, moreover, as high aspirations as do the nonpoor and want the same things, among them a good education and a nice place to live. This study reveals no difference between poor and nonpoor when it comes to life goals and wanting to work.(p. 12)

The pristine clarity of Goodwin's conclusions of course did not settle the matter, as scores of studies were funded thereafter and even today, with gener-ally the same results. See, for example, the various volumes in the University of Michigan's Panel Study on Income Dynamics, a project initiated in 1968 to study attitudinal and behavioral components of economic status.

6. Oscar Lewis, *Five Families: Mexican Case Studies in the Culture of Pov-erty* (New York: Basic Books, 1959) and *La Vida: A Puerto Rican Family in the Culture of Poverty in San Juan and New York* (New York: Random House, 1966).

7. Anthropological field work in black urban ghettos clearly confirms the applicability of Lewis's concept, finding similar attitudes and behavior rooted in long-term joblessness. See Elliot Lebow, *Tally's Corner* (Boston: Little, Brown, 1967); Kenneth Clark, *Dark Ghetto* (New York: Harper & Row, 1965); and especially Ulf Hannerz, *Soulside: Studies in Ghetto Culture and Community* (New York: Columbia University Press, 1969). And in his tracing of contempo-

rary urban ghetto culture to the rural south, Nicholas Lemann shows that the culture of poverty is a rural as well as urban phenomenon. See *The Promised Land* (New York: Random House, 1991).

8. Lewis was so convinced of the culture of poverty's roots in the capitalist structure that in 1969 he and a team of researchers went to Cuba to study firsthand the effects of the transition from capitalism to socialism on the lives of the poor. Unfortunately, he was not able to complete his work first because within a year he was ordered to leave the country and then some of his papers were confiscated and at least one of his principal informants was arrested. Shortly after leaving Cuba, Lewis died of a heart attack, and it was left to his wife and colleagues to prepare for publication the results of his year in Cuba. Although tentative, his papers do suggest that the revolution was making some changes in the attitudes and behavior of poor Cubans. See Oscar Lewis, Ruth Lewis, and Susan Rigdon, *Four Men: An Oral History of Contemporary Cuba* (Urbana: University of Illinois Press, 1978).

9. Edward Banfield, *The Unheavenly City* (Boston: Little, Brown, 1968): 125.

10. There is a parallel between Banfield's time horizon theory and the writings of an early twentieth-century white supremacist. Edward Rossin, writing in a 1901 article, "The Cause of Race Superiority," argued that Europeans, what he called the more "energetic races" were "future oriented," valuing foresight and the capacity to defer gratification, while blacks and others "live from hand to mouth taking no thought of tomorrow." See *Annals of the American Academy of Political and Social Science* 18(1901): 72, 75.

11. Wilson, *The Truly Disadvantaged*, p. 15. To be sure, as I will discuss later, there were other reasons for liberal intellectual disenchantment with research on black poverty.

12. Lee Rainwater and William Yancey, *The Moynihan Report and the Politics of Controversy* (Cambridge: MIT Press, 1967). This volume includes the full text of the report and a good sample of press reports and scholarly and political commentary about it.

13. See E. Franklin Frazier, *The Negro Family in the United States* (Chicago: The University of Chicago Press, 1939).

14. Subsequent research called into question the causal effects of slavery and, to some extent, urbanization in the development of female-headed households among blacks. See especially Herbert Gutman, *The Black Family in Slavery and Freedom, 1750–1925* (New York: Pantheon, 1976). Guttman demonstrates that the black family was not destroyed during slavery and was relatively stable from emancipation until early in the twentieth century.

15. Moynihan, "The Negro Family: A Case for National Action," in Rainwater and Yancey, *The Moynihan Report*, pp. 369, 375.

16. See Mary McCroy, "President Talks Frankly to Negroes," and Rowland Evans and Robert Novak, "Inside Report: The Moynihan Report," in Rainwater and Yancey, *The Moynihan Report*, pp. 369, 375.

17. This view was expressed most forcefully by Joyce Ladner, when she was a young black sociologist just completing her dissertation at Washington University under the supervision of Lee Rainwater. See *Tomorrow's Tomorrow: The Black Woman* (New York: Doubleday, 1971). Professor Ladner, (currently vice president for academic affairs at Howard University) now rejects these notions and sees the problems of teenage pregnancy, out-of-wedlock births, and female-headed households in precisely the same way as her nemesis, Moynihan, writing and lecturing about the crisis of the black family and serving as chairman of the District of Columbia Mayor's Commission on Teenage Pregnancy. In *Tomorrow's Tomorrow* she claimed that early sexual intimacy and childbirth should be understood as an acceptable cultural alternative in inner-city black communities. But see her more recent "Teenage Pregnancy: The Implications for Black America," in *The State of Black America* (New York: National Urban League, 1986).

18. Louis Lomax, *The Negro Revolt* (New York: Harper & Row, 1962): 226–27.

19. The Urban League, given its historic mission and its social work orientation, was ideally suited to deal with these problems, which it did begin to attack in the 1980s but by then the number of female-headed households and the attendant problems had, as Moynihan predicted, gotten much worse. Throughout this period of black leadership silence, the Nation of Islam under the leadership of Elijah Muhammad made criticism of the internal disabilities of the black community and moral reform essential elements of its agenda for the "so-called Negro"—a tradition continued under its leadership by Louis Farrakhan.

20. Thomas Edsal, "Underclass Term Falls From Favor," *Washington Post*, August 13, 1990. Edsal reports that in an interview after his address Wilson said he had not decided whether to give up the word permanently.

21. Garry Ralison, "An Exploration of the Term Underclass as It Relates to African Americans," *Journal of Black Studies* 23(1991): 289.

22. John MacNicol, "In Pursuit of the Underclass," *Journal of Social Policy* 16(1989): 326.

23. Ibid.

24. Gunnar Myrdal, *The Challenge of Affluence* (New York: Pantheon, 1963): 34, as cited in Ralïson, "An Exploration of the Term Underclass."

25. Ibid. In the technical literature on the underclass Myrdal's notion that it results from changed educational and skill requirements for postindustrial employment is referred to as the jobs/skill mismatch hypothesis. See John Kasarda, "Urban Change and Minority Opportunities," in P. Peterson (ed.),

The New Urban Reality (Washington: Brookings Institution, 1985).

26. Karl Marx, *Capital* (New York: International Publishers, 1867/1967): 643. This stratum is distinguished from Marx's notion of the lumpen proletariat, which is a group outside the labor force—"the lowest sediment of the relative surplus population," which he said consisted of three parts, people able to work, paupers, and orphan children who work only in times of prosperity and those unable to work because of their failure to adjust or adapt to the requirements of industrial civilization. To some extent Marx's lumpen proletariat is closer to what some refer to as the underclass, however, it is usually rejected by contemporary analysts.

27. Quoted in P. Passell, "Chronic Poverty," from a privately circulated paper by the Urban Institute's Ronald Mincy. See the *New York Times*, March 6, 1991.

28. Ken Auletta, *The Underclass* (New York: Random House, 1982).

29. See Passel quoting Mincy in "Chronic Poverty" for these estimates. In another statistical definition of the underclass—those who are persistently poor, people below the poverty level in eight of ten years studied—blacks constituted 62 percent of the total. See Greg Duncan et al., *Years of Poverty, Years of Plenty* (Ann Arbor: University of Michigan Press, 1984):10.

30. William Wilson (ed.), "The Ghetto Underclass: Social Science Perspectives, "*Annals of the American Academy of Political and Social Science* 501(1989).

31. Lemann, *The Promised Land.* Although many critics have challenged Lemann's thesis about the southern roots of northern underclass culture, it is thoroughly consistent with anthropological field studies of urban ghetto culture. Hannerz in *Soulside* (p. 177) traces all save one of the ten components of ghetto specific culture to the rural south. The only exception that did not have a clear rural southern origin was "fear of trouble in the environment."

32. Mack Jones, "The Black Underclass as a Systemic Phenomenon," in James Jennings (ed.), *Race, Politics and Economic Development* (New York: Verso, 1992): 53.

33. A. Giddens, *The Class Structure of the Advanced Societies* (London: Hutchinson University Library, 1973), as cited in Rogolin, "An Exploration of the Term Underclass," p. 291.

34. Ibid., pp. 297–98.

35. Passell, "Chronic Poverty."

36. Douglas Glasgow, *The Black Underclass* (New York: Vintage Books, 1981).

37. Good examples in the popular literature are Time's cover story "The American Underclass," August 29, 1977; Mickey Kaus, "The Work Ethic State," *New Republic*, July 7, 1986; and Nicholas Lemann's two- part essay in the *Atlantic*, "The Origins of the Underclass" (June, July 1986), and more generally,

"New Studies Focus on the Very Poor," *New York Times*, December 20, 1987.

38. See Lemann, *The Promised Land*.

39. Richard Nathan and Emmett Carson, "Understanding the Urban Underclass" (Washington: Joint Center for Political Studies, 1982): 3

40. Ibid.

41. Ibid., p. 7.

42. Ibid., p. 18.

43. Ibid., p. 25.

44. Wilson, *The Truly Disadvantaged*, p. 10.

45. Wilson, *The Declining Significance of Race* (Chicago: University of Chicago Press, 1980).

46. See Theodore Hershberg, et. al., "A Tale of Three Cities: Blacks and Immigrants in Philadelphia: 1850–1880, 1930 and 1970," *Annals of the American Academy of Political and Social Science* 441(1979): 55–81. This article is actually a synthesis of the findings reported in three dissertations and several journal articles by five members of the interdisciplinary Philadelphia Social History Project. On the project see Hershberg, "The Philadelphia Social History Project: A Special Issue," *Historical Methods* 9(1976). See also Hershberg et al., *Toward an Interdisciplinary History of the City: Work, Space, Family and Group Experience in Nineteenth Century Philadelphia* (New York: Oxford University Press, 1979).

47. Hershberg et al., "A Tale of Three Cities," p. 65.

48. Ibid., p. 65.

49. Ibid., p. 66.

50. F. F. Furstenberg, T. Hershberg, and J. Model, "The Origins of Female-headed Households: The Impact of the Urban Experience," *Journal of Interdisciplinary History* 6(1975). DuBois made similar observations about Philadelphia's black community in his *The Philadelphia Negro: A Social Study* (New York: Schocken Press, 1899/1965).

51. Hershberg, "A Tale of Three Cities," p. 75.

52. Ibid., pp. 73–74.

53. Ibid., p. 78.

54. Ibid., p. 80.

55. Although Hershberg's model is in most respects entirely consistent with Wilson's, Hershberg is less certain than Wilson about the irrelevance of contemporary racism (writing only that it has "somewhat abated" in modern-day Philadelphia) in explaining the predicament of inner-city blacks and is

more convinced than Wilson of the need for race-specific policies, writing (p. 81) "unless major structural changes and perhaps some form of preferential treatment are undertaken at all levels of public and urban policy, it is doubtful that assimilation and economic progress for blacks will be made."

56. Wilson, *The Truly Disadvantaged*, p. viii. Wilson is somewhat disingenuous here since a careful reading of *The Declining Significance of Race* does suggest social democratic implications; however, when he was asked at a symposium on the book at the University of Pennsylvania he testily denied these implications, refusing to discuss the ideological implications of his work. Thus, he can hardly fault his critics today for misreading his work. In all likelihood Wilson, like most mainstream academicians and politicians, declined to embrace the socialist implications of his analysis for fear it would render him a less effective policy advocate and consultant. Stung by the charge of conservatism and yet wishing to distinguish himself from traditional liberals, he now finds it prudent to embrace democratic socialism.

57. Ibid., p. 6.

58. Ibid.

59. Ibid., pp. 10–11.

60. Kenneth Clark, "The Role of Race" and "Carl Gresham Responds," *New York Times Magazine*, October 5, 1980.

61. Wilson, *The Truly Disadvantaged*, p. 11.

62. Ibid., p. 12.

63. The conservative writers he refers to are James Q. Wilson, *Thinking About Crime* (New York: Basic Books, 1969); Charles Murray, *Losing Ground* (New York: Basic Books, 1984); and Thomas Sowell, *Civil Rights: Rhetoric and Reality* (New York: William Morrow, 1984).

64. Wilson, *The Truly Disadvantaged*, p. 12.

65. Ibid., p. 15.

66. See the list of cases, administrative decisions, and judicial opinions in Kathanne Green, *Affirmative Action and Principles of Justice* (New York: Greenwood, 1984): 87–161.

67. Wilson, unlike most writers on the subject, pays hardly any attention to drugs and the drug trade in his analysis of the problems and disabilities of the black underclass.

68. Wilson, *The Truly Disadvantaged*, pp. 55–56.

69. Ibid, p. 61.

70. Ibid., p. 58.

71. Douglas Massey and Nancy Denton, "Trends in the Residential Segregation of Blacks, Hispanics, and Asians: 1970–80," *American Sociological Review* 52(1987): 802–25.

72. After the 1992 Los Angeles revolt Lawrence Mead, a leading poverty researcher, argued that unemployment was not the problem in inner-city communities; rather the solution, he said, was to "teach the poor how to live." See his "Jobs Programs and Other Bromides," *New York Times*, May 19, 1992. This role model muddle mars Roy Brooks's otherwise useful book on race in contemporary American life, *Rethinking the American Race Problem,* in which he proposes that middle-class black families "adopt" and resocialize poor blacks in appropriate attitudes and behavior. There are several problems with Brooks's proposal. First, it is morally arrogant. Second, it is not practical because most middle-class families, black and white, have enough problems just staying middle-class and properly rearing their own children. In addition, many in the black middle-class have relatives who are not and must provide them with material and psychic support. Also, it would not work even if it was done since ghetto culture is a response to structural constraints and opportunities, and all the role modeling in the world will not substantially change it unless it is coupled with structural change.

73. Teenage pregnancy and single mother families are a problem, although a social and economic, not a moral one, since to the extent that these families and children do not become a burden on the state in terms of poverty and welfare dependency, it is difficult to fix a morally correct age for sexual intimacy or child birth. In reading the endless laments about teenage pregnancy, I recall the line from James Baldwin's *Blues for Mr. Charlie* in which a young girl tells her mother who fears she is pregnant that "I hope I am. I going to have my baby and he is gonna be a warrior." This sentiment isexpressed in a different way in Stevie Wonder's "Living Just Enough for the City."

74. Wilson, *The Truly Disadvantaged*, p. 130.

75. Ibid, pp. 137–38.

76. On "Sorriness" as blacks use it among themselves, see Brooks, *Rethinking the American Race Problem*, passim.

77. Martin Kilson, "Social Classes and Intergenerational Poverty," *The Public Interest* 41(1981): 58–77.

78. See "The Moral Quandary of the Black Community," *The Public Interest* 79(1985): 9–22, and "The Need for Moral Leadership in the Black Community," *New Perspectives* 16(1984): 14–19.

79. On the Loury case see "Harvard Teacher Faces 2nd Police Charge in 1987," *New York Times*, December 3, 1987.

80. See Robert C. Smith, "Black Leaders: Silence on Marion Barry Is a Mistake," *San Francisco Chronicle*, August 1, 1990.

81. See E. R. Shipp, "Notes from Tyson Trial: Prayers and Cheers for the Heavyweight," *New York Times*, February 3, 1992.

82. See Harvey M. Brenner, "Estimating the Effects of Economic Change on National Health and Social Well Being," paper prepared for the Subcommittee on Economic Goals and Intergovernmental Policy, Joint Economic Committee, July 15, 1984.

83. See Jeanne Prial Gordus and Sean McAliden, "Economic Change, Physical Illness and Social Deviance," paper prepared for the Subcommittee on Economic Goals and Intergovernmental Policy, Joint Economic Committee, July 14, 1984.

84. *America's Black Population, 1970–72: A Statistical View* (Washington: U.S. Bureau of the Census, 1983): Table 3, 13.

85. U.S. Department of Labor, *A Profile of the Working Poor* (Washington: Government Printing Office 1989): Table 8.2.

86. Cella Dugger, "Tiny Incomes, Little Help for Single Mothers," *New York Times*, March 31, 1992.

87. See Carter Wilson, "Restructuring and the Growth of Concentrated Poverty in Detroit," *Urban Affairs Quarterly* (forthcoming).

88. Wilson, *The Truly Disadvantaged*, pp. 100–01.

89. R. Cole and D. Deskin, "Racial Factors in Site Location and Employment Patterns of Japanese Auto Firms in America," *California Management Review* 31(Fall 1988): 9–22.

90. M. Turner, M. Fix, and R. Struyk, *Opportunities Denied, Opportunities Diminished: Discrimination in Hiring* (Washington: 1991): 1.

91. Joleen Kirschenman and Kathryn Neckerman, "We'd Love to Hire Them But . . . : The Meaning of Race For Employers," in C. Jencks and P. Peterson (eds.), *The Urban Underclass* (Washington: Brookings Institution, 1992): 203.

92. Ibid., p. 204.

93. About half the employers interviewed openly stated they saw differences in the work ethic between whites, blacks, and Hispanics: 37.7 percent ranked blacks lowest in this regard, 1.4 percent Hispanics, and none whites. Ibid., p. 210.

94. Ibid., p. 212.

95. Ibid.

96. In a convoluted passage Kirscherman and Neckermann try to locate their work within the confines of Wilson's model in spite of its convincing contradiction of his stance on the irrelevancy of racism. They write:

By stressing employer's preconception about inner-city workers, we do not mean to imply that there are no problems of labor quality in the inner-city: the low reading and mathematics test scores of Chicago public school students testify to these problems. But if the quality of the inner-city labor force has indeed deteriorated, then it is incumbent on employers to avoid hiring inner-city workers. This is precisely the result one would expect from William Julius Wilson's account of increased social dislocations in the inner-city since the early 1970s. Because race and inner-city residence are so highly correlated, it would not be surprising if race were to become a key marker of worker productivity.

I don't know how to interpret this passage except as an explanation for racism in the sense that employers are seen to be acting rationally in using race as a marker to disqualify black workers from the inner-city.

97. Rochelle Sharp, "Losing Ground: In Latest Recession Only Blacks Suffered Net Employment Loss," *Wall Street Journal*, September 14, 1993.

98. Ibid. For example, companies added a net 2,719 black managers during the recession, bringing the 1991 total to 248,915 or about 5.2 percent of the total for all races.

99. Carson, "Why the Poor Stay Poor," p. 69.

100. Wilson, *The Truly Disadvantaged*, p. 117.

101. See Robert C. Smith, "Hammering at the Truth: The Civil Rights Era and After," *Transition* 54(1991): 90–103, and Smith, "Politics Is Not Enough: On the Institutionalization of the Afro-American Freedom Movement," in R. Gomes and L. Williams (eds.), *From Exclusion To Inclusion: The Long Struggle for African-American Political Power* (New York: Greenwood Press, 1992): 97–126.

102. Wilson (pp. 158–59) tends to dismiss the role of internal self-help and community development and mobilization because he thinks that the problems are largely structural rather than moral or cultural, and therefore moral or cultural reform cannot be effective (perhaps also because he wishes to dissociate himself from these ideas because they are usually linked to conservative thinkers). But such internal inactives must surely be a part of any comprehensive reform agenda. Nor does Wilson discuss the problem of drugs and the illconceived war on drugs, which also must be dealt with in any comprehensive attack on inner-city problems.

103. Wilson, *The Truly Disadvantaged*, p. 124.

104. In an op-ed essay on Democratic party strategy Wilson wrote, "White Americans have not turned against blacks but against a strategy that emphasizes programs perceived to benefit only minorities. . . . Mr. [Jesse] Jackson who put forth universal themes that highlighted and proposed universal solutions to social problems plaguing all racial groups in America received far more working and middle class support than most political observers thought possible." See "How the Democrats Can Harness Whites and Blacks," *New*

York Times, March 24, 1989. On the first point the evidence seems to suggest that whites (especially the poor and working-class) have turned away from the Democratic party in part because of its perceived embrace of blacks, see Thomas and Mary Edsal, *Chain Reaction: The Impact of Race, Rights and Taxes on American Politics* (New York: Norton, 1991). And Jackson received relatively little support from poor and working-class whites despite his agenda and his sometimes eloquent appeals to their interests and concerns. See Lorenzo Morris and Linda Williams, "The Coalition at the End of the Rainbow: The 1984 Jackson Campaign" in L. Barker and R. Walters (eds.), *Jesse Jackson's 1984 Presidential Campaign*, (Urbana: University of Illinois Press, 1989): 227–48, and Robert C. Smith, "From Insurgency Toward Inclusion: The Jackson Campaigns of 1984 and 1988," in L. Morris (ed.) *The Social and Political Implications of the 1984 Jesse Jackson Presidential Campaign* (New York: Praeger, 1990): 215–30.

105. Wilson, *The Truly Disadvantaged*, p. 121.

106. On the failure of the government to implement even the watered-down Humphrey-Hawkins full employment act, see Augustus Hawkins, "Whatever Happened to Full Employment?" *Urban League Review* 10(1986): 9–12.

107. Ralph Bunche, "A Critique of New Deal Planning as It Affects the Negro," *Journal of Negro Education* 5(1936): 59–65.

108. Charles Hamilton, "Full Employment as a Viable Issue," in *When The Marching Stopped: An Analysis of Black Issues in the 70s* (New York: National Urban League, 1978): 59–61.

109. On the origins, enactment, and implementation of the Humphrey-Hawkins Act see Essie Seek, "Political Decision Making on Full Employment: Implications for Social Work Intervention" (Ph.D. dissertation, University of Southern California, 1981), and Robert C. Smith, *"We Have No Leaders": The Afro-American Freedom Struggle in the Post–Civil Rights Era* (forthcoming); chap. 8.

Epliogue

1. Derrick Bell, *Faces at the Bottom of the Well: The Permanence of Racism* (New York: Basic Books, 1992).

2. Most whites apparently believe that racism in America is a thing of the past. In the most recent survey, for example, 69 percent of whites say there is no discrimination against blacks in education, 63 percent say there is no discrimination in access to skilled labor jobs, 56 percent feel blacks have equal access to housing and 51 percent feel that blacks can get credit loans and mortages on the same basis as whites. See *Taking America's Pulse: The Full Report of the National Conference on Inter-Group Relations* (New York: National Conference Christians and Jews, 1994).

3. Smith, *"We Have No Leaders,"*:

Index